BIRTHING A MOVEMENT

BIRTHING A MOVEMENT

Midwives, Law, and the Politics of Reproductive Care

Renée Ann Cramer

Stanford University Press
Stanford, California

STANFORD UNIVERSITY PRESS
Stanford, California

Printed in the United States of America on acid-free, archival-quality paper

Library of Congress Cataloging-in-Publication Data
Names: Cramer, Renée Ann, author.
Title: Birthing a movement : midwives, law, and the politics of reproductive
    care / Renée Ann Cramer.
Description: Stanford, California : Stanford University Press, 2021. |
    Includes bibliographical references and index.
Identifiers: LCCN 2020021112 (print) | LCCN 2020021113 (ebook) |
    ISBN 9781503609839 (cloth) | ISBN 9781503614499 (paperback) |
    ISBN 9781503614505 (ebook)
Subjects: LCSH: Midwives—Legal status, laws, etc.—United States. |
    Midwives—United States--History. | Social movements—United States. |
    Childbirth—Political aspects—United States.
Classification: LCC KF2915.M5 C73 2021 (print) | LCC KF2915.M5 (ebook) |
    DDC 344.7304/15—dc23
LC record available at https://lccn.loc.gov/2020021112
LC ebook record available at https://lccn.loc.gov/2020021113

Cover design: Derek Thornton, Notch Design

Text design: Kevin Barrett Kane

Typeset at Stanford University Press in 10.5/14.4 Minion Pro

This, too.

TABLE OF CONTENTS

ACKNOWLEDGMENTS

This book owes its existence to Susan Sterett. A few months after Susan ended her stint in the Law and Social Sciences office at the National Science Foundation, we chatted during a workshop on undergraduate legal studies. My grant proposal had not been funded, and when she asked me how my revisions on the proposal were going, I answered honestly that I wasn't doing them. I didn't have time, and the chances of being granted an award were so slim (around 6% of proposals are funded) that it didn't seem worth the effort. Not only was I unlikely to revise and resubmit the proposal, I told her, I was considering dropping the project as a whole.

Susan looked me dead in the eye and said, "Most grants are submitted two or three times before being funded. Women tend not to revise and resubmit. Professors at undergraduate-serving, teaching-heavy institutions tend not to revise and resubmit. You are both. You got good reviews with helpful comments. You need to resubmit."

So, I went home and grumbled a bit, then spent four intense weeks combing through the proposal and the reviews, making difficult but meaningful revisions and rethinking key aspects of the project. I crossed my fingers, resubmitted, and tried to forget about it. As winter break 2014 began, I got word that I had three years of funding from NSF. I don't know that I can adequately express how essential receiving the grant was for the completion of the project.

The funding was key, of course. But even more importantly, the fact that I had earned a grant meant that the project had the high regard of scholars in the field: It was the morale boost I needed to continue the work.

I am grateful to the reviewers for NSF, and to Helena Silverstein and Jon Gould, who were program officers during the period that the award was administered. Both also offered insight and shared conversation throughout the research and writing.

My colleagues in the department of Law, Politics, and Society at Drake University are tremendously good scholars and friends. We meet regularly to talk about each other's work, and I am grateful that Will Garriott, Nate Holdren, and Matt Canfield all read several versions of portions of this manuscript. They each offered nuanced, critical, enthusiastic, and supportive comments—right up until the day before I submitted the final draft. Friends and colleagues at other institutions did the same—among them: Sarah Cote Hampson, Jeff Dudas, Christine Harrington, Carol Spaulding Kruse, Phoebe Clark, and Anna Kirkland. Thanks, too, to Ana Hernandez and Jamie (Wall) Hanna for their generous and insightful readings of an entire draft of this book.

I am grateful for the wide-ranging scholarly and personal conversations I had during the writing of this book—sometimes on the topics of midwives, but often not—with Liz Chiarello, Hadar Aviram, Laura Hatcher, Josh Wilson, Jinee Lokaneeta, Susan Burgess, Dvora Yanow, Jean Carmalt, Erin Mayo-Adam, Amanda Hollis-Brusky, and Julie Novkov. For sharing with me their scholarship, friendship, and commitment to midwifery, thanks to Emily Anesta, Rebecca Spence, Mandi Hardy, Jennifer Block, Indra Lusero, Megan Day Suhr, Susan Jenkins, Monica Basile, and Farah Diaz-Tello. Thanks, too, to Farah for organizing a group of us to put together a reproductive justice playlist; that music (plus a lot of coffee) facilitated the writing of this book.

I have been fortunate to have several outstanding undergraduate assistants working with me—observing and taking notes at meetings of midwives, transcribing interviews, and coding transcriptions and fieldnotes. Erin Mitchell coded all my early interviews as a check on my own coding. For a significant period of time, I had a dedicated team of students conducting interviews and taking fieldnotes; tracking down historical, legal, and journalistic accounts; and meeting regularly to analyze and interpret the data I was collecting. I'm exceedingly grateful to them: Kari Bengston, Samuel Meyer, Maya Bolter, Katie Berger, Gabriella Gugliotta, Kati Seeman, Phoebe Clark, and Jamie (Wall) Hanna. Working with these students—each of whom brought their disciplinary and personal perspectives to the project—provided me with valuable checks on my assumptions and clarity about what needed deeper explanation. It was also simply more fun to accomplish some of this work with colored markers and pizza, in a group.

Several classes of undergrads at Drake University have engaged this as a work-in-progress, among them: Will Garriott's senior seminar, twice, and my reproductive law and politics class, twice. This book benefited tremendously from those conversations, as well as from the conversations that accompanied presenting this work at the Drake Center for the Humanities, the Western Political Science Association, and Law and Society Association.

I am grateful for the funding for this project from the National Science Foundation, the American Political Science Association, Drake University Center for the Humanities, and the Iowa State Historical Society.

I am grateful to the anonymous readers engaged by Stanford University Press at two points during the review process. I am also grateful for the entire staff at Stanford—editorial, production, and support—thanks especially to Marcela Maxfield, Emily Smith, and Jennifer Gordon. And, so many thanks go to Michelle Lipinski for all the work she did to support this project for years, as it came to fruition.

I am so lucky to have several groups of people I can text or message at any hour—about work, about family, about the presidency and the state of the world. Among them: Anna-Maria Marshall, Claire Rasmussen, and Mary Dudas; Santhi Leon and Monica Williams; the Scrappy Scribblers (especially Nikol Alexander-Floyd and Beth Posner Ginsberg); and the Easy Writers (Renée Dineen, Jamie Dubrow Melzer, Madeline Brutus, and Abigail Morgan Prout) and several other women from Jen Louden's Taos Writer's Retreat and Writer's Oasis (especially Amanda Skofstad, Lisa Jones, Ren Powell, Pam Bustin, Laurie Sanders-Cannon, Peggy Hansen, and Jen herself); and the Powerful Women who gather at LSA for dinner once a year (including some already named, as well as Kim Richman, Lori Sexton, Keramet Reiter, Alesha Doan, Danielle Rudes, and Shannon Portillo). Thanks also to good friends for their unwavering support, and occasional distraction: Heather Laporte, Julia Jordan-Zachery, Melissa Sturm-Smith,

Tony Tyler, Craig Owens, Charlynn Rick, Andrew Fowler, Sue Mattison, Carrie Dunham-LaGree, Alejandro Hernandez, Sandy Gustafson, Tatiana Prowell (especially for an amazingly important dinner in Baltimore), Megan Brown, Brooke Kiener, Yasmina Madden, Jennifer Harvey (especially for being there for the final push while we both were writing daily in winter 2020), and Emily Winslow Stark who sent a very well-timed email.

During the final week of revising this manuscript, my stepdad Denny Drew passed away. I want to thank my mom Carolyn and my sister Tami for showing me exactly how important it is to set work aside in order to mourn and celebrate, and then: eat and sleep. I love you both. And, I'd like to thank my husband Aaron, for—at the same time—reminding me to also give priority to the book, and to myself. The connections I have with everyone named here, plus my son Wyatt, constitute the best part of my life.

BIRTHING A MOVEMENT

INTRODUCTION

Knowing About Legality and Illegality in Midwifery Care in the United States

> "I was a sociologist before I was a midwife.
> It's the same. Except some of us touch vaginas."
> —Sarah, a midwife from Oklahoma,
> at the Midwives Alliance of North America Conference

> "Different bodies of knowledge are produced in different settings."
> —Barbara Katz Rothman, *A Bun in the Oven* (2016, pp. 132–133)

> "We tell ourselves stories in order to live."
> —Joan Didion, *We Tell Ourselves Stories in Order to Live* (2006, p. 185)

"IF YOU PRACTICE HERE, you're probably gonna get prosecuted and sent to jail. I've been prosecuted criminally [three times] in South Dakota." That's how Gina describes her thirty years working as an "outlaw midwife" from an "illegal state."[1] In early June 2007, I drove a dusty dirt road east and north across the South Dakota border, a few miles into Minnesota, and down a quarter-mile driveway—past horses, cows, and goats—to Gina's small farmhouse surrounded by several outbuildings and a neat-as-a-pin yard. The home was no different from dozens of similar 100-acre plots in the rural southwestern Minnesota countryside. This uniformity benefited Gina, who has attended more than 600 births and trained at least a dozen apprentices. She used this farmhouse as a safe house and site of practice; in 2007 she operated across state lines to keep herself out of jail. When I drove up that summer day, a visibly pregnant woman was getting into the passenger seat of a waiting car. Gina waved good-bye to her before she greeted me and we walked to the small, two-room outbuilding that was meticulously arranged for her midwifery practice.

In the late 1990s, in Yankton, South Dakota, Gina first went to trial, charged with practicing without a license. Gina had previously trained as a certified nurse midwife (CNM) but was practicing as a "direct-entry" or "lay" midwife, an unlicensed midwife who has become skilled through a mix of apprenticeship and book learning. "They found me not guilty," Gina tells me about those charges in the 90s. This wasn't the end of her legal trouble, though. After the jury's not-guilty verdict, the state successfully sought an injunction against her midwifery practice.

At this point in our conversation, Gina opened a folder to show me the cease and desist order she received from the state, an order that she continued to violate:

> [This one says] I can't practice as a CNM without a license, which I don't believe I've done. But in its definition, [the judge] said since I've admitted to such things as providing food and fluids, and putting a cold washcloth on the forehead and pressure to the lower back, and um, hot moist pads, uh, and a few more midwifery kind of things like listening to fetal heart tones . . . or prenatal massage or cutting the cord. These are things that only a certified nurse midwife can do in the state of South Dakota. And I thought, "That is absolutely ridiculous!"

Gina tells me that after she received the cease and desist letter, "I'm sure that the state of South Dakota thought I had quit." But, after much prayer and discernment, "I continued practicing as a direct-entry midwife."

I had first met Gina at a South Dakota Safe Childbirth Options conference in Custer, South Dakota. The event focused on the lack of access to labor and delivery care in the state, which is especially problematic for rural families living far from hospitals. During the course of an intensive weekend of workshops, I attended a session meant to prepare husbands to handle emergencies that come up during unassisted birth, as well as classes on prenatal nutrition, decisions regarding vaccination, and the history of midwifery in the state. As a participant-observer, I gave a lecture on the laws relating to coercive force during childbirth. While in Custer, I connected with midwives and their advocates. Each told me, "You have to interview Gina." That's how I ended up, a year later, sitting with Gina in rural Minnesota.

After Gina's first acquittal, she was found guilty of violating the injunction against her practice and given a suspended sentence of sixty days in jail and a $5,000 fine. She tells me that she was "scolded" by the judge and told to stop her practice. But her calling was too strong and the need for her skills too great for her to listen to the law. Women would choose to give birth with no assistance at all before going to the hospital—such was the strength of their faith, their desire to avoid a hospital birth experience, or their distance from quality medical care. Relying on her faith, Gina reasoned that she would be there for those women, whether it was legal or not:

> I wasn't sure what to do. I'm a Christian and I love the Lord very much and, and as a Christian I can't just go out and quote "disobey the law," you know, and here they're saying that I'm disobeying the law, which has nothing to do with what I was doing. And I didn't feel I was disobeying it, but I went to the Lord and I said, "Lord, I've got to know why I'm doing this. Am I just doing this because I enjoy being with moms and babies? If that's the only reason, then that's not a good enough reason, and I need to stop." And, so I really prayed about it. I prayed. I fasted. I got counsel from some Godly friends that I knew would understand both sides of the issue. And, and I just waited on the Lord, for Him to show me what He wanted me to do.

Reading her Bible one morning, Gina tells me, she read a passage that made clear to her that God had called midwives to practice with women who needed them. Feeling that this was her ministry, she continued in her practice as a direct-entry midwife in the state.

Shortly after this decision, Gina attended a particularly traumatic birth that culminated in the need to transport her client and baby, in a blizzard and via helicopter, to the regional hospital for emergency care. The baby had been born at home with shoulder dystocia and a cord wrap and was not breathing well but did have weak heart tones. Gina did CPR until the child could be transported and intubated. The baby lived in the NICU for several days before passing away.[2] Gina found herself, again, in court, charged with practicing medicine without a license, in violation of the cease and desist order.[3] She told me, "Well, I knew I was in trouble, not that I was doing anything wrong." She was not charged with negligence or held responsible for the child's death. Rather, she explained, "They charged me with four counts . . . of practicing unlicensed midwifery. And so that's what I was convicted of; I was convicted of all four counts":

> [The judge] could have sentenced me to a year in jail on each of the four counts and $1,000 fine. But, she sentenced me to 180 days in jail on each count and a $500 fine; and the prosecuting attorney wanted a reimbursement to the family for what they had paid me for the birth.
>
> And so she said [I owe] a $500 reimbursement to the family. And the family refused to accept that.
>
> Then she suspended all the jail time but thirty days. And so I had to pay the $2,000 fine, and I served thirty days in jail . . . for being a midwife in the state of South Dakota.

When I asked Gina what that was like, a grandmother midwife spending thirty days in jail, she answered simply, "It was not easy." And then she laughed and told me to read her book.

Gina's exhortation reaffirmed my desire, as a sociolegal scholar, to write my own.

Birthing a Movement: Midwives, Law, and the Politics of Reproductive Care is a sociolegal story that weaves together legal pluralism, legal mobilization, legal consciousness, and legal implementation in order to better understand their constitutive interactions in the creation of professional boundaries and disciplinary knowledge. In it, I examine the multiple ways that midwives and advocates mobilize to expand access to reproductive care, as well as the seemingly contradictory impulses they have in both seeking, and seeking to avoid, the state. The book is also, at its core, an argument about the need for holistic, embodied, and integrative sociolegal research and a reminder for us to take seriously the stories we tell about law in society, as those stories create spaces within which justice can flourish.

LEGAL PLURALISM AND THE STATUS OF MIDWIVES IN THE UNITED STATES

The legal landscape of homebirth midwifery in the United States is pluralistic. I mean this first in the classical sense of legal pluralism, whereby we notice that formal, state-promulgated rules and practices exist side by side—and sometimes in tension with—traditional or folk practices that also have the normative force of law.[4] Midwives use practices handed down through professional generations—a Gaskin maneuver to turn a breech baby, for instance—alongside law that places a breech delivery outside of their scope of practice. And, second, I use the term "legal pluralism" to highlight that the formal, state-promulgated rules and practices are *themselves* pluralistic; a certified professional midwife (CPM) might have a legal and regulated practice in Oregon, but when she moves to Illinois, that same practice is no longer legal and is not regulated. Midwives in the United States participate in legal systems that Boaventura de Sousa Santos might say are typified by "interlegality" and in what Sally Merry has termed the "new legal pluralism."[5]

At its most elemental, this book examines and showcases the legal pluralism that governs those who attend to people who labor and deliver.[6] These midwives go by several different designations that indicate their training, their attitudes, their scope of practice, and their legal status—many of which are determined by the laws (and norms) of their locale and which might shift due to geography or politics. This pluralism necessitates that we take care to articulate a common language and understanding of who attends birth in the United States.

Most births (98%) in the United States take place in hospitals and are attended by obstetrician-gynecologists (ob-gyns) and a nursing staff.[7] Ob-gyns are specialist allopathic doctors who have trained in women's reproductive health. Obstetrics is the medical practice of working with pregnant and laboring women; gynecological practice covers the rest of women's reproductive lives, including menopause.[8] Nurses who work labor and delivery are also specialists, focusing on labor and delivery only; they do not do whole woman health nor reproductive care outside of labor and delivery.[9] These practitioners (ob-gyns, labor and delivery nurses) are experts in hospital birth and the medical model of care. If you labor and deliver in the United States, it is almost certain you will be in their hands.

A small but increasing percentage of hospital births (around 8%) are attended by certified nurse midwives (CNMs),[10] who also attend to prenatal care and do postnatal follow-up. CNMs are accredited by the American College of Nurse-Midwives. They sit for their exams after earning their BS in nursing, achieving an RN certification, and then receiving their MS in nursing. CNMs are authorized to practice in hospitals in all fifty states,[11] and in birth centers in thirty-seven states, plus the District of Columbia.[12]

When I first interviewed Gina, CNMs in South Dakota could practice legally in hospital settings, but not at home; they gained legal status for homebirth in South Dakota in 2013. CNMs may legally attend homebirths in all fifty states, but the vast majority of births attended by certified nurse midwives take place in the hospital, and most CNMs self-select into hospital practices. In 2014, the year of the most recently available data, 94.2 percent of all births attended by CNMs were hospital births; 3 percent occurred in free-standing birth centers, and 2.7 percent were homebirths.[13] As of May 2015, there were 11,194 CNMs registered with the American College of Nurse-Midwives (ACNM).[14] Although the story of how CNMs gained professional prominence and legal status is fascinating and important,[15] this book does not recount that story.

Rather, this book focuses on certified professional midwives (CPMs), direct-entry midwives, and their advocates. CPMs are not nurses. They operate outside of the medical model; they attend *only* out-of-hospital birth. In this book, I use "midwife" generally to refer to any person who is *not* a nurse midwife but who is trained to attend during labor and delivery and to provide pre- and postnatal care. When I am writing about particular practitioners, organizations, or communities, I use the designation that *they* adopt to refer to themselves. Because my primary interest in this book is the fight for and over the CPM credential, most (but not all) of the midwives whom I spoke with are practicing as, or aspiring to be recognized as, CPMs.

There are currently two paths to the training required for CPM certification by the North American Registry of Midwives (NARM). Potential CPMs must hold a high school degree or equivalent and either apply for certification through a portfolio evaluation process (PEP) or graduate from a didactic program approved by the Midwifery Education Accreditation Council (MEAC). Certification of CPMs rests on establishing competency through skills assessment and exams. Potential CPMs going through PEP must undertake clinical training or apprenticeship under the supervision of an experienced preceptor for at least two years. During that training, they must observe ten births in any setting and in any capacity; assist a preceptor in twenty births, twenty-five prenatal exams, twenty newborn exams, and ten postpartum visits; and serve as the primary provider (still under supervision) at twenty births, seventy-five prenatal exams, twenty newborn exams, and forty postpartum visits. After accruing this experience, candidates may sit for the CPM exam. MEAC-accredited programs organize their clinical training to coincide with didactic learning; in addition to the clinical practice as above, MEAC applicants must take a course on cultural competency and must attend at least two planned hospital births.

Until recently, most CPMs were achieving their competency through apprenticeship programs, and apprenticeship is the more traditional route to gaining expertise in midwifery. Increasingly, however, CPM candidates are attending MEAC-accredited schools—in part because federal student loans now cover the expenses of such programs and because many states are beginning to condition legal status on a didactic route to certification. There are midwives who are wary of these didactic requirements. They worry that these requirements will constrain access to the profession for candidates who live far from a MEAC-accredited school or have other barriers to that education. They also worry about the loss of women's ways of knowing and transmitting knowledge, when apprenticeship is no longer the primary mode of education.

CPMs do not have hospital privileges in any jurisdiction; they only attend out-of-hospital birth and provide the pre- and postnatal care associated with it. They almost always practice in a client's home. Only 8 percent of CPMs responding to the North American Registry of Midwives' most recent "job analysis" survey indicated that their primary workplace is a birth center.[16] In 2016, the most recent year for which there are data available, there were 2,069 CPMs registered with NARM and active in their profession.

While the legal status for certified nurse midwives has been relatively stable since the mid-twentieth century, the legal status for CPMs has been contested and in flux since the mid-1970s, and especially since around the year 2000. When I started this research, in 2006, twenty-two states licensed and regulated CPMs; twenty-eight refused to. CPM practice was illegal in South Dakota when I interviewed Gina; it remained so until June 17, 2017. By fall 2019, thirty-five states licensed CPMs, and all but one of those regulates their practice.[17] CPM practice remains illegal in eight states, where it could bring felony convictions and penalties that include imprisonment. CPMs are unregulated, with a confused and confusing legal status in the remaining seven states. Many of those states have active consumer and advocacy movements attempting to achieve legalization, regulation, and licensure for certified professional midwives.

CNMs and CPMs have a long and sometimes contentious relationship. In some states CNMs lobby against legalization for CPMs. But sometimes it is a mutually beneficial relationship, and the CNMs and CPMs support each other's practices.

Finally, some midwives are neither CNMs nor CPMs. Their designations vary according to state law, academic background, and personal preference. These titles include licensed midwives, lay midwives, direct-entry midwives, traditional midwives, and birth attendants. These practitioners have almost always been trained through apprenticeship, though some have gone through nursing or other didactic learning programs but do not identify as CPMs or CNMs when practicing out-of-hospital birth. Some of them desire CPM credentialing and regulation and actively advocate for their state to adopt those standards. Others eschew credentialing for religious, spiritual, or political reasons and vigorously seek to avoid the CPM credential and state involvement with their practice. Some of these midwives actively oppose legislation meant to regulate their practice and license CPMs.[18]

These disparities in legal status and nomenclature, and the rapid movement toward licensure in several states, can be confusing for practitioners and consumers alike. When I lived in California, I had the option of a homebirth attended by a legal, licensed, and regulated CPM or CNM, or a hospital birth attended by either an ob-gyn or a CNM. Now that I live in Iowa, a state that still refuses to license CPMs, I could have either an in- or out-of-hospital birth attended by a certified nurse midwife, and I could also rather easily find a CPM, but she wouldn't be governed by any state body and could find herself charged with the felony of practicing medicine without a license. Just four hours north, in South Dakota, are midwives like Gina, who—until gaining legal status in the summer of 2017—might well have operated out of safe houses in bordering states to avoid cease and desist orders. Four hours south, in Missouri, both CPMs and CNMs operate legally—but CPMs do so without regulatory governance—some in birth centers that do not comport with state ambulatory surgery center laws recently used to limit abortion providers by regulating clinic location, size, and staffing. CPMs in Missouri are also always under threat that legislators will rescind their legal status.

Mapping the regulatory web that midwives operate under within various jurisdictions is partly a project of legal pluralism. In addition, understanding the distinctions in practice, self-perception, and relationship to medicine and state underscored by these designations—as well as grasping how state and medical power have contributed to this plurality—touches on legal mobilization and legal consciousness. Midwives in illegal and/or unregulated states find themselves in a seemingly unsustainable situation and are often envious of their professional sisters in places where regulation and licensure are available. In those states, advocates must work on two projects simultaneously: They must convince state legislators of the legitimacy and safety of midwife attended homebirth, while also building a birth culture that will support them with a diverse set of clients who want out-of-hospital birth experiences. In legal and regulated states, midwives must also create a strong and supportive birth culture while dealing with the existence of barriers to safe practice that result in poorly integrated care, and, often, poor outcomes for moms and babies.

LEGAL MOBILIZATION ON BEHALF OF CERTIFIED PROFESSIONAL MIDWIVES

Legal mobilization scholars, and the movement actors they study, have long recognized that law is sometimes a strategic resource to be used instrumentally for the advancement of movement goals. Movement activists often explicitly acknowledge the instrumental use of law to be part of a multipronged strategy, and frequently these activists acknowledge trade-offs when they adopt legal mobilization as a technique.[19] Individuals within marginalized groups clearly have the ability to knowingly make meaningful compromises while pursuing legal mobilization.[20] Such mobilization holds both opportunities and constraints; through it, activists may knowingly accept otherwise unwanted normalization (or, domestication) of their claims in order to achieve victory.[21] And, there are frequently debates within movements and among movement activists about the decision to pursue legal mobilization at all.[22]

As well, multiple scholars of legal mobilization point in various ways to the constitutive power of law and rights claiming as a partial answer to the question of why social movement actors continue to engage with the legal system, even when it might seem to fail, restrain, or limit them.[23]

When individuals within a group mobilize to use law in order to articulate a rights claim, they participate—even when they fail or when their efforts come up short—in reshaping the content of that right. Social movement actors engaged in legal mobilization often see and understand that law is constitutive of meaning and engage in a process of "legal translation" by which their claims are made legible to legal actors.[24]

As much recent work on CPMs evidences, midwives and their advocates have focused their mobilization efforts since the mid-1980s on seeking professional status.[25] Their advocates have been primarily casting their cause as a consumer movement meant to expand the birth options of moms and families. While some midwives do not welcome, nor want, state regulation, the dominant paradigm for organizing has been to seek licensure and state recognition. Midwives and their advocates are engaged in a multipronged set of strategies to increase access to homebirth midwifery care through expansion of CPM licensure. Their actions range from political mobilization, in the form of lobbying legislators and engaging in electoral politics, to social movement activities meant to change a culture of birth in a given locale through Red Tent events, Labor Day picnics, film screenings, and engaging the media.

Some of their actions can be easily understood as legal mobilization strategies,[26] from the defense of midwives in criminal cases to the tort actions brought by lawyers against doctors accused of obstetric violence during hospital birth. These sorts of cause lawyering activities are joined with legal mobilization that focuses not on rights, but on seeking governance through regulation and regulatory policy.[27] Nationally and locally, midwives and advocates engage in cultural spaces ranging from alternative health fairs to hospital delivery rooms, legislative and regulatory spaces like the state house and the medical board, and in explicitly legal spaces like the courtroom.

As Ronen Shamir has pointed out, it isn't always necessary or useful to distinguish among the various forms of legality that activists and lawmakers engage with, as they create social change. He writes, "Legislation, adjudication, regulations, and enforcement are all part of the matrix of how things get done."[28] In large part because of how they view the roles of law, the state, medicine, and midwifery, midwives "get things done" using a broad range of political, legal, and cultural strategies.

In 2019, midwives in Kentucky and Hawaii achieved legal status; they followed on the heels of Alabama and South Dakota (2017), Maine and Michigan (2016), Maryland (2015), Rhode Island (2014), and Indiana (2013). As I write this in 2020, there are active movements to legalize and regulate midwifery in four states and on the island of Puerto Rico. The bill to legalize midwifery in Iowa just died in subcommittee, but Illinois and Georgia still had bills pending, and advocates were cautiously optimistic. Consumers and midwives in five additional states and the District of Columbia are working toward launching reinvigorated legislative efforts. Though change takes time, midwifery advocates have had steady success in expanding access to care.

LEGAL CONSCIOUSNESS, ACTIVISM, AND PRACTICE

Midwives and their advocates have nuanced and strategic understandings of law, and their varied forms of mobilization makes sense, given that their legal consciousness is multilayered. Legal consciousness is, simply put, "the ways in which people experience, understand, and act in relation to law."[29] Legal consciousness, write Lynette Chua and David Engel, "comprises both cognition and behavior, both the ideologies and the practices of people as they navigate their way through situations in which law could play a role."[30]

Scholars of legal consciousness have been interested in the ways that the "mandarin materials" of legal doctrine impact legal practice and understanding.[31] They have recognized that even those folks not mobilizing law as activists have legal experiences and conceptions of the legal, and that legal consciousness is constitutively developed and expressed through the daily, lived experiences of average people.[32] Legal anthropologists, critical race theorists, and scholars concerned with understanding Indigenous knowledge and law have all grappled with the ways that commonsense understandings become, reinforce, and challenge legal knowledge through processes of legal consciousness building.[33] And, scholars have recognized the need to attend to the legal consciousness of people who interact with, but do not see themselves as mobilizing, the law.[34]

Further, neoliberal governance plays an important role in reconstituting the legal consciousness of everyday and marginalized people as they engage with the regulatory power of the state. Regulatory power, and the economization of that power, constitutes those making claims on the state as vulnerable to being silenced and ignored, once they achieve the very regulatory governance they seek. And, the "imposition of regulations and desire for state funding" post-1980 has pushed advocacy organizations, often against their will, onto "the terrain of the state."[35]

When regulatory governance is promulgated and situated within the contemporary context of neoliberalism, identities of "consumer" and "victim" gain primacy over "citizen." The activism and legal consciousness around those identities is different from rights-seeking or protest-oriented activism. Within neoliberal contexts, activists' access to regulatory governance trumps seeking access to rights. Midwifery is a case in point. My fieldwork shows clearly that women advocating for midwifery care are more frequently seeking regulatory governance, and access to care as consumers, via legal and political mobilization, in what is certainly a shift in legal consciousness from rights-claiming toward disciplinary and economic power.

Though this isn't the whole story, of course. There are pockets of, as Kristin Bumiller puts it, "insurgency." And as she found in her examination of the neoliberal appropriation of feminist anti–sexual violence work, "Women, in their everyday practices [are] reinvent[ing] their relationship to authority."[36] This book details those "everyday practices," as well as the tensions that midwives and advocates face in seeking state regulatory power.

While the implications of moving away from rights talk might seem to de-center law, such a move also proves to make pro-midwifery mobilization unique in the ways that it self-consciously and intentionally cuts across legal, political, and social movement strategies. Indeed, Bruce Hoffman's investigation of pro-midwifery movements at the state level notes that midwives and their advocates are savvy in their "awareness of the dual nature of law, leveraging law's ideals in support of political ends."[37] Activists' legal consciousness understands law as a necessary, but insufficient, way of achieving well-integrated care for people who are laboring and delivering.

Midwives and their advocates believe that the skills, knowledge, and practices of trained out-of-hospital birth attendants constitute an authoritative knowledge that should be respected by policymakers and regulators and should be readily available to those who give birth. The goal of the pro-midwifery activism that I study is to increase access to culturally appropriate, affordable, and safe care for people who desire to labor and deliver outside of the hospital. Most midwives agree that the best way to provide this is to expand access to "physiologic birth"—what many call "natural birth," meaning unmedicated birth not facilitated by medical technologies like continuous fetal monitoring or drugs meant to slow, augment, or numb contractions.[38] Midwives and their advocates organize their activism around three primary issues of access. First, they understand themselves to be engaged in *risk mitigation* in the interests of public health achieved through regulatory governance and professionalization; second, they see themselves as engaged in *empowering* people who are laboring and delivering who seek autonomy through resistance to dominant norms of medicalized birth; and, third, they seek to *increase access* to a wide range of reproductive care by mobilizing for reproductive justice.

It is tempting to think of all of these forms of political, social, and legal mobilization as rooted in a tradition of women's movements, which are "found where[ever] women act collectively to present public claims based on their gendered identities as women."[39] These movements—according to Amy Mazur, Dorothy McBride, and Season Hoard—"provide a means for women, in their full cultural and ethnic complexity, to make their gender-conscious ideas public, to participate in achieving their goals, and to change public policy and the state."[40]

Often, midwives focus on the definition of midwifery as "with woman" and emphasize that theirs is a profession of women, for women. Some of the roots of contemporary midwifery advocacy grow from 1970s feminism in the United States, with midwives themselves referring to their work for legal status as part of the third wave of a feminist project. Similarly, most of the public *receiving* messages about midwives and their clients experience those messages as gendered—birthing bodies are feminine/femininized bodies, and the lactating-lobbying bodies of women in the statehouses simultaneously undermined, and established, the credibility of consumer-activists.

Though I adopt gendered language in discussing the activism and mobilization strategies at the state level, I do want to insert three cautions about considering the movement for midwifery a movement for women's rights. First, not all midwives would align themselves with what is commonly understood to be a feminist political project. Midwives and their advocates are clear in their articulations of the power and knowledge of those who labor and deliver, and clear on the problematic regulations that impact and limit decision making of those people with regard to a range of their reproductive capacity. Most will argue that this particular knowledge is female and feminine. But, midwives and their advocates often hesitate to call their movement "feminist."[41]

Second, by 2019, midwifery organizations, especially at the national meetings and within national organizations, were using gender-inclusive language and widening the scope of practice and duty of care of midwives to include all "people who labor and deliver," in a way that is an important corrective to hegemonic feminism that is woman-body focused.

The third caution relates specifically to "rights consciousness" as missing from the articulated legal consciousness of midwives and their advocates.[42] Indeed, midwives and their advocates in the United States mobilize law, often without mobilizing *rights*. They engage in lobbying and social movement activism, frequently while declaring their cause apolitical. Their considerable success brings them more fully into the state's regulatory gaze—a goal they might personally abhor—even while the regulation often fails to fulfill the transformational promise offered by professional status. Midwives and their advocates rely on particular expressions of legal ideology and relationships to state power because of their understanding of the dominance of the state in regard to women's reproductive choices. Advocates pursue goals of professionalization, legalization, and regulation, even when their individual views of the state and its power understand that response to be a limit on freedom to practice, and attend birth.

At times, state law appears hegemonic: As much as they may wish to avoid it, midwives and their advocates encounter the state when it prosecutes midwives for attending birth; when they advocate for licensure and regulation; and when they suffer the law's failed implementation by running up against regulations meant to constrain access to some forms of reproductive care and some ways of transmitting knowledge about reproductive health and autonomy. Their advocacy opens space for a new cultural politics of birth—one that often explicitly seeks to transform the relationships of women, midwives, and families to state power. The institutions within which midwives and their advocates are located shape access to different framings of law and politics and provide opportunities and constraints related to legal consciousness and legal mobilization.[43]

Even as midwives and their advocates adopt a language of professionalization in order to achieve legality, they do so—as the legal mobilization literature would predict—with an eye toward the potential drawbacks, and certain limits, of such a strategy. This ability to mobilize in multiple and simultaneous ways is rooted in a legal consciousness that is constitutively developed and expressed through their daily, lived experiences as midwives, mothers, people-who-give-birth, and consumers. As they come up against failed and limiting implementation of laws meant to enable their access and practice,[44] their commonsense understandings both become, and reinforce, legal knowledge through a process of legal consciousness building. The legal consciousness literature helps us understand the wide range of legal mobilization tactics used by movement activists[45]—including mobilization tactics undertaken in the face of the limits of law and the persistence of injustice. This is particularly important for midwives, who are often failed by the implementation of the laws they most seek, yet understand legalizing their professional status to be essential to providing care to families.

LEGAL IMPLEMENTATION OF POTENTIALLY TRANSFORMATIONAL LAW

Existing sociolegal scholarship is clear that there are often difficulties in implementing potentially transformational law—those laws that "challenge or contradict social norms."[46] In particular, a review of the literature shows that those laws meant specifically to protect and serve woman-identifying people, and especially to serve them in accessing their reproductive and sexual autonomy, often fail.[47]

These findings feel especially important, when we look at the flawed implementation of laws that decriminalize and regulate midwifery care. Laws meant to help increase access for women to a woman-dominated profession, in the service of their reproductive autonomy, often fail to live up to their transformational promise. Even in states where their practice has been legal for a relatively long period of time, homebirth midwives report that they are, or feel, "illegal" in some of what they do. In some jurisdictions, woman- and baby-serving practices—like stitching tears, using Pitocin to stop a hemorrhage, and carrying oxygen—are construed as illegal and against the rules. In other places, midwives wrongly believe that they are required to have liability or malpractice insurance; they mistakenly but absolutely believe that they must have a collaborating physician or hospital practice agreement. They may be unable to find labs willing to run the bloodwork associated with prenatal care. And, in even the most legal of legal states, midwives and their clients report social disapprobation of their choice to attend and deliver at home; they face harassment from doctors and nurses during emergency transfer situations, as well as family members who call Child Protective Services when they disagree with the safety of an out-of-hospital option.

Just as women continue to seek rights and access law, even as they recognize the limits of those laws for full protection and autonomy, the flawed implementation of regulations meant to safeguard midwifery has not dampened advocates' enthusiasm for legal mobilization. Flawed implementation has, though, contributed to their increased work to change the cultures of birth in their locales. My research clearly shows that achieving greater access to physiological birth requires political and legal mobilization, certainly—it also requires changing the narrative around birth in the United States, often through cultural practices meant to change norms and ideas.

In fact, this book demonstrates that when state-level pro-midwifery advocates engage in legal mobilization and political movement building, three things inform their activism: their (individual and collective) view and understanding of law and politics; their particular strategic interactions and opportunities; and the way that the laws on the books have been implemented to date. These factors operate constitutively to close and open particular pathways for success. Yet they are all embedded within imperatives to commodification of services, regulation of practice, and accreditation of educational pathways. They are further embedded within patriarchal structures of power that dismiss women's ways of knowing and traditional ways of disseminating knowledge, causing further harm to the racialized bodies of Women of Color.

Alternative and simultaneous narratives of midwifery and advocacy can be found in the reproductive justice movement, lawyering on behalf of victims of obstetric harm, the voices of midwives who refuse licensure, as well as manifestos and direct action by birth anarchists, radical doulas, and full spectrum midwives who articulate even more sweeping claims to reproductive autonomy. Their assertions are not distinct from calls for professionalization; rather, they are simultaneous with them, and often articulated in spaces that overlap, by individuals' whose perspectives are fluid. For many activists and practitioners, the goal—access to quality midwifery care and a viable practice—is far more important than the means by which it is achieved. Legal, political, and cultural mobilization share equal importance, are pursued simultaneously, and are often inseparable.

METHODS, STORIES, AND KNOWLEDGE

This book is the culmination of fourteen years of research, funded at various stages by the American Political Science Association, the Iowa State Historical Society, Drake University's Center for the Humanities, Drake University's College of Arts and Sciences, and the National Science Foundation. My research initially focused on identifying and understanding the different regulatory environments for midwifery and activism and was located primarily in three states while being contextualized within the national movement of midwifery advocates. Using triangulation via mixed methods for data collection,[48] my research included collection and analysis of state politics and the legislative record, trial transcripts and legal briefs, and journalistic coverage of homebirth midwifery prosecutions and midwifery activism. My primary methods, though, were participant-observation, ethnographic fieldwork, formal semi-structured interviews, long and unstructured conversations, and online interaction via email lists, Facebook, and Twitter.

I chose to focus on Iowa, South Dakota, and Missouri. I'd moved from California to Iowa in 2006 and chose those three states to study because their legal status for midwifery was different from California's, where I'd begun my work in 2004. In my three primary field sites, I interviewed CNMs, CPMs, and uncredentialed midwives, as well as consumer advocates and lobbyists, both before and after legalization. I also interviewed midwives and activists from Alabama (legal in 2018), Michigan (legal in 2017), and California (legal since 1992).

My informed opinion, based on the research I have read on birth outcomes and experiences, is that out-of-hospital birth in a low-risk situation is as safe as (if not safer than) in-hospital birth and that the safety of such a birth is improved with better integration of care.[49] In many instances (but not all), integration of care happens when CPMs are legal and regulated. Whether regulated or not, out-of-hospital birth is safer when attended by a trained and skilled practitioner. Though I have considerable concern about the loss of traditional and lay knowledge that comes with the certification, legalization, and regulation of a practice like midwifery—those issues are largely philosophical and pale in comparison to the stated desires of families and midwives alike for regulated and legal practice. These concerns also pale in comparison to the preponderance of the public health data. When some families will choose out-of-hospital birth no matter what other options they have, it makes sense to me to help them have access to licensed and regulated midwives.

Therefore, I was happy to engage in participant-observation for this research, in several contexts. In Iowa, I participated as a bill drafter and citizen-activist in the several iterations of a bill to legalize and regulate CPMs and as a member and co-leader of Friends of Iowa Midwives (later called Iowa Birth, under different leadership). I also wrote a scholarly article on the history of the first birth center in the state, using archival and interview data. In South Dakota, I spoke at the 2009 conference organized by South Dakota Safe Childbirth Options (now called South Dakota Birth Matters), attended several SDSCO organizing events, and consulted on film and video scripts for the group. And, I wrote an early methodology piece on the difficulties and pleasures of doing research "on" people I considered friends, as well as people whose professional identities are illegal. In Missouri, I participated and observed while attending pro-midwifery rallies in the state organized by Friends of Missouri Midwives.

TABLE 1 Midwifery Status in Primary Research Locales

State	Status	Route to Status
Alabama	Legal, unregulated	Legislative process (2018) following highly publicized successful obstetric harm suit
California	Legal, regulated	Legislative process (1992)
Iowa	Illegal, unregulated	
Michigan	Legal, regulation to come	Legislative process (2017); judicial reaffirmation (2019)
Missouri	Legal, unregulated	Legislative process (2014); judicial reaffirmation (2017)
South Dakota	Legal, regulated	Legislative process (2017)

I used a multiple case study methodology to organize my research, interpretation, and thinking about these sites. Though the research design itself was not explicitly comparative, the findings do invite and facilitate comparison. Sociolegal research routinely uses case study methodology to uncover legal mobilization strategies,[50] as well as the impacts of regulatory implementation.[51] Leading scholars in the field have recently advocated that comparative methods be utilized for mobilization studies in particular, arguing that studying law and social movements comparatively and cross-nationally—across time, place and cause—will enable researchers to investigate "the variable conditions that give rise to, sustain, and impact legal and political reform efforts."[52]

The research I conducted investigated perceptions and attitudes during periods of regulatory transition and legal change leading to newly implemented policies. As midwifery regulation is changing rapidly at the state level, this research enables a view of recent legalization, actively prosecuted criminalization, and the absence of law in locales where certified professional midwifery is unregulated despite well-coordinated activist efforts for legislation toward licensure. This research also enabled an up-close view of how these new regulatory environments were impacting midwives and consumers. And, through it, I was provided a focused perspective on how they talked about seeking legal status, mobilizing for political action, and avoiding the state's regulatory gaze, all while attending to people who were laboring and delivering.

I also conducted research in several national venues for midwives and their advocates. I attended The Big Push Summit in 2009 in Birmingham, Alabama—both as a researcher and as a state activist for Iowa. I have participated in The Big Push email list since then, in both capacities. I attended the Midwives Alliance of North America conference in 2015 in Albuquerque, New Mexico, and a pre-conference workshop on pro-midwifery activism facilitated by Geraldine Simkins, as well as the entire program of the 2016 Midwives Alliance of North America (MANA) conference in Atlanta, Georgia. My research assistant Jamie (Wall) Hanna attended the 2017 MANA conference in Long Beach, California, on my behalf. I was present for the first BirthKeepers Summit (Berkeley, California, 2015), as well as the inaugural meeting of the Birth Rights Bar Association in Chicago in 2018, where I presented parts of this manuscript as a work-in-progress. I also participated in a multidisciplinary research collaborative headed by Dr. Saraswathi Vedam, at the University of British Columbia, which produced, in 2018, both a website that maps integration of care and outcomes across a range of geographic, legal, and demographic factors[53] and an article that was published in *PLoS One*.[54]

Through this research, I have amassed more than 1,200 pages of field-notes, completed fifty hours of formal interviews with sixteen midwives and pro-midwifery activists, and spent hundreds of hours in well-documented conversation with these participants and dozens of others. Sixteen formal interviews feels a small number—until one remembers that the states I focused on denied practitioners legal status until quite recently, and the population of midwives in each state was exceptionally small. There were two lay midwives practicing openly in South Dakota when I began this work, four that I was aware of in Iowa, and an estimated ten in Missouri. Each state had an activist core of around three to five women and men, and one or two doctors in each state provided valuable assistance to pro-midwifery groups. Out of a universe of thirty or so potential interviewees, I accomplished 50 percent, with additional wide-ranging and long-winded conversations among those I did not formally interview.[55] I consulted dozens of sources including journalistic accounts of midwifery practice and prosecution; amicus briefs and court decisions; midwives' narratives of their professional lives and callings; and historical accounts of midwifery, medicine, and gynecology.

The approach I have taken to analyzing these texts, notes, and interviews has been interpretive. Interpretive methods of data analysis are marked by close observation, undertaken in order to explain complex social phenomena, with a focus on the contexts within which those phenomena are embedded.[56] I am not seeking to predict which states will pass bills, when, why, or how—though I have gotten good at guessing—nor to predict what will happen to lay midwives or CPMs once professionalization happens. Nor am I working to diagnose problems in movement strategies. Rather, I am interested in the ways that midwives and their advocates articulate their priorities and strategies, the ways that they report that their practices have been impacted by legalization efforts, and how those things relate to the enduring power of law and legality.

While interpretive methods do not focus on making predictions, and interpretive data often are not useful for generalization, reflective and interpretive methods do lend themselves to hermeneutic and phenomeno-logical understandings of particular organizations and movements,[57] while contributing to theory building within the disciplines. Interpretive methods alert sociolegal researchers to the contingent, variable, and interdependent relationships among law, practice, consciousness, and mobilization. We can use interpretive methods to "write a story that turns accidents into a well-plotted moral tale," rather than merely "offering an account of just one thing after another."[58] We can use interpretive method to construct a narrative that answers some of these questions:

> How do the pieces make up a whole? Does the law work the same way? . . . What are the stable, recurrent, and consequential patterns of action, if not law-on-the-books, written in the cases, statutes, and regulations?[59]

So, throughout this book, my presentation and analysis of the data I collected relies on, hinges on, takes the form of, a story. I take to heart the work of sociolegal scholars who highlight the power of narratives and stories to both reinforce and undermine hegemonic "tales" told by and about law.[60] A focus on lived experience of law in average people's everyday realities often entails a focus on the stories they tell, and the stories we reconstruct, about their lives.[61] As Susan Silbey writes, "Any one person tells different stories of law. Legality . . . is constructed from cultural tropes and memes circulating within the events of everyday life."[62] And indeed, the very "durability" of law and legal institutions "derives directly from the multiplicity of citizen interests and narratives inscribed in the law."[63]

As a piece of feminist scholarship, this book also takes seriously the insights gained from feminist, critical race, and womanist political theory regarding the power of story and auto-ethnographic accounts in consciousness raising, activism, and understanding.[64] Scholars working within a reproductive justice frame understand, as Rickie Solinger writes in her history of pregnancy in the United States, that "sex-and-pregnancy is more than a biological event."[65] Rather, sex-and-pregnancy is comprised of a set of cultural, social, and political signs to be promulgated through story, interpreted through narrative, and focused on as a lens through which women's emancipation can occur. As such, story and narrative are essential elements of reproductive justice activism and scholarly framing.[66] Given my intellectual and normative commitments—to feminist scholarship, reproductive justice, sociolegal scholarship, and interpretive methodologies—it is only fitting that this book, in fact, is full of stories.

I also retell these stories because, quite simply, when midwives and activists told me about their lives, they tended to tell them to me *as stories*. In fact, a key moment in almost every interview I conducted or random conversation I had was the moment that a midwife, a mom, or an activist told me the story of the birth that made them realize the need to increase access to midwifery care. Sometimes those birth narratives are stories of women's empowerment through out-of-hospital birth; quite frequently they are stories of obstetric violence, physician abuse and neglect, and the disempowerment of people who labor and deliver in hospital settings.

I have heard countless birth stories—and have come to understand the articulation of the birth story itself as a potentially counter-hegemonic practice meant to disseminate particular forms of knowledge about contemporary maternity care. Almost always, these narratives are tied to and used to exemplify structural inequality: Midwives point to the paternalistic chauvinism that Amish and Mennonite women are met with during hospital transfers; the refusal to provide pain relief for African American women in similar situations; the infantilizing use of "mommy" to talk down to laboring women when they enter hospital settings; the moment when a CPS visit is triggered by the immigrant status, marijuana use, or planned homebirth of the family entering the system; the fear that midwives feel when they must drop a client off at the ER doors and leave without ensuring continuity of care.

Some of the most important work toward cultural change done by advocates and midwives is work done in the vein of consciousness raising and storytelling. Storytelling is inseparable from advocacy. Believing that we can change the cultures of birth in the United States by sharing stories of empowered physiologic birth (whatever the locale), midwives and moms are clear about the importance of talking about their births, and many of the classic texts on out-of-hospital birth—written by Ina May Gaskin, Judith Rooks, Sheila Kitzinger, Peggy Vincent, and Carol Leonard—are compilations of birth stories interspersed with memoir, politics, and law.[67]

Simultaneously, advocates and moms believe that sharing stories of recovery from obstetric violence and disrespect during labor and delivery can help highlight the inadequacies of the current medical model for serving women's needs. And, moms and midwives of color, Indigenous women, genderqueer and trans parents work within these narratives to highlight disparate outcomes, gross structural inequality, heteronormative language, and the lack of attention to diverse bodies that come with medical—and some midwifery—care.

Of course, I have my own story—one that, as I reflect on it nearly fifteen years later, I realize is not just a birth story but a legal story. It is also a story of seeking scholarly solutions. And, it is a story of scholarly access—one that I told midwives and moms, routinely, as a way of explaining my interest and my activism. Like the midwives and pregnant/parenting people I interviewed, I use my story strategically to make a point, and to establish solidarity.

In part, the story goes like this:

When I was pregnant with my son, a colleague told me that she hoped I wasn't "one of those women" who approached labor as "an extreme sport." She was referring to the many women in our social circles who were determined to labor without interventions like epidurals or episiotomies, who might want a homebirth or a water birth—or both. These women, she thought, seemed to approach birth as a challenge to their strength and commitment, concomitant with a desire to experience it absent the trappings of medicalization. She disdained them.

I *was* "one of those women"—a White, nearly middle-aged, striving-to-ward-middle class, extremely well-educated cis woman living in southern Los Angeles County in the early 2000s. I went to yoga and ate organic vegetarian food and spent my pregnancy walking briskly on the beach, envisioning dolphins as my guides through what I hoped would be a calm, average—but also transcendent—labor. While I wouldn't have wanted an "extreme sport" birth, and while I certainly bristled at her characterizing my plans in that way, I absolutely did not want an epidural, or an episiotomy. I wanted a "natural birth."

Unfortunately, I had enough student loan debt that I wasn't solidly middle class, and my insurance provider didn't cover certified professional midwifery care, so I labored and delivered for four short but excruciating hours at Harbor City's Kaiser Permanente on industrial north Pacific Coast Highway—despite its name, far from the beach.[68] My son's birth cost me $9—the monthly premium I paid as part of my union faculty job at Cal State Long Beach, no copay required.

It was an experience I'd never want to replicate, beginning with a nurse who asked me to labor quietly because a mom had just had a baby die in the next room, and they didn't want her to feel bad, hearing me give birth. She then tried to break my water forcibly, without my consent; when I said "ouch" and flinched away, she asked how I was going to handle unmedicated labor. I had back labor—with contractions that had no discernible beginning, middle, or end—and they had to "pit me" (put me on an IV drip of Pitocin) as a way of regulating the waves.

The birth proceeded quickly, though, and was ultimately completed with an unmedicated third-degree episiotomy to facilitate an emergency vacuum extraction by an ob-gyn I had never met. Then, the pediatric nurse weighed my son on a faulty scale. Believing he weighed less than five pounds, she took him from me for eight hours—after asking me accusingly what "mommy had done to make him turn out so small"—right before my original nurse reminded me to be sure to fill out a customer satisfaction survey about my care and her provision of it.

My subsequent conversations with other moms, midwives, and their advocates convinced me, in retrospect, that I had experienced a rather typical hospital birth: Hierarchies of power were in place, moderate violence was exerted on my body and psyche, I felt timed and monitored and pressured to perform, and my choices surrounding natural birth were denigrated by all of the medical personnel involved. I was patronizingly called "mommy" when told to push or asked to make decisions regarding my care, and the only parenting support I got while hospitalized was an exhortation to watch several pre-loaded videos from my hospital bed, instructing me on feeding schedules and swaddling. I left with a commitment to breastfeed but without knowing how, and I took home a poorly stitched wound that would become a set of vaginal cysts requiring emergency room attention within a month.

I knew, even then, that midwifery care and out-of-hospital birth offered alternative ways of framing and engaging with the birth experience; I also knew that I wasn't able to access that care, for a variety of reasons. I knew, before I began to study it, that midwifery was about reproduction, childbirth, *and* the law. I knew intuitively what I later read in Raymond DeVries classic text *Regulating Birth*: "In the modern world, medicine and law are constant—perhaps unwelcome—companions at birth."[69]

A HOLISTIC AND EMBODIED SOCIOLEGAL NARRATIVE

During my several years of research, I often reflected on my son's birth story—rewriting it and healing from it, revisiting it with midwives who told me what could have been done differently. And, I reflected as well, on Gina's story. It was one of the first I heard and transcribed—and one that I've revisited through press accounts, conversations with others, and my own changing and shifting evaluation of Gina and her practice. Midwives' work, and the work of birthing, is undeniably *embodied*—messy, tactile, felt-in-the-body. My reflections on the stories I tell about midwives' work remind me that scholarship is also embodied. At least for me, writing and thinking are messy, tactile, felt-in-the-body; at its most vibrant, scholarly writing and reading is, for me, integrative and holistic. This book implicitly argues for the value of that embodied approach to scholarly knowledge production and understanding.

These stories also serve, for me, as terrific examples of the multiple strands of a constitutive sociolegal story that plays out across the country—wherever midwives are regulated and wherever they are not. In 2011, Scott Barclay, Lynn Jones, and Anna-Maria Marshall used the metaphor of two spinning wheels to help readers understand their view that those of us studying social movements and law have too much individual analysis going on—and not enough coordination. They point to studies of legal mobilization and studies of social movement mobilization and show that the two very rarely meet in the middle. And, these authors argued, the field of sociolegal studies is itself at a critical juncture, in terms of the scholarly articulation of the connections between legal mobilization strategies and identified gaps in legal implementation.[70] By attending to birth, I attempt to attend to these connections—with an eye to improving both integration of care for people who labor and deliver and improving integration of theory for those of us involved in sociolegal world and theory building.

Though each individual birth story is unique in its particulars, none is absolutely singular; and, no singular theory explains or illuminates them. Rather, these experiences must be interpreted through several sociolegal literatures. I understand parts of my interview with Gina as a conversation about the legal consciousness of a midwife who operates under a cloud of illegality that had her driving across the South Dakota–Minnesota border for every prenatal visit and every birth. I have come to see our conversation, too, as a mere moment within decades-long legal mobilization and political activism, through which South Dakota advocates recently succeeded in getting the state legislature to legalize the practice of certified professional midwifery. Indeed, almost exactly a decade after I interviewed her, I sat in a diner in Sioux Falls, South Dakota, and met the baby that Gina had most recently delivered: the first granddaughter of an exceptionally important pro-midwifery activist and lobbyist in the state. That activist told me that she hopes that the rest of her eight daughters' children will be born at home in South Dakota, with Gina attending. Regrettably, even in the face of this success, Gina's ongoing story—and the work of other midwives in her state—often tells of flawed and failing implementation of legal reform.

In her elaboration of the legal consciousness literature, Anna-Maria Marshall writes, "Law is not confined to formal rules and legal institutions. Rather, law is an important part of the 'cultural toolkit' . . . providing symbolic resources that organize and make sense of the complexity of the social world."[71] Marshall argues that through engaging with the legal consciousness literature, we see that

> [O]rdinary people draw on frames for legality in making sense of their daily lives; when they act on these interpretations, they re-create the meaning of law itself. Legal culture emerges from this interactive process between meaning and the social and cultural practice of everyday life.[72]

A significant part of the constitution of legal consciousness around birth lies in the telling of these stories, and in understanding both the hospital and the home as informal sites of law and legality.

Birthing a Movement, then, is a law and society story about the often-flawed implementation of potentially transformative regulatory policy, of the legal mobilization of everyday citizens, and of the legal consciousness of midwives and advocates thrown into unanticipated activism and a relationship to the state that they did not originally seek. It also relates the stories that women tell about their experiences in birth, and at birth. In that way, this book is an extension of my son's birth story—which is a legal story, a personal story, *and* a scholarly story. My experience of his birth was a genesis—and a continuation—of sociolegal work on regulatory power, legal consciousness, mobilization, and failure.

Birth stories, like scholarship itself, are both expressions of experience *and* our interpretation of it. The locales of stories matter: Where are they set? in the home? in the hospital? Where are they told? in books? at La Leche League meetings? around a campfire? at coffee in the swankiest part of town? Barbara Katz Rothman rightly insists, "Different bodies of knowledge are produced in different settings."[73]

Pierre Bourdieu wrote that "the constitutive power which is granted to ordinary language lies not in the language itself but in the group which authorizes it and invests it with authority."[74] While "official language" lays down "the dividing line between the thinkable and the unthinkable" (for our purposes, between being born in the hospital and being born at home), midwives' stories of birth and law are constitutive moments in their claim for authoritative knowledge of practices that support reproductive justice. This book is one locale for articulation of a body of knowledge about birth, about activism, about law, and about sociolegal scholarship.

Stories of and about birth, reported in a constitutive register, do what Barbara Yngvesson and Christine Harrington have asked sociolegal theory attend to; they help us understand "meaning construction and the dynamics of power, legal ideology, and knowledge as politics."[75] Stories about birth are stories about the construction of legal subjectivity in midwives and their client families; they are cultural, legal, and political stories of both mobilization and consciousness. They often exist as counter-hegemonic and rebellious narratives meant to imagine new ways of doing *and* knowing. As one midwife I spoke with made clear, "We don't have politics knowledge; we have birth knowledge." Another I spoke with called her practice, and the realities of the women she works with, "cervical disobedience."[76]

The book you are reading is a sometimes disobedient story of attending to birth to expand margins of reproductive care *and* scholarly knowledge. It is a story that I daily live with, and through—as a mom, as a feminist, as a teacher, and as a sociolegal scholar. I certainly hope to contribute to policy conversations and mobilization strategies for midwives. I also hope that this analysis of what I observed and learned will craft a better narrative about the legal status of CPMs, their mobilization and consciousness, and the limits of law. My intent is to offer a law and society story that contributes to the sociolegal literatures that care about the theoretical divisions I have mentioned in this introduction. In doing so, I argue that the kinds of disciplinary knowledge produced and understood by midwives—holistic, strategic, and embodied—is the kind of sociolegal knowledge and approach that enriches our field.

1 HISTORY AND STATUS OF MIDWIVES IN THE UNITED STATES

> "Well, I guess I am going to jail tonight."
> —Ophelia, a certified professional midwife in Missouri

ONE WARM MISSOURI EVENING, in the summer of 2017, I sat in Ophelia's living room for a long and exceptionally wide-ranging conversation about her midwifery practice and her decade of activism in the state. Ophelia, a certified professional midwife living and working in a small city in Missouri, is at the forefront of the fight for legal status in the state and has tremendous knowledge about the legislative process, the subsequent Missouri Supreme Court case, and the process of state activists' political and legal mobilization. She also has a strong memory of what it was like to attend out-of-hospital birth, prior to her practice being legal. This chance to speak uninterrupted for several hours was a much-anticipated and welcome follow-up to the handful of times we had previously met—in Alabama at a Big Push Summit, in a Des Moines coffee shop as she drove through on her way to visit friends elsewhere, and in various online communities. I was exceptionally excited to hear the story of her practice, of the route to midwifery's legal status in Missouri, and to catch up on her life. In the time since we'd first met, she'd married and had two children, had seen CPMs legalized in Missouri, had been with her mom at her passing, and had opened a thriving out-of-hospital birth practice. We chatted while her husband wrangled with their two young boys and as extended family members came in and out with food and news.

Toward the end of our conversation, I learned something about Ophelia that I'd never known: She had been subjected to police investigation for being a midwife, in an investigation that began when a client needed emergency transport. Ophelia recounted that at the time of her significant brush with the law, she was studying toward her CPM and had almost completed the requirements for testing, though the certification was not possible in her state. She had been working for the previous six years as an apprentice to another midwife, who was also unlicensed. As Ophelia put it, "Of course, we were both illegal direct-entry midwives at that point, even though she'd [the other midwife] been to hundreds of births." She explained that the client at the birth that led to her investigation had transferred to Ophelia's care from an ob-gyn practice at thirty-five weeks, in order to try to have a VBAC (vaginal birth after caesarean). While the client "seemed like a good VBAC candidate," Ophelia now told me that taking her on so late in her pregnancy was "a mistake on my part—because I didn't have time to educate her well."

Her senior midwife preceptor lived "two or three hours away" from both Ophelia and the client;[1] Ophelia explained it was "normal at the time" to have such a wide geographic range for midwifery care because there were so few midwives practicing in the state. In this case, though, the labor went much more quickly than any of the women expected. Ophelia called the senior midwife, who couldn't get there in time to attend the birth; she called a back-up senior midwife, who also could not be sure of getting there before the child was born. A third midwife "got on the road right away" to join Ophelia at the birth. Here, Ophelia paused in her story to remind me that most midwives work in teams—some think of it as one for the mom, one for the baby; working as a team is a good way to reduce fatigue, have company, and add a layer of protection and care. Ophelia explained to me, "I had done a hundred births by this point, but I wanted an assistant."

When the baby was born, the cord was "triple wrapped" around the neck. The child was "pale, floppy, and not breathing," but the baby's heart was beating. Ophelia called the ambulance, and, as she resuscitated the baby, the mom began to hemorrhage while delivering the placenta. When the EMTs arrived, Ophelia directed them, appropriately, not to intubate the baby. They responded by asking her, "Who are you and what is your name?"

After giving them her name and telling them she was an apprentice midwife, the EMTs asked Ophelia to identify the midwife preceptor with whom she was working. Years later, Ophelia remembered, "I told them, 'Well, I can't really tell you that. I don't feel comfortable sharing her name. She wasn't here anyway.'" She explained to me:

> I really wasn't sure exactly what to do. I was trying to act casual and not raise their suspicions. I also wanted to text the [third] midwife and tell her not to show up. But she didn't show up anyway, because she saw the ambulances, fire trucks, and police cars [and drove away].
>
> I knew I didn't want them to grab my charts. [I had] twenty [different] people's information in my tote bag. I remember discretely dropping that behind the couch. Then they tried to take my cell phone from me.

The police officers who were present threatened Ophelia: "We can take you to jail tonight—you don't have a right to remain silent in an investigation like this." She remembered, "There were seven police officers, and they kept following me around the house and threatening me with hauling me off to jail." She continued to clean up from the birth and to secrete her records and notes. She told me, "I put my phone in the dryer with dirty bloody clothes and the ringer off." When she took trash out the back door, she also hid her charts "under a lilac bush against the shed." After an hour of watching her clean up, the police officers told Ophelia they were going to go get a warrant for her arrest. Ophelia said, "I thought to myself, 'Well I guess I am going to jail tonight.'" Five of the officers left, telling Ophelia they were going to get a warrant; two remained behind, as Ophelia put it, "to watch me." She retrieved her phone, went outside, and called her father, telling him, "Hey Dad, I just finished a birth, and I think I'm going to be getting arrested. . . . " She told her dad where her charts were and asked him to collect them, adding, "But don't come by here now because the cops are watching the house."

Ophelia then decided to call a homebirth-friendly attorney she knew from her work at the state capitol, where she was a citizen-activist lobbying for legislation to legalize her practice. She smiled at me, "I thought I should call an attorney before they [took me] to jail." The attorney told her, "You're under no obligation to wait for them to come and arrest you. Go over to McDonald's and get a hamburger." She smiled again, "So I started to drive away. And all these police cars followed." Her smile disappeared as she recalled, "I was really unsettled."

Before going to McDonald's, Ophelia and her dad met up in the Walmart parking lot. Police officers were still tailing her. Ophelia laughed, "My dad is hilarious. He likes to give a Bible tract to everyone—the Silent Night Christmas Gospel. And," she told me emphatically, "he conscientiously follows every law." Having just retrieved the client charts that could incriminate Ophelia in any anti-midwifery prosecution against her, her dad "handed the police officers a Silent Night." Privately, Ophelia told her dad to "take the charts and put them somewhere but don't tell me where," and, she directed him, "don't put them anywhere on my residence." She told me that for four months those charts were hidden in a hay barn on a rural property, a location known only to her father.

Next, Ophelia told me, "I was still shaken up and didn't want to go in and sit down [at the McDonald's] so I went through the drive-through." In fact, she was so "freaked out" that she placed her order and drove away without waiting for the food. She recalled that what followed was an exceptionally long night:

> I just kept driving around [the city]. I didn't know what else to do. I didn't want to stop because the conversation at the house was very uncomfortable, and I wanted to avoid another one if I could. I called a friend and said "I really need a place to sleep until I get arrested." [When she got to her friend's house, her friend said,] "We might as well lock the door. [The police] should at least have to knock."

When Ophelia woke up and hadn't heard anything from the police, she said, "I was like 'What do I do with my life?'" She called her client at the hospital to check in on the baby and offered to visit. The mom told her that both she and the baby were fine (the child was in the NICU for four days before going home, healthy), but she added, "I don't think you should come over here. The hospital staff is asking all kinds of questions." One bit of bad luck was that the doctor who was in the ER at the time of the transfer from Ophelia's care was one of the primary opponents of the bill to legalize her practice. She knew that the doctor, and others who opposed the bill, were heavily invested in getting a midwife charged with, and found guilty of, practicing medicine without a license.

Knowing that she was a woman with a strong Christian code of ethics, I asked Ophelia, "Did you feel weird lying?" She answered with a smile, "I never really outright lied to anyone." Then, she elaborated:

I felt weird not telling my friends that I was being investigated and might go to jail. Every day I'd wake up and wonder if I'd be arrested. The baby's parents were questioned, and they wouldn't tell the police anything. The police didn't have a way to prove I was the midwife. [They couldn't prove I was anything other than] a Good Samaritan.

Ophelia continued to wait for her arrest:

For weeks, every time I was [in that city] I waited to be followed. I didn't hear from anyone but I could tell I was still being watched. Nothing happened for three months. . . . In October, I felt like I could go back to births. In November, I got a call from someone who identified himself as an investigator with the police. [He said to her,] "We know that you know stuff, and you're gonna tell us. We need more information from the birth you were at." I just kept repeating the bare bones facts of the story.

"We will find a way to make you talk," he said.

"And that," she smiled as she told me, "is the last I ever heard."

HOSPITAL BIRTH AS HEGEMONIC COMMON SENSE

Where were you born? If you have labored and delivered, where did that take place? Among those readers who are younger than seventy (or who have children who are), and were born in the United States, more than 98 percent of you answered "the hospital." Even those readers who labored with or were delivered by midwives likely had that birth take place in a hospital, or hospital-associated birth center, attended by certified nurse midwives. There are around 4 million babies born a year in the United States, and, as the national rate of 0.9 percent homebirth would indicate,[2] hospitals have become the de facto locale for birth. Labor and delivery is the number one reason for hospitalization in the United States; almost half of all hospital procedures are obstetric, and ob-gyn visits are the fourth most common reason for an out-patient visit.[3]

Giving birth in a hospital is simply common sense, and has been since the 1950s. What's more, those readers who were born at home, or who delivered at home in the United States, understand that their experience is outside of the mainstream. Indeed, we all know, without even thinking about it, that in the United States hospital births are "standard practice."[4] Hospitals are hegemonic in the medical practices of birth in much the same way that legality is hegemonic in our day-to-day life. Legality, Susan Silbey writes, "lies submerged within the taken-for-granted expectations of ordinary life."[5] Hospital birth is common sense, taken for granted, and expected; out-of-hospital birth is not. As lawyer and activist Indra Lusero puts it, this hegemony of the hospital means that homebirth with a midwife has become both structurally and conceptually "impossible" in the United States. "The present-day structure of maternity care diminishes the viability of home-birth midwifery as a profession," they writes, "and as a consumer choice."[6]

If hospitals were also the safest and most comfortable place for low-risk births to take place—and if they were also the place where women were not belittled and where women of color were not put at heightened risk—perhaps midwives and their advocates would not have such a compelling case to make in questioning the norm. However, although the United States spends more money per person on health care than other developed nations, we have shockingly middle-of-the road outcomes for women and babies; though we have all the technology money can buy and at our disposal for birth, our rates of neonatal mortality and maternal mortality are stunningly bad, when compared to other developed nations. And, the disparate care and outcomes for women and babies of color? Unethically bad.

Indeed, there are solid reasons that women would rationally desire less technologically intense experiences of labor and delivery. Midwifery advocates emphasize, in every conversation, that our commonsense understanding of hospital birth as the safest place is "just not true."[7] They point out that while infant mortality has declined by 13 percent in the United States since the advent of sterile hospital birth, maternal morbidity rates (the rates at which women die from postpartum complications) have been increasing. Since 1986, when the Centers for Disease Control and Prevention (CDC) and the American College of Obstetricians and Gynecologists (ACOG) teamed up to begin tracking data on it, the maternal morbidity rate has increased nearly 27 percent in the two decades since 2000.[8] While other industrialized democracies have experienced steadily declining rates of maternal morbidity, birth—midwives argue—has become more dangerous for women in the United States.

In 2015, Deirdre Cooper Owens reports, the United States was ranked 46 out of 184 countries for which the World Health Organization has data, with "a maternal mortality rate double that of Canada."[9] Even when care doesn't result in death or maternal injury, most women find that the care they receive is subpar. "It is unsurprising that many of the women in the study reported that their prenatal visits with ob-gyns were hurried, pressuring, and impersonal,"[10] all the more if they are women of color.

The United States and the UK had identical morbidity rates (10 women died for every 10,000) in 2000. By 2018, the UK rate had lowered, to 9.2;[11] Ireland, Sweden, Denmark, Italy, and Finland all have maternal morbidity rates below 5 per 10,000 live births.[12] According to the Centers for Disease Control, in 2018, women in the United States died at a rate of 26.4 deaths per 100,000 live births (a rate higher than that experienced by women in Libya, Turkey, and the Islamic Republic of Iran), with at least 20 percent of those deaths from preventable causes.[13] The racial disparities in maternal outcomes are shocking. African American women experience maternal morbidity at a rate four times the rate of White women nationwide.[14] And, some individual states having shockingly poor outcomes.

It is worth noting that those states with the worst maternal morbidity rates are also those states with the most restrictive laws on abortion. For instance, Georgia's rate is 46.2 deaths and Louisiana's is 72 deaths per 100,000 live births.[15] In 2019, shortly after publicity surrounding the state's closure of several women's health clinics in an attempt to stop abortion, the Texas Medical Association noted that the state had a higher rate of maternal morbidity than the rest of the United States and argued that "serious problems" persist.[16] Amnesty International,[17] the United Nations,[18] and the World Health Organization[19] have all pointed to the maternal morbidity rates in the United States, and disparate impacts for women of color, as human rights problems. These organizations acknowledge that we have a maternal health crisis in the United States.

Part of the explanation for the increased risk American women have faced while giving birth since the initial public health gains of the industrial era is that the move to hospital birth has meant that the level and types of interventions into normal physiological birth have increased exponentially. Contemporary hospital birth in the United States begins with "the formal medical acknowledgment of pregnancy and classification of a woman as a patient" and continues with a series of "complex ritual[s] used to regulate and de-sex pregnancy and birth and turn them into medical processes."[20] This technocratic management of birth introduces new risks to people as they labor and deliver. From the timing of contractions, to the internal fetal monitor that requires laboring people to lie prone, to the epidural that makes pushing without the assistance of the monitor difficult—this "cascade of interventions" becomes a "package deal."[21] Jennifer Block writes:

> With Pitocin comes amniotomy, internal fetal monitoring, immobilization, epidural, and urine catheter; oftentimes a blood sample will be taken from the fetus's scalp to confirm a heart tracing, and an intrauterine pressure catheter will be inserted to measure the contractions' strength within the womb. Intervention leads to intervention.[22]

These interventions are exceptionally commonplace. Childbirth Connection, supported by the Kellogg Foundation, deployed three national "Listening to Mothers" surveys of childbirth experiences. The data from the most recent, 2013, show that 53 percent of women surveyed had experienced labor induction; 89 percent of laboring people experienced electronic fetal monitoring; 83 percent used pain medications; 50 percent were administered synthetic oxytocin; 36 percent had their membranes ruptured artificially; 31 percent had C-sections; and 11 percent had a vacuum- or forceps-assisted delivery.[23] Other research shows that these interventions "are often premature, and . . . in retrospect, may be viewed as unnecessary."[24]

There is the perception among critics that many of the interventions are done for the convenience of the hospital staff. For instance, Elizabeth Kukura argues that interventions are initiated because hospital care providers are extremely concerned with how long labor and delivery take, and they expect those processes "to progress from first to second stage labor and through the pushing phase within certain periods of time."[25] Many hospitals, concerned with liability, don't allow women to walk around in labor; for the comfort of the obstetrician, most labor rooms have beds that force women to labor on their backs, with feet in stirrups (the worst physiological position for birth). The "Listening to Mothers" report shows that only 43 percent of women who labored and delivered were permitted to walk around after admittance to the hospital, and 68 percent "reported that they lay on their backs while pushing."[26]

Contrast all of this with Jennifer Block's eloquent description of "natural" or "physiologic" childbirth:

Normal, spontaneous childbirth is an automatic sequence, a series of internal and external movements, voluntary and involuntary, that a woman's body makes in order to have a baby. The pituitary gland releases the hormone oxytocin, which causes the smooth muscle lining of the uterus to contract rhythmically, and those contractions gradually accelerate and intensify. The lower portion of the uterus, the cervix . . . softens and opens into the vagina; the pelvic joints and ligaments become pliant; the amniotic sac . . . ruptures. The baby descends into the pelvis and through the dilated cervix, and, with the aid of muscular efforts, bodily movement, and the stretching of the pelvic anatomy, is expelled from womb to world.[27]

Why, then, intervene in normal and low-risk childbirth? Innovations and interventions have become dominant, midwifery advocates argue, because doctors are enamored of, and reliant upon, the technology they can use during otherwise routine pregnancy, labor, and delivery. Medical professionals see pregnancy as pathological, not healthy; they see labor and delivery as flawed, not natural. Judith Pence Rooks notes:

> As a specialty of medicine, the main focus of obstetrics is the diagnosis and treatment of pregnancy complications and the management of diseases affecting pregnant women and the fetuses they carry. This focus is vital because, although most pregnancies are normal, serious complications and diseases are not uncommon and can be deadly. However, physicians have expanded the proportion of pregnancies considered abnormal or pathologic by using monitoring devices that over-diagnose complications, by basing diagnosis on overly narrow definitions of normal, and by treating variations from those definitions as pathologic.[28]

Much of technocratic birth culture resides within a culture of fear, which is a topic that sociologist Barbara Katz Rothman elaborated on in her keynote address to the Midwives Alliance of North America (MANA), the professional organization for non-nurse midwives, in 2016. "We are in a risk society," she told those of us gathered for her talk on midwives as providers of an artisanal birth experience. She explained that in contemporary medicine, no one is considered "healthy" anymore; we are merely, occasionally, "low risk." Medical anthropologists agree. Doctors define these risks, and medical science offers a range within which "normal" and "deviant" states of health can fall.[29] While there are objective measures for health and risk, and midwives employ them in their decision making about clients, Rothman argues that "risk perception may not be about quantifiable risk so much as it is about immeasurable fear."[30] "Our fears," she writes, "are informed by history and economics, by social power and stigma, by myths and nightmares."[31] Doctors experience pregnant bodies mediated through cultural myths, norms, and stereotypes. These often heighten their fear and potentially diminish the care they provide.

In the United States, women's reproductive capacity has long been something to "manage," and, depending on the race and class status of the woman, "protect." From doctrine that posited women as too weak to properly breed without labor laws limiting their access to work, to cases that posited teenagers were too weak to be exposed to the "potentially leaking, bursting," and "embarrassing" pregnant body of a teacher—Supreme Court decisions have reinforced cultural assumptions about women's fragility and pregnancy's illicitness as a result of sexual activity.[32]

In an attempt to temper fears of "unruly" pregnant bodies,[33] medical models of birth standardize, instrumentalize, and regulate pregnancy—and especially the pregnancies of women who, for racial reasons, evoke cultural fear and anxiety. The technocratic model and medicalization of birth for poor women and women of color has particularly pernicious effects; such medicalization ensures, according to legal and medical anthropologist Khiara Bridges, "a constant, third-party surveillance of the pregnant body." Bridges notes that our culture "fetishizes the fetus and venerates medical science," pitting woman against child in medical decision making. "Women desiring less technology-intense prenatal care must act as careful consumers and locate these providers through other channels."[34] These women, Bridges notes, are often seen to be acting selfishly, against the best interests of their children.

Additionally, doctors who learn to rely on interventions are not trained to see physiological birth as it unfolds normally. They are trained to believe that interventions are better than nature. The routine—unnecessary, and harmful—cutting of episiotomies is a good example (episiotomies are straight line cuts to the vagina to assist in delivery). When midwife Peggy Vincent explained to an ob-gyn colleague in the 1980s that she "will only do an episiotomy if [she] think[s] the baby may be in trouble and [she] want[s] it to be born quickly" because she would "rather repair a jagged tear than a large cut any day," he replied that "he was taught [incorrectly] that women will suffer from uterine prolapse and incontinence in later years if they are not routinely cut."[35]

Episiotomy was the norm from the 1950s to the early 2000s. But the straight cuts of physician-made episiotomies really don't heal as well as tears that occur naturally through the process of birth, and tearing isn't even an inevitable by-product of labor and delivery. Realizing that, doctors changed their practice, and by 2016, Robbie Davis-Floyd reports,[36] episiotomy had again become rather uncommon in US hospitals. This was an exceptionally rapid change in practice, in response to clear evidence of the potential harm from a medical intervention.

Unfortunately, we've not seen the same progress in response to the exponential growth in the rate of caesarean section. The World Health Organization estimates that 85 percent of all pregnancies could officially be considered "low risk"—meaning the person is experiencing a healthy pregnancy, with no diabetes or high blood pressure, is having a single baby (not twins or other multiples), and is nearing her full-term due date with the baby presenting head down. As midwife Ina May Gaskin has so clearly stated, and as statistics from her midwifery team bear out, "Spontaneous labor in a healthy woman cannot be improved upon."[37] The WHO agrees. Given what we know of pregnancies and birth, WHO guidelines say that the global C-section rate should be between 12 and 15 percent. The C-section rate in the United States in 2018 was an alarming 32 percent.

Some have felt that, because male doctors have been shown to be more likely to initiate C-section delivery,[38] increasing the rates of female ob-gyns practicing hospital birth would improve the experiences of women in labor and delivery. These expectations have proved largely false; even as more women have become labor and delivery doctors, the C-section rate at US hospitals has risen. The system itself, the expectations and understandings it articulates, and the larger cultural paradigm seem to be the problems, not the personnel choosing to work in hospital settings. Rothman puts it this way:

> Many people thought that the increased numbers of women obstetrics would bring the C-section rates down, but no, women are yet more rushed, overburdened by their own double shifts as doctors and as mothers, and their C-section rates are even higher.[39]

Pro-midwifery advocates point to all of this data and argue that, even though hospital birth is now common sense and hegemonic, and despite public health gains and progressive strides in care, hospital birth isn't necessarily the best option for low-risk people as they labor and deliver. And, they argue, citing studies based on the statistics gathered by MANA, that—for low-risk women—planned out-of-hospital birth attended by a professional midwife has stunningly good results.[40]

HOW DID WE GET HERE?

Peggy Vincent begins her memoir this way: "Women have been having babies forever. Through the centuries, the basic process hasn't changed at all."[41] Indeed, for most of history, women have been attended by midwives as they labored and delivered. So, how did we get here? To Missouri in the mid-2000s, where a good-outcome birth attended by a trained professional could bring the midwife months of police involvement and worry? To Georgia in 2018, where maternal morbidity for African American women is at crisis level? To upstate New York in 2019, where a woman with a long record of service to Amish communities is arrested for "pretending" to be a midwife? To Iowa, where the hospital-by-hospital C-section rate can't be determined, because hospitals won't answer questions put to them by consumers?

Understanding the roots of the medical profession and its relationship to law—and how that has contributed to the contemporary legal pluralism of midwifery and midwives' criminality—is not an abstract project. Neither is it solely an academic project. Rather, a key part of the movement to revitalize out-of-hospital birth is the movement among midwives and their advocates to offer a critical history of obstetrics-gynecology and a critical view of the commonplace assumption that the hospital is the best (that is, the safest, most family friendly, most empowering) locale for birth. At every national gathering of midwives and advocates that I attended, from The Big Push to MANA annual meetings to the BirthKeepers Summit, breakout sessions highlighted midwives' re-telling of the history of their profession and its relationship to medicine. In local contexts, midwives and advocates embarked on a project of educating consumers that highlighted their profession as distinct from medical doctors, offering speakers and films that gave positive views of out-of-hospital birth, from multiple cultural perspectives. Knowing and telling this history is itself a piece of pro-midwifery advocacy.

The problems with hospital birth, and the medical profession, is a well-known story to midwives and their advocates, leveraged as a way of helping pregnant people see that there are other options. It is a story told by scholars from various disciplines—history, women's and gender studies, African American studies, sociology, sociolegal studies, and anthropology—and a story told often (but not always) as part of a self-consciously emancipatory political project.

I find very little to argue with, when I read and hear these accounts of the growth of the medical profession, the delegitimation of midwifery care, and the consolidation of hospital power; but I find it important to remind readers that, like narratives of individuals' births themselves, the story of the birth of the medical profession and the temporary decimation of midwifery in the United States is also told for strategic reasons. I take the self-narration of certified professional midwives and lay and/or direct-entry midwives as the starting point for understanding this history, even though I am aware of gaps and lapses in their recounting, because I find these stories about their history to be a key component of their mobilization for and against legal status.

The story of how we got here, as told by pro-midwifery advocates, goes like this:

Prior to the turn of the twentieth century, birth happened at home, attended by women. For centuries, women have passed down their knowledge of birth through oral tradition and apprenticeship, transmitting their essential understanding of women's bodies-in-labor and care for those bodies. The practice of midwifery has been present as a practice in every culture on earth, whether it has been practiced by shamans with an expertise in childbirth, by family members who attended to their nieces and daughters and sisters, by women going away with each other, removing themselves to a sacred spot to give birth.

Sometimes, those attendants have explicitly called themselves "midwives." The historical records show that these women—midwives—have often organized themselves to provide this care and to transmit knowledge. And, the records show, the scope of midwifery care has historically and geographically been varied: In some cases it has extended to vaccination of infants, provision of prophylactics and contraception for women, and postnatal care; in other times and places, midwifery has focused only on attending women as they give birth.[42]

In addition to being organized, midwives have often been regulated. For most of recorded history, their practices have been permitted, facilitated, and governed by a combination of state and religious power. In his history of women healers, Thomas Forbes offers photos of the formal licenses for midwives from the Middle Ages on.[43] The valence and tenor of the regulatory practices have varied, again by time and place. In locales and time periods where the practice of midwifery has been prohibited or restricted, those prohibitions and restrictions have taken on the tone and ethos of the age and place within which they occur. In Europe in the Middles Ages, for example, prohibitions on midwifery took place, in part, through the burning of them as witches.[44]

In a very different context, "Although Parisian midwives came under some degree of regulation during the late 1300s, only those who wanted to attract wealthy clients applied for certification," and no comprehensive examination and licensure requirement was passed until 1560. That regulation stipulated that "applicants had to provide a character witness and pass an examination conducted by two senior midwives, one physician, and two surgeons." Those midwives who received certification "pledged to report practice by uncertified midwives," as well as "to call a more experienced midwife or physician or surgeon to help with difficult cases."[45]

In Britain, the church controlled midwifery longer than on the Continent, with regulation extending until the mid-eighteenth century. In their comparative survey of the modern history of midwifery, Hilary Marland and Anne Marie Rafferty note that Britain had "struggles over [the] registration" of midwives and argue that

> The debates [over midwifery] and their outcomes hinged on the long-term historical development of the obstetric professions, levels of institutional provision, systems of health care, particularly maternity services, economic forces, urbanization, changes in family life and the employment of women, religion, maternalist policies, the input and interests of various pressure groups—midwives and medical practitioners, public health reformers, politicians and governments, and mothers and their families—and on perceptions of particular national problems.[46]

And, Marland and Rafferty note, in every jurisdiction—but especially those of post-British colonial rule—topics of contention that recurred often were "competition, institutionalization, regionality, the public health challenge and the clash between 'traditional' and 'modern' midwives."[47] Judith Rooks demonstrates that midwifery and medicine evolved together in most locales. "Medicine and midwifery are," she reports, "inherently complementary" but "distinct" professions that engaged fruitful collaborations, in the normalization of midwife-attended birth and even homebirth, and in the development of models that serve women's needs while offering good results.[48]

In the United States, however, competition from the medical profession resulted in restrictions on midwifery that took several forms. Midwives in the United States were in every era "violently denounce[d]."[49] This is a largely untold and unknown history. We rarely hear this story of midwives, the presenters on a panel titled "The Real Story" at the Midwives Alliance of North America meetings in 2016 told a large group, in part because the story is *so* multi-valent. The *real story* is one of multiple points of the consolidation of medical and state power over women's birth. That story/ those stories are only recently being reclaimed—as part of a larger project of professionalization to increase access to out-of-hospital birth. And, midwifery advocates believe, we very rarely hear the full story because to hear it would cause women and pregnant people to question not only how birth happens in America, but why it happens the way that it does, and why our outcomes and experiences are not better.

Doctors and medical associations paid for racist advertisements discrediting immigrant and Black midwives in the progressive era, and "field matrons" were sent to American Indian reservations to teach Indigenous women "better" birthing practices. Physicians benefited from the decimation of Japanese American midwifery through the executive order that interned them during World War II; and, they benefited from outright criminalization and selectively aggressive prosecution as midwives began a renaissance in the 1960s and 70s. In the United States, from the late 1800s to the late-1900s, prohibitions against and regulations upon midwifery took place through laws that criminalized its practice, combined with, and in the service of, social and medical norms that reinforced a fear of labor and delivery; a mix of disgust and embarrassed reverence toward women's reproductive capacity; and a sensibility that appeared to protect middle- and upper-class White women while certainly exploiting the bodies of poor women and women of color. The context that shaped these prohibitions and state actions against midwives is a complex one—one that combines the consolidation of professional status for obstetrician-gynecologists with the medicalization (and eventual industrialization) of birth, all embedded within an overriding governmental interest in the use of women's bodies for nation-building purposes.[50]

The regulation of women of reproductive age, and limits on their access to reproductive health care, have been recurring interests of nation-state lawmaking in the United States, in the service of state formation.[51] Though the focus has been on female bodies and the governance of women's behavior through female fertility, that focus has often been articulated in ways that racialize the subject. Rickie Solinger's excellent history of reproductive politics in the United States makes this case through every era of US social life—showing how, from the enslavement of African women and their use as gynecological test subjects, to the forced sterilization of Indigenous women and White women deemed "unfit" to reproduce, to the focus in the progressive era and beyond on motherhood and the creation of the citizenry as the height of women's moral subjectivity, motherhood has been configured to advance state ends.

PROFESSIONALIZATION AND CONSOLIDATION

In his history of the development of the contemporary hospital, Charles Rosenberg writes this about specialization, "until recently . . . the healing function has been widely diffused through society."[52] Through a cultural process of "medicalization," which Rosenberg defines as "a long-term trend in Western society towards reductionist, somatic, and—increasingly—disease-specific explanations of human feelings and behavior as well as unambiguously physical ills,"[53] doctors began to specialize. With specialization, even those conditions that are not diseases—for example, pregnancy—have become reduced to mere physicality and are particularized as illness or harm, over which individual medical professionals could gain expertise and power.

In the process of medicalization, Rosenberg tells us, "boundary setting was always a priority." Physicians organized themselves into a professional organization—the American Medical Association—in 1847, and increasingly sought to define the boundaries of the field.[54] Physicians, Rosenberg writes, sought to "define and lay claim to" medical practice and to "rationalize [their boundary] policing in terms of the mastery of specific bodies of knowledge and adherence to a code of ethical and gentlemanly behavior."[55] Legitimacy for these medical professionals rested on social status and access to higher learning and linked technical mastery with moral responsibility.[56] Part of the project of moral authority for obstetrician-gynecologists, Kristin Luker's work so clearly shows,[57] was the establishment of their authority over quickening, and their power over determinations about when abortion was necessary. In consolidating medical power over decisions regarding termination of pregnancy, ob-gyns also consolidated power over places and practices of birth. As part of their attempt to gain status, obstetricians and gynecologists colluded in state projects of sterilization of Indigenous, African American, and Latinx women—as well as the prescription of birth control in ways that maintained White privilege.

Rosenberg's historical analysis is persuasive: Certainly the legitimacy of the medical profession and its various fields of specialization rested on access to claims of expertise rooted in higher education. His analysis does not, however, connect the ways that legitimacy also rested on practices that disempowered and exploited women, nor on practices that facilitated the racialization and feminization of midwives, nor on the ease with which doctors' professionalization project meshed with state projects of population control. In fact, even though he talks about alternative and holistic practitioners, Rosenberg never once mentions midwives or gynecologists. Pregnancy doesn't appear in the index.

His history of the hospital, and other similar histories of gynecology-obstetrics, are, Deirdre Cooper Owens notes, "triumphant." But, she argues, "If studied closely, this history evidences how race, class, and gender influenced seemingly value-neutral fields like medicine."[58] Her project traces the roots of American gynecology-obstetrics in the slave system of the southern plantation and documents how women in slavery were used as living test subjects for the development of the professional field, while those African women who served their communities as "granny midwives" were both coopted by the plantation system and delegitimized by the medical profession. As Owens writes, "There is a long history of African American midwifery, dating back to the West African captives who brought traditional birthing knowledge to the Americas. These women . . . delivered the majority of babies in the South during slavery and post-emancipation."[59] Under slavery, these midwives had to serve the interests of slave owners and, later, physicians by acqui-escing to the complete authority that these men exercised over them and their charges. As White men became involved in midwifery cases, Black midwives began to bear physical witness to the surgical treatment and repair of enslaved women who had given birth.[60]

As such, during slavery, granny midwives provided a controlled means for regulating Black women's reproductive capacity.

After slavery ended, however, those midwives constituted competition—not for profits (there were none to be made) but for bodies upon which to experiment and learn. As the medical profession grew, doctors-in-training needed bodies upon which to learn, and experiment. And, with the abolition of slavery, the bodies of enslaved women were no longer readily accessible to professionals-in-training. Hospitals in urban centers, serving primarily poor and marginalized women, could provide those living test subjects en masse—as long as the midwives serving them (granny midwives and immigrant midwives) were not granted access. Police forces in many urban areas simply knew to "provide free transport" to bring laboring women into the training hospitals.[61]

Further movement toward professionalization came with the 1910 pub-lication of the Flexner Report, which recommended science-based training for all doctors and medical professionals. Luker writes that the publication of the Flexner Report "signaled the end of open competition among Amer-ican healers," and that after 1910,

> [T]he closing of the proprietary medical schools, the spread of state licen-sure laws, and the vigor of local medical societies affiliated with the AMA meant that healing was restricted to a smaller number of licensed M.D.'s who had graduated from "approved" medical schools.[62]

By 1913, the AMA had created the Propaganda Department, which helped to develop, by the 1920s, a campaign to eliminate midwifery.[63] Coinciding with the growth of hospitals and medical schools, and using the power of their professional associations, doctors launched a vicious smear campaign to delegitimize the practices of African American and immigrant midwives. They were called "dirty" and "disease-laden" in advertisements meant to steer women toward hospital birth.

On behalf of the growing specialization of obstetrics-gynecology, the AMA also worked with state lawmakers to develop scope of practice and medical practice acts that outlawed other providers, including midwives.[64] Massachusetts passed the first law to make lay midwifery a criminal offense, the 1894 Medical Practice Act. That law eventuated in the first case brought by a midwife against any scope-of-practice law; and the outcome was a defeat for midwifery. In the case, *Commonwealth of Massachusetts v Porn*, the court was swayed by legal arguments that "midwifery was synonymous with obstetrics."[65]

The wave of legislation meant to criminalize lay midwifery was swift, and it successfully decimated previously thriving cultures of midwifery. By 1917, the only legal midwifery practices in the United States were those "recognized by both medicine and the state"[66]—in other words, practices regulated by the state (a difficult lift for lay midwives); this meant, often, only those practices undertaken by nurse midwives, those women with access to formal education along a medical model. Professionalization was further consolidated with the 1933 dissemination of *The Principles and Practice of Obstetrics*, which, as written by Dr. Joseph DeLee (the godfather of modern obstetrics) both pathologized birth and established standardized practices for its control.[67]

Of course, at the time, birth at home was not ideal—and women clearly did suffer. In the years leading up to the progressive era, there was indeed a crisis in maternal health and child welfare. Women had good reason to fear childbirth, as Judith Walzer Leavitt notes in her history of maternity in the United States from 1750–1950. Leavitt writes of the late 1800s and early 1900s, "The medical evidence reveals that women, rich and poor, suffered in childbirth, died in childbirth, and were at risk for a multitude of health problems that potentially affected their childbearing and may have short-ened their lives."[68] Prior to routine handwashing and the use of antibiotics, women died of puerperal fever at astounding rates. Newborns frequently went blind due to being infected by gonorrhea and/or syphilis in the birth canal, until the use of silver nitrate drops to treat their eyes immediately after birth became routine.

Though there were "midwifery" schools opened by the 1880s, primarily by and for immigrant women in the Midwest, the first *nurse*-midwifery school was the Manhattan Midwifery School, opened in New York City in 1925. In their excellent history of nurse midwifery, Helen Varney and Joyce Thompson argue that from the first, midwifery and nursing were understood as separate but complementary professional fields and practices. Nurses weren't midwives, and midwives weren't nurses—their scopes of practice differed—but nurse midwifery flourished within the realm of public health because the state prioritized the provision of services to laboring and delivering women in poor areas. The Sheppard–Towner Act of 1921 was critical to the project of nurse midwifery in this era; the act offered funds directly to the state in the advancement of maternal health.

A majority of the states used funds made available through the Sheppard–Towner Act to employ nurse midwives as public health educators in poor communities and communities of color, primarily to educate granny and immigrant midwives on safer practices for attending childbirth. In some jurisdictions, especially those served by the Frontier Nursing Association, nurse midwives developed strong and supportive relationships with lay midwives. In others, though, states explicitly endeavored to use Sheppard–Towner to solve what was increasingly called "the midwife problem":

> [This] was a contrived hostile debate that was fueled by wretched maternal and infant mortality and morbidity rates, a serious concern about what to do about them, the drive of physicians for control of childbearing women and female practitioners of midwifery, the developing specialty of obstetrics, the need of physicians to elevate the status of obstetrics, and the need for sufficient clinical "material" for medical student experience. The "midwife problem" became a crisis by the early 1900s and a topic of heated debate into the 1920s.[69]

Sheppard–Towner "solved" that problem, through education and supervision of public health nurses. Because of racism inherent within US educational policy, the only women with access to formal schooling were White native-born women with class privilege. Their access to nurse-midwifery education served to further marginalize midwives of color and immigrant women and to decimate the numbers of women serving their own communities.

So, at the same time that nurse midwives were beginning to professionalize through their service to women in Appalachia, the rural South, and the immigrant communities of the Northeast and Midwest, hospitals and ob-gyns were beginning to be an important part of the public health landscape in the United States. This put providers of care for laboring women into conflict with each other, and lay midwifery paid the price. As the medical model over pregnancy and childbirth "gained the upper hand in the United States during the early part of the [twentieth century],"[70] midwives in the United States were pressed "almost to extinction."[71] Simply put the development of public health initiatives that grew nurse midwifery, obstetrics-gynecology, and hospital care also had the impact of "abolishing granny and immigrant midwifery practices," which "both saved, and doomed, midwifery."[72]

For example, in Georgia at the turn of the twentieth century, nearly 6,000 midwives were registered with the state; most of them were African American women serving African American populations. In 1925, the Georgia Board of Health began governing the practices of the reported 9,000 midwives in the state.[73] In 1941, the state discontinued certification of midwives, assuming competent replacements for their care (that is, labor and delivery nurses, nurse midwives, and ob-gyns) were available, and by 1944 the number of state-registered midwives dropped to 2,200. The move to hospital birth was near complete by that time, and homebirth was not available again in Georgia until 1979 when a certified nurse midwife, Linda Segal, opened her practice in Fayetteville. Debbie Pulley, a CPM pioneer and movement leader, began her homebirth practice in the state in 1981 in Atlanta, despite lack of state licensing. As of 2015, there were 500 CNMs at work in the state and a scant "dozen or so CPMs" who continued to practice "despite lack of legal recognition," i.e. illegally.

In Alabama, when the legislature enacted a 1918 law requiring all midwives to pass an exam and register with the state board of health, the Tuskegee Institute responded by instituting training programs for the hundreds of Black midwives operating within the state. Lay midwifery practice continued in the state, though it was impeded by racial attitudes, until 1976 and Alabama's Act 499, which outlawed midwifery. Stacey Tovino reports:

> [L]ay midwives' non-underground practices all but ended within five years of the passage of Act 499. . . . [M]ore than 150 Alabama midwives, all of whom were black, received letters or visits from physicians or nurses informing them that they could no longer practice midwifery. . . . [And] the elimination of lay midwifery in Alabama was effectuated with little organized resistance.[74]

The state of Washington offers a similar example of the reduction in the numbers of midwives, and the disparate impact that legal changes had on midwives of color. From 1817 to 1925, there were sixty licensed midwives in the state of Washington; forty of them were Japanese or Japanese American. Those midwives formed an organization called the Sanba Kai and provided care for anyone who needed it, in racially diverse neighborhoods. Although revered in their communities, beyond those boundaries these Japanese American women were marginalized. And, after World War II and the policy of internment, combined with the move to hospital birth, these midwives of color became nearly impossible to find. In 2016, there were 149 licensed midwives or nurse midwives operating in Washington;[75] and there was only one licensed midwife of color in the entire state.[76] In all of these cases, as Rebecca Spence notes, "Registration and licensure of midwives has been documented as a part of efforts to eliminate midwifery," not to save it or make it safer.[77]

To their credit, though, hospitals were not merely considered "more efficient" places for labor and delivery; there were significant improvements in maternal and fetal health in the 1920s and beyond. Doctors credited these improvements to the hospital locale and their interventions, and the improvements certainly eased fears—never mind that the bulk of the improvement came simply from better antiseptic practices, adopted after doctors could be convinced to wash their hands in between seeing patients. In response to better outcomes, hospitals gained prominence and popularity.

New Deal legislation further solidified the role of the hospital in the community. The federal government consolidated the power and presence of hospitals via the Hill–Burton Act, which, in 1946, provided states with funding to build public facilities. These hospitals were largely (nominally) desegregated—serving populations from all communities within their walls, and by the 1950s, as a result, middle-class Black birth joined middle-class White birth in being moved decisively out of the home. In 1935, the first year that place-of-birth statistics were gathered and reported by the federal government, 36.9 percent of births took place in hospitals; by 1955, 99 percent were accomplished there.[78]

This shift to the hospital was untroubled by a new wave of woman-centered innovations in childbirth coming to the United States from the UK and Europe, as hospitals seemed able to accommodate small but important changes in the way they facilitated birth. The local losses of midwives and growth of medicalized care translated into hospitalized—and, eventually, industrialized—birth for women in the United States. Birth had moved into the hospitals first for poor women and women of color, and later, as anesthetized labor and delivery became possible, for women with higher socioeconomic status.

Where public health initiatives moved the first group to the hospital, the availability of scopolamine, which put women into "twilight sleep," made all the difference for middle- and upper-class women. Women had long been told, and long believed, that the trials and pains of labor were divine punishment for the sins of Eve. The thought that women could eliminate the suffering and pain they felt during labor and delivery was almost sacrilegious. But, as suffragettes and first wave feminists began to redefine their understanding of the role and nature of women, they also began to reject the idea that pain in childbirth was simply their deserved lot in life. Scopolamine, widely used in Europe and the UK at the turn of the century, gave women the illusion (via amnesia) that the birth of their children had been pain free, and women clamored for access to the drug. Varney and Thompson report that twilight sleep "could not get here fast enough," for US women;[79] after its arrival in 1914, upper-class women made its use fashionable, and as middle-class women accessed it, teaching hospitals began to use it on all laboring and delivering women, in order to learn from and about it.

Certainly, twilight sleep enabled women to feel less fear of childbirth, in large part because they had absolutely no memory of what occurred during their labor. In addition to being an amnesiac, however, scopolamine loosened inhibitions, and women on it were reportedly often "out of their minds" with pain, hysteria, and hallucination. Though they'd never know it, women who labored under twilight sleep were often strapped down, stripped naked, and left alone to moan, scream, and cry until they were delivered.[80]

Aside from agitating for access to scopolamine, and resisting the idea that they should feel pain in childbirth, women also participated in the move to the hospital for labor and delivery as part of a response to the pathologization of birth and the fear that surrounded it. As Varney and Thompson explain,

It is impossible to know whether births around 1920 were really more pathological or whether doctors saw more pathology in birth because they were looking for it and had more means to prevent and cure it. Doctors believed, however, that women should deliver in hospitals in order to receive the preventive treatments that seemed to protect birth from itself. Interventions grew steadily in number after 1900.[81]

As Lusero writes, "Maternity care was set up in and inadvertently shaped by the industrialization of medicine."[82]

However, there began to be, even before the 1950s, some dissatisfaction with aspects of this industrialized model of care. Dr. Grantly Dick-Read, a British obstetrician, visited the United States for the first time in 1947, bringing with him an advocacy for more natural childbirth. Dick-Read's book, *Childbirth Without Fear,* lauded women's natural ability to labor and deliver and became an international bestseller. Importantly, Dick-Read argued that women needed to be conscious partners with obstetricians and nursing staff in the birth of their children. Dick-Read also advocated for midwives to become more commonplace in the United States; they practiced widely in the British context. This advocacy—combined with the death-in-childbirth of one of the most active proponents of twilight sleep, Frances X. Carmody—contributed to the eventual end of scopolamine's use and a reawakening of a natural birth movement, which sought medical pain relief that allowed women to remain conscious during childbirth.

This reawakening continued into the second half of the century. Methods like Lamaze gained popularity from the late 1950s on. Betty Friedan, in her 1963 classic *The Feminine Mystique*, argued that birth should be experienced by the couple—it was a way for husband and wife to bond while recognizing the woman's feminine power. These cultural moves facilitated the call to bring husbands into the birthing chamber as partners in labor and delivery—though their presence was not widely accepted until the mid-1970s. Midwife Carol Leonard tells a story of a man in New Hampshire who handcuffed himself to his wife's emergency hospital bed so that they would be transported together by ambulance to the only hospital in the region (in Boston) that would allow him to be present for the birth of his child. My mother-in-law has told me proudly that my husband, born in 1971, was the first baby born in her part of West Virginia to have a father present in the room. She was also allowed to pioneer the use of nitrous oxide (laughing gas) for her labor and delivery.

The rise of "scientific motherhood"—facilitated by modern medical advances like the epidural and the unquestioned authority of doctors, coupled with feminism's call for conscious pain relief in childbirth—made it easy for American women, as a cultural position, to accept that birth is a medical event.[83] Even "natural" childbirth, they believed, should be accomplished in a hospital—not at home.

But dissatisfaction was also brewing.

As practices of biomedicine became even more fashionable and stratified in the 1970s, through medical specialization and disparate availability, a reconfigured landscape of health care and hospital care became "quite complex and multilayered."[84] The story of the growth of hospitals and specialization, the expansion of health care access, and the rise of more technological and scientific medical practice are all often seen as part of a generally laudatory story. But, as the widely acknowledged contemporary crisis in rural health care attests, the consolidation of this care in the 1980s resulted in smaller hospitals closing in favor of larger regional medical centers in urban areas. As a result, birth moved even farther out of the home—in rural America that meant moving from the farm, to the town, to the city, to the regional medical center.

Rooks argues that the centralization of hospitals and regionalization of care negatively impacted prenatal care, labor, and delivery in rural areas especially, in large part because regional hospital centers took the place of local family doctors and small-town hospital care.[85] Women had a harder time receiving pre- and postnatal care, let alone making it to a regional center for the labor and delivery of their children. In 2019, the American Academy of Family Physicians put it this way:

> We have lost more than 100 rural hospitals in this country in the last 10 years, including 10 already this year. More than 400 other hospitals are at risk of closing. This has created medical and obstetric deserts where there is no medical care for hundreds of miles. Most of these have been in communities with largely minority populations. These closures have greatly affected those living in poverty and those with low incomes, especially in areas where transportation poses challenges. Women and children in

particular have been experiencing the brunt of this change in the health care landscape.[86]

Rooks also argues that this regionalization and centralization "contributed to over-medicalization of childbirth and to the high financial costs associated with excessive use of high-technology obstetric care."[87] Also, regrettably, with the move to the hospital and the rise of surgical intervention came a loss of particular skills. Peggy Vincent, a certified nurse midwife with a hospital practice in California, identifies this loss of skill as something that happens when hospital birth is so tightly managed. She writes, "Vaginal delivery of breech babies is becoming a lost art. And it's a shame, because a well- managed, hands-off delivery of a breech is a thing of beauty."[88] Barbara Katz Rothman, who has been a researcher and advocate within alternative birth movements since the late 1970s, calls the US system of birth "industrial." She argues that such care is

> managed no more in the interests of birthing women and babies than industrial food is managed in the interests of its consumers. Industries run in their own interests. . . . Industrially processed food stops being food, and in a way, *industrially processed birth stops being birth.*[89]

This idea—that the birth process loses something essential to it when it is medicalized, standardized, and industrialized—became central to midwives' efforts to reclaim birth as natural part of many people's life cycle. They argued strenuously that birth is not a medical event—let alone a medical crisis—and that care for laboring and delivering women could be accomplished at home, by trained and skilled professionals.

This revitalization of out-of-hospital midwifery in the last third of the century was not met happily by medical professionals and hospital associations. As the move to managed care in the 1980s and 90s led to increased physician turf guarding in general, ob-gyns needed to continue to articulate their expertise in the field of birth. The major publications of doctors and medical professionals pointed out, accurately, that there was a paucity of validated research in the North American context to verify the claims of midwives and their clients that homebirth was, indeed, safe. In the absence of such research, they argued, hospital birth should continue to be the norm—to do otherwise would be to go backwards.[90] And, in an attempt to both maintain what they believed were important strides in public health that could only be accomplished in-hospital *and* to maintain a monopoly on birth for the economic well being, the professional associations of doctors, nurse midwives, and hospital administrators all moved to endorse statements against out-of-hospital midwifery care, while waging a public relations campaign on behalf of "baby friendly hospitals."

As they listened to the reasons midwives and advocates offered in support of homebirth, hospitals also heard, loud and clear, that the way they were structuring the birth experience had not been serving moms and families. To the extent that they were competing with each other for valuable patient-clients (and to the extent that some ob-gyns were open to innovation), many hospitals became responsive to demands to allow men in the labor and delivery room; to allow babies to "sleep in" with new mothers, who also received support in breastfeeding; and to allow women some limited options in terms of where and how they would labor and deliver.

As part of a move to maintain monopoly over birth, while still engaging in best practices, nurses no longer routinely shaved women and made them undergo enemas; women were no longer strapped down to hospital beds. Rather, laboring people were offered "walking epidurals" and constant external fetal monitoring that allowed them limited mobility in rooms that had been painted and decorated to resemble nurseries. These are not small changes—and they were hard won by consumers and sympathetic labor and delivery nurses and nurse midwives. Even the most cosmetic of changes made a big difference in women's labor and delivery experiences.

And, even the seemingly cosmetic changes were often difficult for hospital staff to understand and accept, as they represented a paradigmatic change in the way ob-gyns would approach their role in labor and delivery. In New Hampshire, for example, the midwife Carol Leonard, who was married to the head of obstetrics and gynecology at the local hospital, witnessed this process as her husband began to make changes. She tells her readers that in the mid-1970s:

> This is no walk in the park. One of the earliest and most significant changes that Ken proposes is the use of the labor rooms for labor *and* delivery, all in the same bed. This meets with fierce resistance from the other obstetricians. Frankly, they think he has lost his mind. They respond

by saying they weren't trained to do primitive bed deliveries. They say it is barbaric not to use a delivery table. His colleagues are quite vehement about this, until they get a tidal wave of positive feedback from the women themselves. They slowly come around. I'd like to say the conversation happens in response to women's demands, but it is strictly monetary. . . .

. . . Unfortunately, it is the same old practitioners, just in a hip, new disguise. They still don't trust or particularly enjoy birth.[91]

Part of being "baby friendly" meant offering options to women in childbirth that ob-gyns had historically not provided, and it did entail the solidification of new personnel being welcome in hospital birthing. In response to consumer demands and the organizing done by the American College of Nurse-Midwives, hospitals grew their staffs with certified nurse midwives, which were, by the middle of the 1980s, "legal, licensed, regulated, and able to obtain insurance coverage from private companies and Medicaid in all fifty states and the District of Columbia."[92]

Disrupting the medical model in this way required that hospitals and doctors to learn their limitations. As she became an official affiliate with a hospital in the San Francisco Bay Area, Peggy Vincent recalls a grueling conversation among the ob-gyns as they considered her application. They asked her why a doctor couldn't be a midwife and why midwives were necessary in a hospital setting. She responded by asking them how long a doctor usually stayed with a woman in labor, knowing that doctors usually attend only the last part of birth—often the last half hour or so of labor. She continuing by telling them:

> When a midwife cares for a woman, she stays without interruption through active labor, the birth, and for about two hours afterwards. I spoke about a midwife's skill at administering Verbal Anesthesia: talking a woman through the hard parts of labor. Mostly, I emphasized the difference between the Art of Midwifery and the Science of Obstetrics. . . . [I told them] A doctor can no more be a midwife than a midwife can be a doctor. The real question is: shouldn't a pregnant woman have the ability to make a choice between the two?[93]

Vincent's intuitive response—grounded in her lived experience—that doctors and nurses operating within a medical model simply don't spend enough time with laboring women to "midwife" them, is confirmed in data. Sheila Kitzinger noted in 2005, "In the USA research shows that in some hospitals labor nurses only spend 6% of their time on duty giving support to women in childbirth."[94] In 2013, the Childbirth Connections study showed that women felt barriers to communication with their hospital-based care providers; specifically, 30 percent of survey respondents indicated "that they had held back from asking their provider questions" because their provider "seemed rushed."[95] A woman entering a hospital for a birth will almost certainly not know the nursing staff, may not know the doctor attending her delivery, and will be on a standardized timeline for delivery, but a woman having an out-of-hospital birth with a midwife will, ideally, have had all of her prenatal care with that provider and will be able to labor at a comparatively leisurely pace. Midwives at a homebirth don't leave their clients until hours after the birth has happened; they serve their clients from the start to finish.

At the beginning of the midwifery renaissance, and as states began taking small steps toward being more hospitable to mothers, medical associations and professional organizations continued to advocate against homebirth and in favor of laws that restricted and criminalized homebirth midwifery. The American College of Obstetricians and Gynecologists, the American College of Nurse-Midwives, and the American Hospital Association all endorsed organizational statements against the practice of homebirth midwifery. And, the attorneys general of several states began to actively prosecute lay midwives in their jurisdictions, using laws that had been dormant until the visibility and vocality of lay midwives raised their profile. As prosecutions brought media attention to their cause, midwives and their advocates used the press to differentiate themselves—and their way of attending to birth—from hospitals. Combined with the horror of the prosecutions, midwives argued that hospital birth is industrial, mechanical, unskilled, and depersonalized; both messages have contributed to the renaissance of midwifery since the 1970s.

2 MODERN AND PROFESSIONAL

Legitimating, Marketing, and Reimagining Midwives

"Your ideas are no good, if you don't market them correctly."
—Thomas, publicist, The Big Push for Midwives

FOR ALL OF THE IMMERSION in birth I got as this research project unfolded, the first national gathering of midwives and advocates that I ever attended had no sessions on birth, none on herbs or pharmaceuticals, none on client care, none on charting. The first national meeting I attended focused instead on messaging, marketing, and mobilizing for legal status. I went to The Big Push Summit in Birmingham, Alabama, in 2009 as both a researcher and as a representative from Friends of Iowa Midwives, as we were preparing to launch a legislative drive for legalization of non-nurse midwifery in the state. My goals were to learn more about the national movement, to see how much (and how little) coordination there was between federal and state activism, and to make connections with advocates from around the country. Over the course of the weekend, fifty activists from several states shared resources, strategy, and stories. We met in the ballroom of a downtown hotel and took frequent walks in the muggy Alabama heat, solidifying friendships and alliances. We had good conversation about the best ways to support midwives in our states, the best ways to converse with legislators, and the best ways to motivate consumers and activists. We learned the roots of the renaissance of midwifery—in counter-cultural movements from the 1960s and homeschooling families of the 1980s—and we learned that legitimacy for the profession rested on a different image—the image of a modern, professional midwife.

One full afternoon of the Summit was dedicated to marketing and messaging. Organizers stressed the importance of story and narrative and the multiple platforms that advocates could use to get those stories out—from T-shirt slogans to YouTube videos to websites and email lists. One session, led by a professional publicist, was particularly energetic and fast paced. John advised the midwives and advocates to create a "messaging grid." He told us, "Ask yourself: What we are saying about ourselves, what are they saying about us, what do they say about themselves, what do we say about them? Then, go to the thesaurus." When midwives and advocates make that messaging grid, it very often looks something like Table 2.[1]

After the message-clarifying exercise, Thomas, an expert in product marketing, explained that ideas aren't good if they're not marketed correctly and that the best marketing strategies do not come from focus groups. "Don't ever listen to people," he told the assembled advocates. "Focus groups cause people to say what is reasonable but wrong." Rather, good marketing strategies rely on long-term movement building and mobilization; you need to know your families, he told us, in order to successfully market to them. Building relationships—a skill midwives value highly—would help them build clientele. At The Big Push gathering, midwives and advocates learned about success stories in order to explain them to others; we attended the Summit hoping to bring home the key to passing legislation in our states. Admittedly, many of us were focused on legislators and "the opposition."

At the end of the Knowledge Exchange session, John cautioned against that focus. He argued that before anything, we needed to go to the consumers. "Go to the grassroots first," he emphasized, "not the legislators." This was a seamless transition to the next session, where we brainstormed about ways to connect with consumers, making lists of places to meet them: Holistic health fairs, yoga studios, La Leche League meetings, food cooperatives, and farmer's markets figured prominently. Bars did not make the list of places to connect with homebirth consumers. But that didn't stop us: We ended the day in the grassroots, in a dusty bar in suburban Alabama, dancing.

THE RENAISSANCE OF MIDWIFERY IN THE UNITED STATES

Several cultural factors have converged to contribute to a renaissance in and revitalization of midwifery. Simultaneously, women were organizing as feminists around issues of reproductive care and as pro-choice activists around issues of abortion and gynecological self-help. Among pro-life groups, women were organizing around the sanctity of the fetus and the sacred role of women in birth and parenting. Subgroups within both feminist and pro-life communities shared a counter-cultural disdain for and distrust of a medical model that was no longer serving them. Among both sets of activists came the call to advocate for midwifery and access to midwifery care, as a political project.

Three books published in the 1970s became central to the politics and understandings of activists, each in a particular way: the Boston Women's Health Collective classic *Our Bodies, Ourselves* (1970), Barbara Ehrenreich and Deirdre English's *Witches, Midwives and Nurses: A History of Women Healers* (1973), and Ina May Gaskin's *Spiritual Midwifery* (1975). Ehrenreich and English were among the first to articulate a connection between the economic power of medicine and the marginalization (and fear) of powerful women. It is a connection that continues to resonate with pro-midwifery advocates. Midwifery advocates also, early on, articulated a need for women to engage in self-help and self-education to meet their own reproductive health care needs.

TABLE 2 Midwifery Messaging Grid

What midwives say about themselves	**What doctors say about midwives**
We are safe, well trained, careful, and licensed. We provide high-quality prenatal, birth, and postnatal care. We empower women to experience birth on their terms. For healthy low-risk women, we are a terrific option. Our slogans are: "Midwives Change Community" and "Midwives Deliver."	Midwives are unsafe, unregulated, dirty, uneducated, radical witches. "Home deliveries are for pizza."
What doctors say about themselves	**What midwives say about doctors**
We are necessary. We are safer. We are "baby and mom and family friendly." You will get a healthy baby out of the experience.	Doctors are unnecessarily intervention-heavy and provide routinized, impersonal, industrialized birth processes. Doctors view birth as a medical event, not a natural process. They want a monopoly on birth. But, they are great for emergencies.

The other two books provided some of the knowledge and means by which to resist. *Our Bodies, Ourselves* gave women a new understanding of their anatomy and physiology, and a way to understand their relationships to their bodies as political. *Our Bodies, Ourselves* provided women with the information they would need to take charge of their sexual and reproductive lives.

Gaskin's *Spiritual Midwifery*, a collection of birth stories narrated by the midwife herself, helped women understand their power in labor and delivery. It also highlighted and brought publicity to what happened on The Farm, the countercultural commune she and her husband Stephen founded in Tennessee, where birth was a community event, and outcomes were terrific. Accompanied by photos of long-haired, peaced-out women and men, Ina May's recounting of practices at The Farm changed the language of birth. She didn't talk about "contractions," she wrote instead of "rushes." She didn't call birth "painful," but instead encouraged women to experience the "sensations" of labor and delivery. Rather than focusing on the fear that came with childbirth, Gaskin focused on the power of women in labor. The stories in *Spiritual Midwifery* showed a diversity of birthing styles and positions. They celebrated the eroticism of some birth and the gentleness of others. The stories in that volume were handed down from woman to woman, as midwifery began its renaissance.

Since their publications, the organization of midwifery as a profession has been done in the light on midwifery cast by these books—and in the light of the cultural, economic, and structural phenomena and possibilities that they point to, especially the counter-cultural and back-to-the-land movements of the period. Raymond DeVries and Rebeca Barroso write:

> In the light of this new cultural atmosphere, midwives could renew their identity as a "low-tech, high-touch," women-centered occupation. The very image that had weakened the profession earlier in the century now gave them a niche in the medical marketplace.[2]

These books helped to renew midwives' identity as experts. It helped that midwives were reporting outstanding birth outcomes; those in practice at The Farm reported a 1.4 percent C-section rate after 2,028 births over thirty years, zero instances of maternal mortality, and eight infant deaths.[3]

By the 1970s and 80s, women had also begun to establish networks to help each other access midwifery care in the majority of states, even—especially—where it was not legal. Much like the Jane Collective and other organizations by which women provided abortion access to each other during prohibition, as well as self-help networks of women teaching each other how to do cervical self-exam and track their fertility,[4] these collectives and networks operated through friends and family who referred each other for care and vouched for the quality of the provider, as well as the identity of the person in need.

Peggy Vincent recalls that one day in the late 1960s or early 1970s, "A woman came into the hospital in San Francisco and the doctor wasn't there." There had been a tremendous lapse in communication, and Vincent had to find a midwife to deliver the baby. She did so by making "a quick call to Pat, the midwife, whom I'd certainly heard of. I knew she was unlicensed, one of those clandestine midwives who practiced on the fringes of the medical establishment, always aware she could be arrested at any moment. But I'd also heard only good things about her skills and integrity."[5]

The cultural movement also relied on and reinforced a wider feminist practice of research and publication as a political project of narrativity engaged in telling "better truths."[6] Books about natural birth disseminated these "better truths" about women's bodies, about women's experiences in hospitals, and about potential alternatives. The stories about hospital birth that began to be disseminated publicly were particularly poignant. Some of the most bitter truths found their voice in articulations of the sexism and disempowerment women encountered in hospital locales—both as nurses and as laboring people.

For instance, in her memoir of working as a nurse midwife in California, Vincent tells how a male medical resident continually harassed her and ultimately attempted to rape her, during their shifts together in a major Bay Area hospital. The year was 1962, and she was a nineteen-year-old nursing student.

Scholarship as early as the 1970s and 80s found that medical school textbooks and classrooms evidenced demeaning ideas of women, used demeaning language to describe them, and exhibited sexism that could cloud patient care.[7] Medical anthropologists and sociologists who study the discourses and conversations in exam rooms and among colleagues find that—regardless of their gender—doctors often use their power in the doctor–patient relationship to reinforce patriarchal and discriminatory attitudes and make assumptions about women, and especially women of color and women in poverty.[8] When feminist scholars studied power inequalities in these doctor–patient interactions, they found, "quite simply [that] gender was a part of the interaction."[9]

This felt especially true in interactions surrounding labor and delivery. Barbara Katz Rothman argues that medical expertise in hospital and clinical settings renders women "speechless on our own behalf, unsure of our own certainties." She locates this specifically in gender oppression, writing "One of the ways science silenced us was with that voice, that educated upper-class white guy's voice, making us all answer back with our accents, our screechy, uneducated, uncredentialed voices."[10] These screechy feminine voices were often overlooked during hospital birth, a practice that was disempowering when it happened, but that women turned into empowerment for activism around birth.

In Carol Leonard's memoir of becoming and practicing as a midwife in New Hampshire,[11] she recalls the birth of her son as *the* moment that she decided to change how birth happens—precisely because of how she was treated as a woman, and not as part of a counter-cultural politics or pre-formed feminist stance. She writes that she was joyful all day before she gave birth, knowing that she was about to deliver her child. Even though she was in labor, she hosted a planned dinner party for a group of construction workers who had spent the entire day building the house she and her husband would soon live in. After one particularly strong contraction, she told her husband it was time to go to the hospital—and told the guys to feel free to clean up after the dinner.

Leonard showed up at the hospital in a big flannel shirt, joking to her husband that she was a "tough mountain woman." She recalls that the older obstetric nurse "liked" her and was content to sit to the side when she labored. She remembers further that the contractions were horrible and she was unmedicated, and loud, and that the shift change to a newer, younger nurse was a low point in the delivery. Worse, though, was that the doctor on duty was her least favorite doctor in the practice; he was, she recalls, "a cranky, efficient, and officious man." Throughout the delivery, she experienced him as rude, cold, and even mean. As she birthed her son, she reached down to feel his head, and the doctor slapped her hand away, telling her he didn't want her to touch anything in the "sterile field."

As he stitched her after the episiotomy he performed for the vacuum extraction of her son, the doctor told her that she was lucky, he would do a "husband stitch" to make sure she was "tight enough" to make intercourse pleasurable for him. Even with the rush of oxytocin accompanying the birth of her son, Leonard was stung by his attitude. "I was pissed" she writes, and she asked herself, "what the hell is wrong with this picture?"

Within hours of giving birth, and against medical advice, she and her husband left the hospital, returning home, she writes, to regain her self. As Ina May Gaskin had noted in the preface to *Spiritual Midwifery*, "Women have been taught to believe that they must sacrifice themselves in important ways in order to have a baby,"[12] including acquiescing to major surgery, loss of autonomy in medical decision making, and loss of self in the process of birth. Leonard was uncomfortable enough to refuse that sacrifice. Reflecting on the experience in her memoir, Leonard recounts:

> Even though my delivery was considered a natural birth because I wasn't drugged, I've come to believe there was nothing "natural" about my experience at all. The rote hospital routines have mechanized the naturalness of birth until it is unrecognizable. There is nothing spontaneous or even sensible about being flat on your back with your hands tied down, like a restrained animal.

She felt belittled during the most sacred time in her life and vowed "to help other women have a more positive birth experience than I had." "This," she writes, "was the beginning of my life's work."[13]

Within a year, Leonard began working at a Woman's Health Center, training as a gynecological health care practitioner, and learning on the job; she found and connected with a family practice physician who attended homebirth. He let her shadow and apprentice with him. Between the two of them, a revitalization in out-of-hospital birth occurred in the region. "From 1973 to 1980," Leonard reports, "home births in New Hampshire will increase by 300 percent."[14] By the time Leonard's son was six, he had attended around 500 homebirths with her.

The experience of homebirth's growth in New Hampshire is not outside the norm. Relying on data from the US Institute of Medicine, Robbie

Davis-Floyd explains, "In 1970 the proportion of women giving birth in hospitals reached an all-time high of 99.4 percent . . . but between 1970 and 1977, the percentage of women giving birth at home more than doubled, from 0.6 percent in 1970 to 1.5 percent in 1977."[15] Quite simply, similar moments of radical self-empowerment had started other women on the path of midwifery, all around the country.

For example, in her memoir of her time as a midwife for Amish women in Michigan during the same general period, Kim Osterholzer also tells about how the medical model, and its disservice to families, instigated her practice through the birth experience she eventually had. Osterholzer's husband knew that she wanted to become a midwife but was surprised when she said she wanted to give birth to their first child at home, with a midwife in attendance. He initially refused the idea. But, he was a police officer, and one day he and his partner had to take an abandoned infant into the hospital. Osterholzer writes:

> Hour after hour, Brent stood silently in the shadows of the birthing floor, watching as doctors and nurses entered and exited the rooms of laboring families. He never told me exactly what he saw. I don't think he actually saw anything specifically objectionable. What he described for me when he returned, shaken and aged at the end of his long shift, was attitudes, perspectives, philosophies—attitudes and perspectives and philosophies out of step with ours [Osterholzer and her husband are born again Christians]. "Call the midwife, Kim," he said wearily, rubbing the kinks from his neck, "We're having this baby at home."[16]

Her pregnancy with her second child solidified her understanding of the limits of the medical model; after losing twenty-five pounds in four days from "morning sickness," she called the doctor for help and was told by a nurse "lots of new mommies feel yucky." When she used her expertise to try to access a particular treatment (one that became state of the art a decade later), she was ignored. And, when an IV line caused her tremendous pain, her protests were disregarded. She laid in the hospital bed and, she says, prayed for a miracle to enable her to leave.[17]

After her recovery from the ordeal of her second pregnancy, and the delivery of a healthy baby, she began her apprenticeship in earnest, studying from books required by her preceptor and attending at least one prenatal visit and one birth per month. During her first year, she recorded her presence as an apprentice at thirteen births, thirty-seven prenatal exams, and twelve postpartum visits. Like many midwives that I interviewed, Osterholzer insists that her practice is a "calling"—in her case, as she writes, "I knew without a doubt that God created me to be a midwife among the Amish."[18] The publication *From Calling to Courtroom* documents similar stories from midwives across the country who felt called by God, by goddess, by universe, and by self to serve laboring and delivering people as midwives.[19]

Often this coincided with the feminist health movement and was articulated as a process of consciousness raising and empowerment. Gaddey, a nurse midwife with a homebirth practice in Iowa, explains her entry into midwifery to me in this way during our 2008 interview:

> I think really what sparked my interest in women's health was just what was going on in the mid-seventies which was that kind of women's liberation movement. Women taking charge and, you know, I went to groups where we did our own pelvic exams on each other and on ourselves.
>
> And we'd talk about feminist issues. We joined NOW. . . . That's when I started entertaining going back to school to become an ob-gyn nurse practitioner.
>
> So . . . to make a long story short, I went knocking on the door of this now little grassroots group. These aren't people that you would hook up with.
>
> And I, uh, told them that I didn't really know anything about birthing centers but that I had been reading a lot about nurse midwives. And I understood . . . one of them was a nurse midwife and I said, you know, maybe I could do something in their effort. Didn't know what. And so they really said, "You know, gosh, thank you for your interest. We'll take down your number and we'll call you back."
>
> They never did. Months went by; I called them back. "Hey, I'm still around. I'm still interested. Isn't there something I could do? Stuff envelopes? I could do something." And once again, "No, don't think so." And . . . I just didn't let go. I kept calling every few weeks and finally they said, "Well why don't you just come to one of our board meetings which is gonna be at Sandy's house over on the East side." And I went.
>
> And that really was the turning point; because, it was—it was watching the midwives work, attending births, seeing another model of care

that I had never seen before. And then, within a year of the Birth Center opening, I became pregnant with our fourth. And so I had her with the midwives in attendance at the Birth Center.

> . . . It was the way it ought to be; you know, family focused and totally non-medical. . . . I had her at five in the morning. By three in the afternoon I was home. By seven that night I was making grilled cheese sandwiches for the family. And by 7:45, we were at the door with babe in Snuggly to the opening for the Botanical Center.[20]

I asked her if that birth was empowering; she responded "oh yeah." And from that birth, on, she was committed to becoming a nurse midwife.

As Gaddey's conversation with me illustrates, midwives in this period understood themselves as viable alternatives to the medical model and were convinced that, with their practice, women would be able to have better outcomes and better birth experiences.[21] Consumers from across a wide spectrum of American life agreed. Helen Varney and Joyce Thompson make clear that the growth in the number of community midwives was a direct response to consumer demand in the 1960s, 70s, and 80s.[22] This demand came about in large part through newsletters on alternative birth, childbirth education classes that taught Lamaze and other methods, the memoirs written by midwives profiled here, and consciousness raising among women and their care providers. Key among the insights that midwives and their advocates insisted upon was the understanding that *birth is not a medical emergency.*[23]

Though they may have read Ina May Gaskin's collection of birth stories, and they may be acting like feminists from the self-help movement, it would be wrong to think of the population of homebirth moms at this time as only made up of hippies, revolutionaries, or radicals. Some were, certainly, but many women who made the choice for out-of-hospital birth were not at all counter-cultural. Anthropologist and expert on out-of-hospital birth Robbie Davis-Floyd notes:

> The homebirth mother of the late 1960 and 1970s was as likely to be a childbirth educator or a conservative preacher's wife reacting against a negative hospital experience as a feminist seeking self-empowerment through birth or a hippie rejecting the hegemony of the medical establishment. Then, as now, she was likely to be middle class, which meant in

part that she was used to exercising her right to choose. Perceiving little room for choice in the standardized hospital births of the time, women across the country began to decide to give birth at home.[24]

Yet midwives' lack of legal status got in the way of their practice, and got in the way of consumers' accessing their services. So, simultaneous to growing their services, non-nurse midwives began state-level organizations to seek decriminalization and regulation. Carol Leonard became head of New Hampshire's pro-midwifery organization and writes that in 1981 she was

attending a birth in Manchester when our midwifery bill passe[d] the Senate. . . .

We have worked hard and by the time the bill reaches the Senate it is unopposed. I am proud. New Hampshire is the 9th state in the nation to legalize midwifery. I believe one of the reasons we are successful in our legislative efforts is because the Nurse Midwives and apprentice-trained midwives have all worked together as a sisterhood.

Governor Hugh Gallen is beaming at us. . . . [A]s far as he knows, NH is the only state in the nation with a voluntary midwifery certification program.[25]

In her exceptionally comprehensive history of nurse midwives and professional midwives in the United States, Judith Rooks points out that the "history and culture of the direct-entry midwifery movement" is "locale specific"—by which she means:

[T]he most rapid process toward establishing standards occurred within specific states through the work of local midwifery organizations, some of which developed their own certification processes. The standards developed by state midwifery associations vary with local circumstances, including licensing laws in states that have them.[26]

So, though New Hampshire was one of the first, and its bill was championed and passed because of the unique circumstances in the state, the model of working locally to achieve professional status was standardized across the United States. Within a few years of the New Hampshire law, more state legislatures moved to enact licensure bills that regulated midwives while permitting their practice. Others remained intransigent, and out of those, the contemporary social and political movement for legal status was born.

It was appropriate, too, that The Big Push met in Alabama in 2009, as that state was the ongoing site of attempts by midwives to gain legal status. Advocates in Alabama attempted legalization in 1983, which, according to a midwife involved in the struggle, "went over like a lead balloon." After being prosecuted for midwifery by Alabama, that midwife began the practice of driving to Tennessee to work with moms; Tennessee midwives have been legal and regulated since 2000. But, under risk of prosecution still in Alabama, she soon moved to Louisiana, which had licensed CPMs in 1985. They were the "fifth or sixth in the nation" to do so, she recalls.[27]

PROFESSIONAL, INDIVIDUALIZED AND UNIQUE

Almost all commentaries on contemporary certified professional midwifery in the United States agree that the early 2000s saw an expanded "emergence of traditional midwives who are claiming the *profession* of midwife."[28] Midwives have used both organizational and individual strategies to maintain relevancy in today's marketplace. While those strategies have "varied by context," in the United States, these strategies have included, overwhelmingly, "an emphasis on professionalization."[29]

This movement for professional status is both "meaning seeking" and "meaning making."[30] Robbie Davis-Floyd argues "Direct-entry midwives' efforts at professionalization and commodification contrast in fascinating ways with the ongoing value they place on their relationships with their clients and their grassroots social movement fervor."[31] This tension makes midwives uniquely poised to fill people's needs for authentic experiences of birth and family. When we understand this meaning seeking as a set of legitimation practices, which take place for midwives as everyday practices of their professional lives[32] and are especially fraught when undertaken within a "patchwork of legality,"[33] we see that the activism undertaken by midwives and their advocates fits rather seamlessly with the professionalization project of midwifery. Further, this project often benefits synergistically with national professional organization activities to legitimate the CPM credential, and midwifery as a whole.

One of my goals in this research has been to understand how midwives and their advocates view themselves as legal and political actors, and as positioned within a particular ideology of law and governance. For midwives and their advocates, the social practices surrounding professionalization and the legal and political practices surrounding regulation are in constitutive relationship to each other.[34] Professionalization is the ideology that brings legal consciousness into mobilization and constitutes the heart of the contemporary mainstream movement for midwives. By understanding themselves as reliant on legal status for the safety and expansion of their practice, midwives and their advocates understand that they need to be seen by the state, and by consumers, as professional. In the name of professionalization, midwives have:

- Sought legitimation of non-nurse midwifery, via national organizations, educational accreditation, industrywide standardization, and the development of best practices for assessment and peer review
- Responded to the increasing commodification of the birth experience by critiquing the medical model and constructing laboring women as, primarily, consumers who constitute a market for professional midwifery services
- Accepted (even welcomed) regulatory power and governance, such that pro-midwifery advocacy focuses on state-level legislative efforts to achieve legal status.[35]

This project of professionalization has been undertaken by national organizations like Midwives Alliance of North America and the North American Registry of Midwives. It has also occurred at the local and state level as midwives and advocates lobby for legislative change. And, this professionalization has taken place at national meetings of grassroots activists, like the one from which the opening vignette of this chapter draws: The Big Push, which attempts to facilitate communication across state-level organizations.

LEGITIMATION

Carol Leonard's early experiences with the growth of non-nurse midwifery in New Hampshire—plus quite a bit of serendipity—brought her to the forefront of national midwifery organizations, where she noticed early on a potential for the deep divide between nurse midwives and those seeking accreditation as professional midwives. Leonard was present at the first ever meeting of the International Conference of Midwives, held in El Paso, Texas, in 1977. Of that gathering of around 150 midwives, she writes:

> This meeting will prove to be the historic beginning of the renaissance of the world's oldest helping profession. Many of my heroes are here, the women who are the foundation stones of this new movement. They are charismatic, skilled, feisty, articulate, opinionated, wild, and beautiful midwives. Even with all the diverse backgrounds, what we find most inspirational is our commonality—our steadfast dedication to improving the health and welfare of mothers and babies, and our mutual respect and admiration for each other.[36]

Simultaneously, the American College of Nurse-Midwives became aware of the movement by direct-entry midwives to gain recognition and achieve legal status in the states. A key to legitimation for CPMs is helping the public understand their training as professional, but also distinct from the training received by CNMs. The growth of professional organizations distinct from the American College of Nurse-Midwives was deemed essential.

As Leonard tells it, Sister Angela Murdaugh, president of ACNM in the early 1980s, decided that nurse midwives and lay midwives needed to have a better relationship, even though, according to Leonard, Murdaugh met with tremendous resistance from her base. At Murdaugh's invitation, Leonard, Ina May Gaskin, and several other prominent lay midwives attended an ACNM meeting in Lexington, Kentucky, in 1982, where they hung home-made signs in an elevator that jokingly invited midwives to attend meetings of "The New AMA"—a play on American Medical Association. Their posters brought 100 women to a meeting. Leonard writes:

> Not surprisingly, many of the older and more seasoned certified nurse midwives express grave misgivings and resistance to allying with the "fringe midwives" citing their own long history of arduous years, working to garner respect and inclusion from the male-dominated medical profession.
>
> And yet the younger nurse-midwives stubbornly stand their ground. They are butting heads with authority. They express their belief that nursing should not necessarily be a mandatory prerequisite for midwifery study. Midwifery is a separate profession in its own right, of which nursing is only one component.[37]

From that spring gathering, the Midwives Alliance of North America (MANA) was born. In fall 1982, twenty midwives gathered in Boulder, Colorado, to write the bylaws for the new organization. DeVries and Barroso reflect on the founding of MANA:

> Repeated failures of state organizations to gain licensure, and increased prosecution of non-nurse-midwives for violation of medical practice acts, led to the creation, in 1982, of a new, national organization, the Midwives' Alliance of North America (MANA). The founders of MANA saw it not just as an organization of traditional midwives, but as an opportunity to promote the profession by connecting with other, more established midwives. Membership was open to all midwives, be they nurse-midwives or traditional midwives, and efforts were made to connect with midwife organizations in other countries and with the International Confederation of Midwives (ICM).[38]

And so, non-nurse midwives began to form national organizations for sharing knowledge, and, eventually, professionalizing. In the fall of 1983 they held the first official MANA national meeting in Milwaukee, Wisconsin—home of one of the first lay midwifery colleges in the nation, which was opened by and served European immigrant women in the late 1880s. Of this meeting, Leonard writes:

> It is an overwhelming success but not without its challenges. The most notable confrontation comes at the Open Meeting, where many of the midwives attending express fear and concern about MANA's attempt to define standards of practice for midwives. They are worried that we will be elitist or exclusionist somehow, and it will restrict their practices. . . . The angriest group, by far, are the midwives from West Virginia. . . . They are madder than a bunch of wet hens. They say "who the hell are you to try to tell us what to do?" I can see that they are just sick of being overlooked and disempowered—that causes them a lot of pain.[39]

Many of the controversies were nominally organizational—midwives debated what it meant, for instance, to write bylaws and a code of care and conduct, what it meant to adopt, as the young MANA did, the standards of the International Confederation of Midwives (ICM). At their core, these controversies were also about identity and practice, about legitimacy and power, about who could be recognized as a "midwife."

MANA's founding organizers understood that to the extent that the young association could build on its diversity as strength, it would be more successful. Member midwives made early agreements with each other to focus on the ways midwives provided labor and delivery care, to speak across difference, to recognize each other's expertise, and to support the work of legitimating their profession. Almost all who chronicle those early years stress that diversity again and again. In her book *Bun in the Oven,* Barbara Katz Rothman recalls

> walking into a lunch room at a meeting of the Midwives Alliance of North America sometime in the 1980s and looking at the interest groups that were gathered at round tables to discuss their concerns: Amish women with their traditional costumes, the hippies with their tie-dye costumes, the lesbian separatists in their flannel.[40]

To the extent that midwives respected each other, shared their stories, and built common cause, they believed MANA would flourish.

However, at the same time that diversity in the organization was both a strength and a challenge internally, MANA was finding that the heterogeneity of its membership was a difficult liability to overcome with nurses, nurse midwives, and other medical professionals. Tensions with ACNM continued. In 1984, Leonard, who had been elected vice president of MANA, traveled to Australia to begin the process of affiliating MANA with ICM. Leonard explains, "Our membership bid is controversial because we have midwives, like me . . . who are not nurses."[41]

Indeed, the American College of Nurse-Midwives took a position against including MANA in the ICM, on the grounds that MANA members lacked appropriate and legitimate professional knowledge. Leonard writes:

> I get into a quasi-friendly verbal fisticuffs with the president of the ACNM at a wine-and-cheese reception. She states that her opposition to us is that some of our members are apprentice-trained and lack formal schooling. I say that I will defend to my dying day the validity of hands-on apprentice training as equal, if not superior to, theoretical, didactic book learning.[42]

By the end of the ICM meeting, the vote was overwhelmingly in favor of allowing MANA to affiliate. The only negative vote, out of all of the nations with representation at the meeting, was the vote from the United States, via the ACNM.[43] "Because they had re-created midwifery in two different ways, it proved difficult for MANA and ACNM to work together. Each claimed," DeVries and Barosso argue, "to represent the true tradition of midwifery in the United States."[44] In fact, as Robbie Davis- Floyd chronicles these developments, ACNM sometimes worked at cross-purposes to MANA, at its sister organization, the North American Registry of Midwives (NARM):

> NARM began work on national direct-entry certification in the early 1990s and had its process [for the CPM] up and running by 1994. . . .
>
> But in 1994, after countless hours of deliberation on their own part, the ACNM passed a motion to develop its own direct-entry credential, which was later named the Certified Midwife (CM).[45]

MANA leadership, Davis-Floyd writes, did not see compromise with ACNM as possible. Rather, leaders "saw it as fundamentally detrimental to mid-wifery to require that midwives become nurses first, because they deeply believed in the value of a non-medicalized approach to birth."[46]

A further step in legitimation came a decade later. In May of 1996, representatives from MANA and NARM, joined by members of the Midwifery Education and Accreditation Council (MEAC) and the advocacy organization Citizens for Midwifery (CfM), gathered to write the Midwives Model of Care that those four groups adopted for their mutual use. The Midwives Model of Care charges practitioners with these standards:

> Monitoring the physical, psychological, and social well-being of the mother throughout the childbearing cycle; providing the mother with individualized education, counseling, and prenatal care; continuous hands-on assistance during labor and delivery; and postpartum support.

This model of care has been transmitted to midwives through publications, conferences, and the websites of these national organizations, and it serves a key role in delineating professional practice.

Davis-Floyd and Christine Barbara Johnson have edited a volume of essays that each focus on a different aspect of the "mainstreaming" of the midwifery movement, which they demonstrate has been the emphasis since the 1990s. Meetings of The Big Push and MANA have emphasized the modern and professional nature of evidence-based midwifery care. NARM has worked to standardize the requirements for credentialing and assessment, based on the evidence provided by midwives. Their professional organization has also helped state activists understand the benefits of licensure and regulation.

One important contribution of the Midwives Alliance of North America and the North American Registry of Midwives has come from their ability to speak in a more unified voice about CPMs as professionals and to engage in scientific legitimation. CPMs mobilize a discourse of evidence-based or evidence-informed practice that is essential to the construction of legitimacy for the profession. MANA session organizers adopted these terms after a "modified community café" with midwives and used them to express how midwives themselves view their relationship to data. Proponents of this terminology argue that it gives them more credibility with consumers and is useful in dialogue with other professional health care providers. They also assert that finding the "sweet spot" between clinical expertise, the best research evidence, client values, and individualized needs advances midwifery practice and promotes midwifery's values.[47] As a presenter at MANA noted, "The better the research evidence, the more confident we can be in our clinical decision making."[48]

Through the MANA Stats project, midwifery researchers and advocates can access important data regarding care, safety, and practice—which they can use to highlight CPMs as qualified health care professionals. As Sheila Kitzinger noted in 2005:

> Redefining the identity of the midwife must be linked with knowledge
> of research taking place internationally that has direct bearing on ways
> in which women experience birth and early motherhood, and the role of
> the midwife in creating a facilitating environment for a major life process.
> The new midwifery is *evidence-based.*[49]

The MANA Stats project currently includes at least twenty ongoing projects, including Melissa Cheyney's "Perspectives on Risk" project that has data from 15,660 cases entered by midwives nationwide from 2009–2012; as Cheyney explained in her talk at MANA, she has collected "data on every single thing you ever thought about doing in a birth." Her study features 1,000 data points for every course of care—individually, state-wide, and nationally—with her stated goal being to "leverage policy with data" in an effort to increase the visibility and legitimacy of the profession.

Formally, the movement toward professional status for midwifery has moved along three intersecting pathways: the adoption of the Midwives Model of Care, the development of a list of professional competencies for certification, and the growth of accredited midwifery educational programs. These pathways are interactive and mutually constitutive. They are not without controversy, as each carries with it the potential that some forms of knowledge, and knowledge transfer, will be lost. But, the growth in the numbers of certified professional midwives—after the CPM accreditation became widely available—has been significant. Davis-Floyd notes:

> In January of 1995, there were twenty-five CPMs. By June of 1998 there were approximately 400 CPMs; as of December 2005 [the year that I began researching midwifery in the United States] there were 1,095.[50]

And, as midwifery was growing as a profession, there was also a growth in the "certification economy" around it and around other alternative practitioners.[51]

Even in documentaries that are pro-homebirth, advocates note that, because there is no single qualification for midwifery education, there are fears about uneven midwifery training.[52] Therefore, the most important recent contribution of the national organizations that were engaged in the professionalization project and legal mobilization has been their participation in the US Midwifery Education, Regulation, and Association (US-MERA), with a nationwide attempt to standardize not only the competencies necessary to earn the CPM credential but the pathways for training by which those competencies are achieved. Over the course of more than a decade of fieldwork, I have witnessed no change with as great an impact as the adoption, since 2016, of US-MERA language in state bills.

The agreement, known simply as "US-MERA," is that by 2020, all newly registering CPMs would be required to have taken a MEAC-accredited educational route to their practice. CPMs who already have certification through a portfolio (PEP) process could ask to be "grandmothered in" with a "bridge certificate" prior to 2020. This bridge certificate, issued by NARM, is the culmination of a "process for CPMs to meet new professional regulation requirements in states with legislation requiring an accredited education by 2020 that will allow [portfolio accredited] CPMs to qualify for licensure."[53] PEP and apprentice-trained midwives wanting the bridge to US-MERA and CPM accreditation should have fifty hours of continuing education and coursework in maternal and peri- and prenatal emergency. These requirements, US-MERA advocates note, are very similar to what is already required by the CPM in terms of continuing education.

US-MERA wrote model legislation in 2016 and made it freely available to state organizers to tweak. Most of the states that had not achieved legal status for CPMs by 2016 indicated a willingness (albeit sometimes a reluctant willingness) to adopt US-MERA standards to move their bill forward. This was absolutely a case of a national agreement having local consequences.[54] The work toward the US-MERA agreement far predates the formal process by which it was ratified, and in fact, arguably dates back to the Homebirth Summits—small, invitation-only facilitated gatherings of practitioners (including ob-gyns) designed to discover if consensus could be reached around any of the key issues surrounding out-of-hospital birth. Partnerships formed at these summits included organizations that previously fought over out-of-hospital birth; the meetings brought together diverse groups like ACOG, NARM, MANA, and ACNM for productive conversations—a process that critics called "deal brokering."

The explicit US-MERA coalition formed in 2011. In summer of 2012, the US-MERA Steering Committee hired a consulting group and coach to facilitate the difficult conversations needed by these partners, establishing ground rules and mission. By fall of 2012, the group had undertaken a "gap analysis" to understand any misalignment among the constituent credentialing bodies, and ICM global standards—standards to which members of all the bodies would eventually adhere. And, in April 2013, the group held its first in-person meeting, with the goal of building trust and filling in knowledge gaps about practice. Because ACOG and ACNM have long had anti-homebirth stances, it was particularly important for stakeholders from NARM and MANA to feel respected and heard. A year later, five members from each stakeholder group that was a part of US-MERA met to begin their work to ensure the future of midwifery in the United States; at the end of their meeting, they'd agreed to develop and implement MEAC or ACME-accredited direct-assessment midwifery programs by 2020. In 2015, they reconvened at the Homebirth Summit to make that happen.[55]

The US-MERA agreement was reached via good faith consensus with the national stakeholders at the table, including a MANA representative (though the president of MANA at the time, Marinah Farrell, did not attend the 2015 meeting to protest the lack of Black women and women of color present). Simply put, US-MERA is a big deal. Undoubtedly, in the years I have studied movements for midwives, the most important event to change the landscape of legislation came from this self-regulation via a national movement of consensus building for credential changes.

Indeed, it is "huge," as an NACPM organizer said at MANA, that MEAC education is recognized by the United States Department of Education—as it means that midwives can get federal aid and student loans for undertaking their education. MEAC accreditation also provides protection for students; it gives them the capacity to hold educational programs accountable to benchmarks and standards, to delivering what they promise and advertise. And, the compromise brokered in US-MERA brings former opponents to the legislative table and makes passage of bills more likely. In South Dakota, just before legalization, an advocate told a group of volunteers at an information session, "Accredited schooling is going to be good for getting votes."[56]

In Iowa, after years of stalled progress and a refusal to negotiate, nurse midwives and nurses reached out to pro-CPM advocates, asking for a meeting to talk about legislation that would incorporate US-MERA language. The nurses said that they would be in favor of any scheme whereby "new states" (those not yet legal, including Iowa) would all adopt US-MERA language, with a bridge for portfolio process midwives allowed until 2020. They specifically told gathered stakeholders that the US-MERA educational requirement was what had moved them, and specific legislators, to support the CPM credential after dozens of years of vociferously arguing against it.

The legislators also saw US-MERA as a potential economic boon: Community colleges were willing to lobby on behalf of midwifery education. They realized that the nearest MEAC-accredited program was in Wisconsin and hoped that at least one of the state's two-year colleges would be able to start a viable program, keeping students in the state and drawing others to the region.[57]

At that 2017 summer meeting at Grinnell College, Iowa stakeholders made a list of all of the reasons that a bill to legalize, and perhaps regulate, made sense in the wake of the compromise. After more than a decade of organizing, "It's time," one participant said. Another added "Homebirth is going to keep happening," and regulation will "keep moms and babies safe." Legal and regulated homebirth, those gathered agreed, "is better for mom and baby." Even some of the midwives who had previously sought mere decriminalization and wanted to avoid state regulation were coming around to the idea, based primarily on the unsafe practices of some of their peers. One midwife spoke angrily of another, who was not present: "She delivered a footling breech a few weeks ago and posted it on Facebook." And, even the representatives from the ACNM, who had long been against legalizing CPMs in Iowa, were newly in favor of legislation.[58] One of the ACNM representatives present noted that she had had too many bad experiences with emergency transfer situations; legislation, she believed, would "make homebirth more transfer friendly," and thus, safer for moms and babies. In Michigan, the US-MERA language had allowed pro-CPM activists to get a coveted "neutral" position on their bill from both ACOG and the AMA.[59] Indeed, after years of inaction on several bills in numerous states, all of a sudden I witnessed compromise from former opponents and movement toward legal status.

US-MERA clearly served to legitimate CPMs to audiences who were previously suspicious. Just a few days before I sent this manuscript for publication, the Iowa Senate Committee on Rules held a hearing on a 2020 bill to legalize midwives; though we were optimistic about its potential, the bill died in committee in February 2020. One of the sponsors sent an email to Friends of Iowa Midwives leadership, expressing his regret that the hospital lobby had come out so strongly against the effort and showing his confidence that "there is a light at the end of the tunnel," with high hopes for next year.

COMMODIFICATION: MARKETING THE MIDWIFE-ATTENDED BIRTH EXPERIENCE

Advocates have multiple ways of messaging about midwifery. They use movies, speakers, letters to the editor, rallies, and websites to disrupt the hegemonic assumption that hospitals are the best and only place for birth to occur and to offer midwifery as a professional and attractive alternative.

Midwifery advocates make a wide range of assertions concerning hospitals, especially focusing on how women experience birth in the hospital setting. Most arguments against hospitals as the best locale for low-risk birth point out the risks associated with medicalizing birth and having it occur in an intervention-heavy environment; they focus on the fact that hospitals are vectors for disease and assert that pregnancy is not an illness, birth not an emergency. They focus, as well, on the discomfort women face in hospital settings—from an unwanted and unsafe cascade of interventions, to a lack of family-friendly spaces, to the birth violence that a stunningly large number of women report at the hands of doctors and nurses. The hospital birth experience, advocates rather convincingly argue, is extremely problematic.

Further, out-of-hospital birth advocates argue that the literal price women pay for these births is too high. In 2017, the pre-insurance bill for an average hospital birth in the United States was around $18,000; the average bill for a C-section topped out around $28,000. In the popular 2016 documentary *Why Not Home?*, the narrator tells us that the US birth care system is "a $22 billion per year industry." Midwives contrast these figures to the cost of an average homebirth, which, the film tells us, averages $4,000— and is significantly less expensive than that in rural areas. In states where Medicaid and private insurance companies reimburse for birth attended by CPMs, the out-of-pocket cost is even less.

Bringing attention to the lower cost of midwifery, and serving economically marginalized clients, are not sufficient, however, to the project of professionalization. Nor does doing so enable a midwife to earn an independent living. Barbara Katz Rothman writes, "Talking about midwifery and home birth as cost-savings is good—but when we have something that saves costs, it also fails to generate revenue."[60] Midwives, she advises, should go after elite clients, too—and make a name for themselves as highly skilled and artisanal.

Nor is it sufficient to bring to light the problems associated with in-hospital birth. Legalizing midwifery and expanding access to out-of-hospital birth involves bringing these problems to light, while *simultaneously* raising awareness about alternatives. Midwives and advocates must also include in their messaging the fact that well-regarded research indicates the "health, cost, and quality of care outcomes in midwife-led maternity care are comparable with and in some cases preferable to those for patients with physician-led care."[61]

Finally, midwives must differentiate themselves from hospital birthing centers and family-friendly rooms. They are often quick to point out that while those places might be comfortable, the comfort merely masks the technology. And, they might add, "Home is where a woman can be *herself*."[62] The message sent by advocates is clear: Families don't need to skimp on safety in order to save money and experience out-of-hospital birth.

All of this involves imagining (and selling) contemporary midwifery care as offering an "artisanal," "empowering," "individualized," and "woman-centered" experience. Like the "slow food movement," Barbara Katz Rothman argues, pro-midwifery movements are focused on consumption (of experiences), not production; they organize consumers, not workers.[63] The midwife-attended birth experience becomes a commodity. Commodification of this sort may well be an essential part of any route to legitimation and a regulated market for formerly illegal or out-of-the-mainstream products and practices.[64]

Nor is commodification of motherhood and the birth experience particularly new.[65] As anthropologist of birth Robbie Davis-Floyd noted as early as 2006, there has been "intense commodification of reproduction," in both hospital and out-of-hospital birth circles.[66] Partially in response to cultural cues, she writes, "Commodification forms a major part of the strategy that midwives and their consumer allies employ to obtain legality."[67]

Commodification of midwifery services is constitutive with movements to legalize midwifery, especially now that those movements have been cast as "consumer organizations." As a media and public relations consultant noted at The Big Push Summit in 2009, midwives must organize their consumer base for both purposes, as activists and as clientele, and market to them appropriately. Rothman goes even further, writing:

> Take something exotic, make it in a commune (think soy ice cream at The Farm), talk about peace and love, the planet and vegetarianism and all that— watch it get branded, sold, and brought into the marketplace. It's not a bad thing—it's the kind of success I only wish we'd see for the birth movement.[68]

As we can expect given the shift to an "experience economy" in post-industrial capital,[69] pregnant and laboring women have been re-imagined as "health care experience consumers." It is a move that shifts the conversation from rights to services, and often high-end services at that.[70]

While many women will end their stories of uncomfortable and disempowering hospital birth stories with a statement like, "But, we got a healthy baby out of it!" others say, "I don't think you can separate the experience from the outcome."[71] Rothman wants midwives to speak in a way that values their own skills—even as she acknowledges that this can be at odds with the way that they talk about birth as a natural experience, with expertise about birth resting in the hands of the laboring mother. As she notes, in reality, it takes thousands of hours of training and practice to be a strong midwife. She argues that we need to recognize the practice as an "artisanal craft," and stresses, "Midwives are not mass-producing births: each birth is focused on the individual woman, her needs, her life. The process is important, and not just the product."[72]

Almost uniformly, successful marketing of homebirth has been done by focusing on the out-of-hospital birth experience as *safe, unique,* and *personal*—a *birth experience* that has a positive impact on moms, babies, and families. In the film *Why Not Home?* one homebirth client tells viewers, "It was the best experience I ever had." Even her prenatal exams exceeded her expectations; talking about those experiences she says, "I get choked up. . . . All moms should experience this. . . . It was a really nice experience."[73] One of the most popular of all of the pro-midwife documentaries, *The Business of Being Born,* features, in part, model-beautiful women having serene water births with supportive partners in chic New York City apartments.

Of course, not every client has a pregnancy or health history appropriate for out-of-hospital birth. Proper client screening, coupled with well-documented informed consent, mitigates risk of legal trouble for midwives. In fact, much of a midwife's initial intake and continued interactions with a potential client centers around her determination that the client doesn't have a condition that "risks her out" of her midwifery practice. Level of risk is determined oftentimes by regulatory governance—some states will not allow breech births at home, or VBACs, for instance. Diabetes, obesity, and high blood pressure are all conditions considered to be dispositive against out-of-hospital birth. And, some midwives are simply uncomfortable with providing services to particular clients given their medical history or presentation—and will deem their risk profile unacceptable to their practice, perhaps suggesting alternative care providers for her and offering referrals.

When a midwife does accept a client, and at every step of her care, the principle of informed consent is paramount. Midwives consider their role as educators to be central in the provision of service; many midwives offer information about nutrition, exercise, and preparations for labor and delivery. They are also clear on the need to inform clients about the various tests and procedures relevant to pregnancy—such as amniocentesis, ultrasound, and fetal heart tone monitoring—as well as to provide information about routine prenatal and postpartum care.

Many midwives consider it their duty to provide information and then allow parents and clients to make decisions regarding their care. Documenting informed consent is not merely a means to avoiding legal trouble: It is a foundational principle of quality care for midwives, that their clients are educated about birth, nutrition, and their bodies as part of the process of serving them. It is also a way to begin the personalization of the birth experience.

Such personalization is especially important for marketing out-of-hospital midwifery as artisanal and skilled. Rothman writes, "Someone is pregnant, thinking about the kind of birth she wants. . . . She picks the one that feels most like her, like the kind of person she is, the kind of family she wants to be making."[74] She explains:

> Rather than settling for an industrialized hospital birth, midwifery offers an alternative, a hand-crafted, individually made, and personally catered birth. Midwives can do that because they have the skills, the craft, to individualize the birth to the woman, to meet her physical, psychological, and familial needs.[75]

Midwife and long-time activist Susan Hodges likens midwifery to artistry. It is "painstaking, patient, unique." Hospital birth, she says, is like being in a factory, with an emphasis on efficiency, money, and management.[76]

In her presentation at MANA in 2017, Rothman told the assembled midwives, "What you're selling is your values."[77] Midwives' values are skilled labor in attending to birth, empowerment of the laboring person, and a view of birth as a normal (not a medical) event. As she notes, we must value "expertise, true traditional skills and knowledge, a shared, communal, cultural heritage embodied in the worker."[78] Though some have pushed back at this language of "selling values" to "consumers,"[79] many midwives are becoming more comfortable with demonstrating the value of their expertise and knowledge through commodification; this is in large part because they see that it works to build clientele, grow legitimacy, achieve legal status, and change birth culture one consumer at a time.

Certainly, like Rothman, midwives often see the marketing and commodification of birth as central to the push for legalization. As Rothman said at MANA, to applause, "As much as we need to be in DC and the statehouse we need to be in Hollywood." And, midwives need to cultivate a professional image that plays well with legislators and consumers, an image far removed from cultural stereotypes of midwifery and more in line with Hollywood's. Framing their advocacy within a project of professionalization, and adopting a professional "look," has been part of their success in engaging both consumers and the state. Indeed, a growing comfort with professionalization is part of the legal consciousness within which midwives and advocates operate.

A PROFESSIONAL IMAGE

In her memoir, Carol Leonard includes several stories that speak volumes about the negative image that midwives have had to fight as they sought respect for their profession. She tells of one notable interaction with a doctor she calls Dr. Faith. After having a client give birth while en route to the hospital during an unplanned transport, Leonard brings her in for a postpartum check, and Dr. Faith is enraged. "Who the hell are you?" she recalls him asking her. After she explains she is her midwife, he explodes: "Her *what*? Her midwife? What's that? Like a witch doctor? You just drum and chant and burn some sage, and pray the baby comes out all right?" No shrinking violent, Leonard tells him off—before he turns away from the interaction, he spits in her face.[80]

Leonard tells another story that occurred much later, after legalization of midwifery in New Hampshire, while she and her ob-gyn husband attended an ACOG meeting. The wife of another doctor, upon learning that Carol was a midwife, exclaimed, "Midwife? Dear God! Wasn't that made illegal at the turn of the century, along with prostitution?"[81]

These experiences are not outliers. Leonard's recollections are reinforced by other midwives' memoirs and by my interviews with them. Peggy Vincent remembers, in the mid-1990s, a doctor asking her, "Jesus, what is it with you midwives, never medicating your patients? Is it some kind of ritual female bonding? Something about suffering?"[82] Sue, a CPM in California, told me:

I've had doctors say to me in Orange County, "If it wasn't for people like you, people like her [a client she transferred for care] wouldn't attempt this at home," which is ridiculous. . . . If it wasn't for people like me . . . I'm trained . . . licensed to carry Pitocin and anti-hemorrhage drugs; I'm trained to notice when things go out of the range of normal, you know. If it wasn't for people like me, people like her would try it at home unsafely.

These midwives came to understand that remaking midwifery and gaining legitimacy had to be accomplished at least partly by remaking their image. This quite often literally began with their clothes.

In her memoir, Vincent recalls a conversation with one of her clients, a plaintiff's malpractice attorney who specialized in obstetric claims. As they talked about the meetings Vincent had to attend regarding the authorization of her practice to receive hospital privileges, her client asked, "What do you wear to these meetings?" Vincent remembers, "I thought it was an odd question, but I said 'just this usually,' pointing to my loose pants and T-shirt. 'Oh, no no no no no' she said, 'You've got to look professional. Powerful. Strong.'"[83]

Reading this, I recalled the time our lobbyist pointed at me and said, "Leave the backpacks at home. Carry a good purse, or a briefcase." He went on, telling everyone else, "Don't show up looking like witches or hippies." An organizer in Michigan recalled that she had been told a bit more kindly, "You need to dress for government to see and understand you."[84] And, a member of South Dakota Safe Childbirth Options/Birth Matters remembers a legislator telling her, after her first session lobbying in Pierre, that it was important to project a particular image: "You need to show," he stressed to her, "that there are professional women who want and need homebirth."[85] For him, part of this was about the visual representation of homebirth moms at the capitol—not wanting them to seem fringe; it was also, crucially, a way to highlight that the very small number of families that would be impacted by the law—seen by many legislators as boutique legislation—are families that vote, constituents who donate.

Sometimes, too, the understanding of the power of professional image making came through interactions with opponents. Leonard writes about one of these particular interactions in her memoir. In the late 1990s, she was asked to film a conversation about birth for Dartmouth Medical School's closed-circuit television program. Leonard was one of large group of invited speakers; the others were "several obstetricians, a few nurse-midwives, and me, representing apprentice-trained midwives":

> To this day I can remember what I wore for that discussion, because of the conversation that ensued with the MD, a perinatologist from Vermont, who was seated next to me. I was wearing a conservative Harris-tweed suit in a beautiful mauve heather. He is the joker whose car in the parking lot has a bumper sticker that reads:
>
> HOME DELIVERIES ARE FOR PIZZAS
>
> The doctor leans over to me and whispers, "There's going to be a lay midwife here today, you know."
>
> I feign surprise, "Really?"
>
> He says, "Yes, and I have it on good authority that she bites umbilical cords with her teeth to sever them, instead of cutting them with scissors. Some kind of primal, animal thing I guess."
>
> . . . Obviously, this man assumes that I must be a nurse-midwife, probably because I look more professional that he has anticipated.
>
> I can't resist. "So what does she look like?"
>
> He looks around. "I don't think she's here yet. You know those lay midwives all look alike. They all have greasy, stringy hair and wear ill-fitting dresses and big work boots. And they all have a violent hatred of the medical establishment."
>
> It is my turn to present my talk. As I am introduced and get up to speak, my neighbor looks stricken.
>
> I flash my teeth at him. Biting cords, indeed.
>
> Bite my pizza.[86]

In order to be seen as professional, Vincent and Leonard and others came to understand that midwives must not be seen as witches, wild women, hippies, or grannies. This changing image is a key part of the legitimation of midwifery. This would be a recurring theme when advocating on legislation and when marketing midwifery care.

With professionalization came national instructions about how to cultivate a particular image, often defined more in relationship to what CPMs and their clients are *not*, rather than what they actually are. At a Big Push Summit in 2009, one organizer told the group assembled, "Don't say 'activist' or 'advocate'—those are not good words. Say 'consumer' or 'constituent' instead." She continued, "Also, we don't say 'homebirth' anymore because it's too fringy; we say out-of-hospital birth." Another speaker at this event told advocates, "You can be passionate and emotional—but don't be crazy. Back everything up with data." He then launched into an hour-long presentation on how to use YouTube, Square Space, and other social media that was met with avid attention.[87]

The engagement of midwives and consumers with professionalization is a project that, at its core (and like so many political projects), mobilizes a desire to be seen and recognized by the state.[88] Activism on behalf of certified professional midwives is similar to previous generations' activism around the recognition of the expertise, scope of practice, and social standing of lawyers and doctors, as well as chiropractors, massage therapists, aestheticians, and dieticians. Midwives are following in the footsteps of professionals globally; and, especially in the context of their criminal status in several states, it should not be a surprise that midwives and their advocates want legitimation and acknowledgment of the status of their profession, even when such recognition brings state regulatory policy.

Contemporary political currents within individual states matter to this process of professionalization, as do the broader contexts of contemporary feminisms and neoliberal discourse. The states where midwives remain illegal or unregulated are quite often red states; they are states with legislative bodies and executive branches that are controlled by the Republican Party. As such, in their conversations with state legislators, midwifery advocates don't usually seek reproductive freedom or justice; they don't talk about health care as a right and women's reproductive autonomy as a desirable goal. Rather, they talk about safety, public health, self-funded regulatory agencies, and cost cutting.

Yet even in these jurisdictions, midwives and their advocates necessarily, and actively, seek the state's regulatory gaze; they speak a language of science ("evidence-based care") and professionalism (calling themselves "modern midwives" who serve "clients"). And they realize that even after legalization, mundane issues like the composition of the regulatory board (how many doctors? how many nurses? how many consumers and midwives themselves?), sunset provisions, and scope of practice rulemaking become increasingly and incredibly important. Therefore, legal consciousness in the form of legitimacy-seeking professionalization and regulation is enacted via complex and overlapping political and legal mobilization strategies.

The political and legal mobilization that midwives and their advocates engage in is most frequently centered on helping families gain access to their services, which also helps ensure that midwifery is a vibrant and viable profession. When families can find midwives, they can pay to hire them; when midwives can be paid, they can practice their craft and expand their client base. The more midwives attend out-of-hospital births, the more normalized such births become, and the wider the potential client base.

Access to certified professional midwifery depends on an ability to market midwifery as both safe and unique, which in turn depend on the decriminalization of the practice, its assurance of safety via accreditation and educational requirements, and—quite often—the regulation of the practice by the state. In sum—as many scholars have previously, and convincingly, argued—the political and legal mobilization of midwives and their advocates often centers on "making midwives legal"[89] and "mainstreaming midwives"[90] via practices of professionalization.[91]

Pro-midwifery advocacy involves political mobilization, social movement activism, legal mobilization via obstetric violence litigation and criminal defense of midwives, and legal mobilization through engagement with regulatory bodies—almost always, from the 1980s through the contemporary period, through a frame of professionalization. Such mobilization, advocacy, and activism also include cultural work: picnics and community building, screening films and hosting speakers, as well direct action and political mobilization meant to disrupt commonsense notions of hospital birth and midwifery care. The next four chapters detail the unique, savvy, strategic, and often joyful ways that midwives, moms, and others have been mobilizing for midwives.

3 MOSTLY HAPPY ACCIDENTS

Successfully Mobilizing for Legal Status

> "You guys learned how things are done! Sneaky! Sneaky!"
> —Legislator to the Missouri Midwives Association, after their bill passed

OPHELIA'S EXPERIENCE as the subject of police investigation in Missouri was an impetus for the legislation that she helped to shepherd through the statehouse, but the story of her becoming a midwife, and then midwifing the bill through the legislature, encompasses so much more than that incident. In fact, Ophelia, one of the people most responsible for the legalization of midwifery in Missouri, was born at home herself, in 1982, in an unassisted labor and delivery, because, as she told me, "In the 1980s in Missouri, illegal midwives would do checks, but not births." At the time, out-of-hospital midwifery was a class C felony and carried a potential seven-year jail term. But, after attending her sister's birth as a teenager, Ophelia decided birth was "cool." She finished high school and attended Midwifery School of America via distance education.

In Missouri at the time Ophelia began to practice, there was only one certified nurse midwife openly practicing, but "everyone I knew had had an illegal birth." By the mid-2000s, an estimated 1,000 homebirths took place every year in Missouri, the vast majority of them attended by illegal lay midwives.[1] Her friends asked Ophelia, "Are you sure you want to do that? You can go to prison in Missouri." She reflected on the answer she gave her friends: "I said I'd move, or maybe the law would change." Serving women in her community, she felt, was "doing the right thing." And, doing the right thing,

Ophelia continued, "really appealed to me, *in spite of what the law said.*"
Ophelia knew that midwives couldn't just change the law on a whim. She
told me: "People would say to me, 'Why don't you just go change the law?'
And I would think, Why don't you just go change the speed limit."

Without a robust peer group in her state, Ophelia attended national conferences to network and learn. And, she spent time in Illinois with CNMs—
CPM practice was then, and still is, illegal in Illinois. One certified nurse
midwife in particular caught her attention:

> She was very professional and really supported women in breastfeeding.
> It was weird to me that she was a midwife, and everyone knew. In Mis-
> souri, the conversation would be more like "I can't tell you who my mid-
> wife is, but she's a nice lady."

Back in Missouri, a direct-entry midwife told her that she'd heard Ophelia
had worked with a CNM in Illinois and offered her a job, "She said: 'I'll pay
you $200 to attend and assist.' During this time, I also had a nanny job for a
doctor and I could not tell him what I was doing. They just thought I was a
nice little nineteen-year-old." Over the course of three or four years, Ophelia
attended births with "two or three midwives in a 200–300-mile radius." In
doing so, she realized, "Births would be safer, if moms could find midwives."

Soon enough, Ophelia was introduced to the president of the Missouri
Midwives Association. The organization became very important to her, but,
she smiles when she tells me, before that introduction, "I didn't even know
there was one." When she heard about it, Ophelia remembers thinking,
"That sounds like a professional organization that I should just be able
to join." In fact, people couldn't attend MMA meetings unless they knew
someone in the group; a midwife had to vouch for her and secure her an
invitation.

There were fifteen women at the first meeting she attended, and Ophelia
heard things that concerned her. She tells me, "Some of the ladies there said
things like 'I don't even chart or anything; there's never a paper trail.'" And,
at a business meeting, they discussed a request from an outside anthropologist who wanted statistical data to help in the national case for legalization. The request was too controversial to be met, and the conversations,
according to Ophelia, were "contentious." It seemed to her, she told me
years later, that sharing data should be encouraged. Instead, midwives in

Missouri "had basically made a pact to stay quiet," because "whenever they shared things, someone got arrested." They subscribed to the view that they "shouldn't pursue legislation, because if people at the capitol know there are midwives, they'll just go after us."

The decision to maintain the status quo and stay below the radar might not have been disrupted had it not been for a chance encounter. According to Ophelia, Missouri Constitution Party gubernatorial candidate and House Representative Cynthia Davis was on an airplane, seated next to Ina May Gaskin and Robbie Davis-Floyd—absolute giants in the field of midwifery care and physiologic birth. Upon learning where she was from and the constituency she represented, Gaskin told Davis, "Your state has a horrible law for midwives." It turns out that Davis herself had had seven children by caesarean section and had wanted to attempt a VBAC, but could not find a doctor to support her. She had no idea that legalizing midwifery would have given her more options early on in her childbearing years, and, as a Constitution Party libertarian, she was in favor of unregulated and decriminalized practice.

Upon return to Jefferson City, Davis took immediate action. She wrote and filed a bill without consulting anyone. Everyone—doctors and midwives—showed up to oppose it.

The next year, 2004, Davis told midwives: "I'm gonna file a bill again to make you legal." She further specified, "It has to be a small bill that doesn't add any words to the state law—which is a personal rule of mine." Ophelia laughs, now, saying, "I think she was originally going to just take laws off the books, but then she realized you sometimes have to make law, too." A consumer and a midwife co-hosted a meeting in St. Louis to iron out the language of the bill. After five hours, they came up with this: "No Missouri law shall encroach on a mother's right to give birth in a setting she wants with whomever she wants." Davis loved it—it was the best, for her, in offering small government and no regulation—and it would presumably keep midwives out of jail. The bill was filed as HB36 in 2005 with enthusiastic support of the Missouri Midwives Association and Friends of Missouri Midwives.

Ophelia remembers, "Most of us, in 2005, didn't know anything about lobbying." She adds, "If someone had suggested I go lobby I'd have said that's ridiculous." Representative Davis told them that the most important thing was to fill up the room at the committee hearing, so the next Missouri

Midwives Association meeting was held at the capitol. Ophelia brought "two random friends, one of whom was a "homebirth mom who wanted an adventure." The plan was simply to give a two-page fact sheet to the state representative, or better yet for these nervous newcomers, to the representative's assistant. But, the first office they stopped at, the assistant wasn't there, and Ophelia and her friends "ended up in a mortifying conversation with the rep." She tells me, "I left there thinking, 'I'm *never* going to do that again.'" She instead looked forward to the committee hearing, where she says, "I thought, 'All I have to do is warm a chair.'" In fact, though, Davis arranged for Ophelia to have a private conversation with the chair and vice chair of the House Children and Families Committee, prior to the hearing before that body. Ophelia was grateful that the forty-five-minute chat was "really nice" and that the vice chair of the committee was a former La Leche League leader—"She was just fine, too, to talk with." In fact, that day, "We had eight great conversations. I know now how rare that is."

During that first hearing, midwives and legislators heard "really good, really convincing testimony from [two medical doctors], one of whom told the legislators, 'Everything I learned [about birth], I learned from midwives.'" "We had real MDs testifying," Ophelia tells me, "and the medical opposition was caught unprepared with just a lobbyist, no docs there on the other side." Ophelia continues, "The bill was voted out of committee; as it went to the House floor, Cynthia said 'Now we have 163 people to educate!'"

That began a two-month period in Jefferson City, with Ophelia and her colleagues spending two or three days a week "having good conversations and gaining confidence." At that time, there were "four core ladies" working to pass the bill. They were: "just a homebirth mom," a college student who was a "passionate supporter," Ophelia, and the president of Missouri Midwives Association. "We got a great political education," Ophelia tells me, "because before then none of us had any idea of how to do politics. The legislators would ask 'Are you a midwife?' and I would answer 'I hope to be.'" This was her answer, even though she was attending homebirths, illegally, as an apprentice midwife in the state.

The bill died in the Senate's General Laws Committee that year, without so much as a hearing or a vote. The head of the committee was a "stodgy lawyer, single, with no kids." Ophelia opines, "He listened to the doctors because they were the only experts he knew. We packed the room for the hearing, but he killed it." One senator, though, had a homeschooling wife who wanted to learn more about midwifery; she brought her kids to Ophelia's house and chatted. She told Ophelia, "I loved my C-section, but I have friends who have homebirths in my church." And, she disclosed that she had been having trouble with miscarriages early in her pregnancies. Ophelia used her expertise to help this mom understand what was going on in the pregnancies and how to potentially mitigate the problem. When she carried her next child to term and had a healthy (hospital) delivery, her husband the senator considered himself in true debt to the midwives of the state. He told Ophelia, "I will do anything you want me to do," even as he also acknowledged, "I'm kind of a far-right guy, not the most popular person around here."

Indeed, he was far to the right of even Missouri conservatives at the time, running on a two-plank platform: anti-abortion and anti-gambling. Midwives understood his liabilities across partisan lines but also recognized him as strategic, entrepreneurial, smart, and articulate. That senator made good on his promise by helping the midwives think more strategically about the legislators, and advising them to connect legislators with constituents that cared about what they cared about. One senator, for instance, was married to a teacher and cared about education; to meet with him, they found a teacher constituent who was also a homebirth mom.

For several more years, different versions of a bill to legalize or decriminalize CPMs floated through various committees of the Missouri Senate and House. Ophelia says that even the senator who frequently carried the bill to committee "didn't really care about" it—"it wasn't his priority." He seemed to think of the midwives as merely "cute little housewives with a bill."

And, legislators (almost always with no medical experience) were often incredibly patronizing to them. One told Ophelia, "I understand you want moms to do what they want—but some moms make bad decisions." In her role as the leader of New Hampshire's midwifery organization, Carol Leonard had often attended legislative hearings in states where folks wanted to legalize midwifery and had experienced the same thing. She writes, "These hearings, along with the self-aggrandizing, upper-class, middle-aged white men who are so belittling and patronizing, *make me so angry.*"[2] Leonard recalls being asked to give testimony in Louisiana, a state early to legalize; she was

> shocked at how sexist and condescending the puffy legislators are. My testimony is based on data compiled by the Louisiana midwives in conjunction with the state's Bureau of Vital Statistics. . . . One of the "good ole

boys" . . . says, "now, don't you worry your pretty little head about nuthin'
darlin. We'll take care of everything. We don't need you botherin' with all
these numbers and such."[3]

Back in Missouri, decades later, perceived allies abandoned the pro-midwifery cause, exacerbating the tensions surrounding the image of midwives
and homebirth moms. A liberal pro-choice Democratic senator threatened
to filibuster the bill, in Ophelia's opinion, in order to keep the medical lobby
from ousting him from office after his vocal opposition to tort reform. In
response, his constituents reacted angrily: "Columbia [a university town]
hippie homebirth pro-choice moms came down [to Jefferson City, the state
capital], furious." He refused to meet with them. Their high-profile presence
also angered legislators who were nominally supportive; after they left, a
legislator called Ophelia and told her:

> You've gotta look good up here. No nursing three-year-olds. This is a pro-
> fessional building. I want you to do your hair nice. I want to see you all
> up here in pantyhose and suits. No more paisley skirts; that's what hippies
> wear. I want pencil skirts.

So, Ophelia says, "We spiffed up our looks and told everyone to please dress
up." She smiled ruefully as she told me, "We really cleaned up our image
when we went to the capitol."

But, angered at these directives, the Columbia people had a rally—and
"of course the press focused on a lady with dreadlocks belly dancing." The
legislator who had originally called Ophelia was *beyond mad.* He called
her again and yelled into the phone: "You make sure your people wear
deodorant—the good kind—not the hippie kind!" She was living in Jefferson City five days a week by this time, working round the clock to both
deliver babies and birth a bill. Recalling his anger, she looks me in the eye,
"I wanted to know, do any of the other lobbyists get lectured on what kind
of shoes they wear?"

But help was on the way, in the form of a young policy director for one
of the legislators interested in the bill. She came up with a novel approach:
"Why not," she asked Ophelia, "just amend a bill—get yours attached to
something else?" She went on, "The opposition's guy is lazy. . . . Why don't
you just come up with ambiguous language that doesn't say midwife?" She

thought again for a moment, and directed Ophelia, "Just think of a word that means midwife that isn't 'midwife.'"

As it happens, one of the folks helping out at the capitol was a homeschooling teenager who wanted to learn about politics and tagged along with her dad—an attorney and lobbyist who was offering the group free advice and strategy. A few days after this conversation, she came up to Ophelia, very excitedly, and said, "I think I know a word! I get an email every day with a new word to study for the SAT, and I saw this one . . . 'tocology': the branch of medicine concerned with childbirth!" They ran the idea to legalize "tocology" by amending a separate bill past their bill's sponsor, who okayed the strategy and added, "Just add some federal code that references midwives. No one ever looks up federal code." Ophelia went and googled federal code: "We worked on it like it was a job, or a secret project," she smiles.

Under Missouri law, amendments to bills must be germane to the topic amended. A supportive senator was pushing a big insurance bill; his staff agreed that the provision of birth services via a trained attendant was a matter that was germane to insurance, so they added this language to the bill:

> Notwithstanding any law to the contrary, any person who holds current ministerial or *tocological certification* [emphasis added] by an organization accredited by the National Organization for Competency Assurance may provide services as defined in 42 U.S.C. 1396 r-6(b)(4)€(ii)(I) "services related to pregnancy (including prenatal, delivery and post-partum-services").

Ten years later, Ophelia tells me about what happened when she attended a birth in 2007:

> I remember the mom was laboring on her hands and knees and I was holding a warm compress on her perineum and my cell phone was buzzing. . . . I emerged from the birth [hours later] and found out [the language made it] into the Senate bill, no one questioned it and it's gone to the House.

She looks at me a bit incredulously:

> We thought the lobbyists would go through the bill and people would notice. . . . But no one noticed. So, we just acted like normal. They *did not read the bill*; and didn't even know that "tocology" was in there.

The bill passed both houses, and went to the governor for his signature. Ophelia laughed as she told me, "The House Rules guy said to me, 'You guys learned how things are done! Sneaky! Sneaky!'"

POLITICAL MOBILIZATION STRATEGIES: LOBBYING FOR LEGISLATION

The original thrust of legislative organizing around certified professional midwifery was simply to pass bills to decriminalize their practice. In its first years, the motto for The Big Push organization was "Legislation, Not Prosecution." CPMs and their advocates hoped that decriminalization would reduce the likelihood of prosecution, increase the cost of "hunting down . . . midwives," and, where outright decriminalization could not occur, lessen the charges from felonies to misdemeanors. However, as Ida Darragh pointed out in her address to The Big Push gathering in 2009, the decriminalization of certified professional midwives, and indeed decriminalization in general, "is really really hard."

One of the main difficulties for any legislative mobilization on behalf of midwives is the need to convince legislators that homebirth is safe. Without regulation of practice and integration of care, however, that claim is harder to make, and doctors and hospital associations could easily oppose unregulated practice. Increasingly, state-level efforts to legalize midwifery practice began relying on bringing it within the regulatory gaze. At the very least, the conversation around the table among state activists usually began with a discussion of whether a "decrim" bill was sufficient to the task at hand. Most state activists, with the support of national organizations, and well aware of the prosecution of the 90s and 2000s, moved forward with regulatory bills, arguing that mere decriminalization was not enough.

National organizations like The Big Push, the Midwives Alliance of North America, and the National Association of Certified Professional Midwives provided important support to consumers and midwives in their fight for legal status.[4] In varying degrees, these organizations provided technical, nuts-and-bolts assistance, help with coordinating a message, a space to share strategies, and help in framing the profession. The Birth Rights Bar Association, after its founding meeting, performed similar functions around a wider range of reproductive justice issues; and organizations like Childbirth Connection and Citizens for Midwifery provided grants to assist in research and advocacy.

Big Push leaders provided essential nuts-and-bolts support in Missouri, where, I was told, one person in particular "helped with media and wrote press releases" while an affiliated attorney and a team of eighteen law students wrote an amicus brief when the law was challenged at the Missouri Supreme Court. Some advocates and midwives also praised the members of The Big Push (some were themselves founding members) for providing a nationwide virtual space for information sharing and strategizing. As a vetted and members-only mix of public relations professionals, midwives, lawyers, and advocates, The Big Push email list was a consistently valuable space for information gathering—and at almost all times, incredibly active. As a member of that list, I would consistently get nine to ten emails a day during the legislative session, from activists asking and answering questions, sharing resources about the safety of out-of-hospital birth, or responding to media requests and stories.

But, ultimately, national advocates did not know the lay of the land in individual states. "We know more about our state legislators than Big Push does," said an advocate from Missouri. An activist from Michigan told me, "I wish I could say that we got a lot of help from national organizations, but we didn't." One national leader from Midwives Alliance of North America (MANA) came to Missouri to "help answer legislators' technical questions," but "she didn't seem to understand our legislative process as much as we did." And, while "it was fun to swap stories" with a different national leader, Ophelia told me that woman "didn't know our state like we do."

Certainly, state-level activists have been successful in part because of the already organized network to help defend midwives in criminal prosecution and civil litigation,[5] and because of the organized presence of MANA and other groups who can certify, license, and develop best practices. Big Push list members learned from hearing others' experiences that they were in for a long haul of a fight. Iowa advocates, for instance, have been seeking legislation since 1984, when a bill was introduced that led to a Scope of Practice Committee, which in 1999 recommended legalization and licensure. Bills stemming from that committee went nowhere, often dying in committee, or on the calendar at the close of session. From 2010 to 2015, both the Republican and Democratic parties had planks devoted to legalizing midwives in the state but didn't get it done. Currently, midwives acting as CPMs in Iowa understand that they risk being charged with practicing medicine without a license. In those states where legislation was achieved, organizers explained that their success rested in part on their ability to maintain consistent crowds at the statehouse; lobbying their legislators to pass bills to legalize and regulate midwifery was a vitally important use of their time and resources.

In their study of successful pro-midwifery organizing in Indiana, Katherine Beckett and Bruce Hoffman also note the importance of a strong presence of community members at the statehouse:

> The virtual, visual, and aural presence of an enthusiastic group of midwives and home birth consumers has had a powerful impact on these debates; in this case, the female identity of the resisters (and their association with a most powerful cultural icon, motherhood) has worked to their advantage.[6]

In some states, the Amish, Hutterite, and Mennonite constituencies were quite important. Organizers in South Dakota and Iowa told stories about seeing the Wisconsin bill pass in 2005.[7] As a South Dakota organizer explained, "Amish filled the gallery," and Wisconsin was "one of the rare states that got a bill that year."[8]

Ophelia agrees with these assessments of the importance of a strong constituent presence, telling me that in Missouri, "The consumer angle is how we made things happen at the capitol." Organizers of the Missouri movement would look strategically for people to send to particular representatives, saying things like "We need a homebirth mom in Koster's district who works at a hospital."

I witnessed organizers in all of the states where I conducted research taking copious notes on their conversations with legislators, detailing their connections, their constituent interactions, and their particular concerns about midwifery care. In Iowa, organizers had a grid of all the legislators mapped out and taped inside folders to hand to consumers when they came to the capitol for lobby days, including talking points specific to each. Organizers in South Dakota, Iowa, and Missouri would all send blast emails with details about legislators' inquiries, asking specific moms and families to reach out on particular issues. Midwifery advocates in these states organized in-district meetings during the summers while the legislators were at home, often getting forty to fifty people to show up. In Missouri, legislators told organizers that they were "blown away with their organization."

In Michigan, organizers had an enormous phone tree, which began all the way back in 2008 when Michigan hosted the annual MANA conference, which had energized consumers and midwives alike. They began "Monday conference calls," which lasted two hours each week—and continued for the eight years required to get the work done. It was absolutely necessary to build a group of loyal consumers and clients, even though (or perhaps because) it was a constant struggle to keep the whole state involved. One organizer told my research assistant that when they heard there wouldn't be a vote they had planned on, they called everyone they knew and asked them to call their legislators; staffers came in and told their bosses that it was important to them. This activity instigated a vote. Ultimately successful, this organizer told a group gathered to learn about state legislation at a MANA conference session, "You never know what it's going to be that gets it done."[9]

In Missouri, relying on grassroots mobilization, the group chose not to hire an outside lobbyist after the first year. In South Dakota, the paid lobbyist was the key organizer in the state who stayed in Pierre during session and lobbied for the midwifery bill, while simultaneously working for a South Dakota pro-life organization, for which she was also a paid lobbyist. In Iowa, organizers hired a professional lobbyist for one year, then a doula and homebirth advocate was employed by Friends of Iowa Midwives for several years of intensive lobbying.

These lobbyists—whether homegrown or hired—often served important educational roles. An advocate for Michigan midwifery noted that, very early on, they met with a lobbyist simply "for an overview of how state government works."[10] But experiences with lobbyists were also mixed. Representatives from North Carolina told members of The Big Push, "We had a lobbyist approach us. He hadn't been in health care before. He told us we were stupid and he was gonna fix it for us, and it would be tens of thousands of dollars." Folks from Idaho recalled that they had a midwife whose aunt was a citizen lobbyist, and she took on the group and shepherded them through the process. She volunteered her time but allowed the Idaho organization to pay her expenses. "She wasn't really the right person for the job," the advocate acknowledged:

There were a few embarrassments around it. But all in all she got us started. The next year, we did it ourselves and wore ourselves out. We were burnt, exhausted by it. So, the third year, we said let's talk about a professional lobbyist.

Like advocates in Idaho, those in Michigan eventually hired a professional lobbyist who also believed in the cause. One of the Michigan organizers told us, "She's like a pair of ruby slippers. She gets me into places I never knew I could go." Most of the fundraising they did in Michigan (nearly $75,000) went to pay the lobbyist. Volunteers paid untold costs in time, mileage, lunch money, lost wages, and parking. If people wanted to donate, but cash and food weren't options, organizers would ask them to donate phone minutes and cell plans. Sometimes state organizers got very lucky with either deep-pocket donors within their consumer base or with a "very specific group of people from one community," who donated because of their ties to particular midwives.[11]

Ophelia remembers, "We asked around . . . 'Should we hire a lobbyist?' Everyone emphatically said no. It will change the dynamic of how people will feel about you. Right now you're these helpless little housewives, everyone kinda feels sorry for you and wants to help you."

They compromised in the first year by hiring an attorney to help them navigate the legal and political waters, and to keep an eye on the range of bills relating to birth and midwifery that were coming before the legislature. He was a homebirth dad and "gave us quite a deal" off his regular "high end" fee structure. Through the course of the year with that lobbyist, Ophelia noticed, "He can do stuff we can't do. He can swagger in and say, 'I don't like that language . . .'" She continued, "The fact that [midwifery] is personal to us really bothers [the legislators]. They just want to talk about the issues." And ultimately they feel more comfortable talking to a lobbyist. Advocates in Missouri eventually realized that the expense of a paid professional lobbyist, coupled with most lobbyists' lack of deep knowledge about out-of-hospital birth, made it worthwhile to hire one of their own and support her work in the capitol.

Most state activists also learned to be media savvy in order to use the press to get the right message out to consumers. Sometimes this meant avoiding the press altogether. During the legislative session, organizers in Idaho made a conscious choice not to link into the media. An activist from Idaho told The Big Push gathering, "Even when things passed, we did not put it in the newspaper. The day we were up for a vote in the Senate, the Boise newspaper didn't even mention it. . . . That served us very well."

Activists elsewhere took a different tack. Ophelia told me, "I'd write letters to the editor in small papers," in order to educate readers about homebirth midwifery, the legislative process, and the Friends of Missouri Midwives efforts to mobilize. As a strategy, most pro-midwifery advocacy groups tried very hard to keep ahead of media reporting. They would organize to be ready to make positive comments on the web pages of newspapers that ran any advocacy letters to the editor or homebirth-related articles. And, they worked to communicate quickly with each other so that "people who are contacted when something bad happens, can be on the same page" in talking with the media. In lingo introduced at The Big Push Summit, midwives and advocates learned to use their "conversational capital" and do a "big push for branding." They became adept at online social networking to dramatically build capacity for organizing their base and influencing journalistic treatment.

Though the original organizing for midwifery happened in person and on the phone, by the late 2000s, social media had become an exceptionally important technology that midwives and their advocates weren't yet fully exploiting. Many groups—from North Carolina, to Iowa, to The Big Push itself—found themselves on increasingly outdated AOL servers and Yahoo e-lists. Facebook hadn't yet become the organizing tool it now is, and Twitter wasn't even discussed.

In South Dakota, the lead organizer explained, "We've really been working to amp up social media." Doing so, as midwives and advocates found in later years, sometimes came with a cost. In one state, organizers report, "We have a hostile consumer who wanders around social media to see if midwives are incriminating themselves." And midwives who made poor decisions and then posted about them (for example, the unlicensed midwife in Iowa who had posted on Facebook about the footling breech she had delivered), could hurt the movement's credibility.

If the online work was sometimes fraught, the in-person work was often grueling. Ophelia recalls that she would spend forty to sixty hours per week volunteering in Jefferson City, while still attending several births per month. Sometimes, it was difficult to know how to effectively use the people who signed up and how best to deploy fundraising.

To keep the community of volunteers together, Michigan activists told us, they encouraged those in the core of the organization to "treat it like work," to "treat each other like sisters," and to schedule annual retreats for strategy and community. Many Michigan midwives were also farmers and serve farming communities—they and their clients had already been active around food justice issues. They saw an easy transition from natural foods and food justice to natural birth and birth justice. Added to the mix, there were many homeschoolers among the consumer advocates—some of them already had considerable legislative experience.[12] But, by and large, most of the women active in this movement were not political operatives—in fact, pro-midwifery organizing was very often their first interaction with state government and politics.

The work that advocates did to make their presence known to lawmakers also helped them attract and build a community of consumers. Midwives and their advocates designed, and took delight in wearing, cheeky T-shirts— like the Wild West–themed "Wanted Poster" garment sold by South Dakota activists in 2006 and 2007, meant to highlight the felony criminal status of midwives in the state after two of them were jailed, or ones with the slogan "Midwives: They Help People Out," sold at The Big Push Summit. In New Hampshire, pregnant women showed up to hearings on the legalization bill wearing T-shirts that said "I want to be born at home."[13] Iowa midwives and clients wore black T-shirts with the boundaries of the state, within which were the words "Make Midwives Legal" in bold white print.

Advocates made calendars featuring photos of children born at home via unattended birth in states where midwifery has been illegal, and baby quilts with the names of those children, to raffle and sell as fundraisers, as well as to display to legislators on the fence about legalization. In Michigan, advocates got photos of babies born at home who shared birthdates with legislators, and then sent those legislators Happy Birthday cards, featuring photos of those kids. In Iowa, activists planned a calendar project—each month would feature a picture of a baby born at home, whether unattended or with an unlicensed midwife, representing the month of their birth. Several states' advocates reported sending postcards with little baby footprints and the words "a new voter was born at home in your district." They reported that senators "loved" those postcards; some consumers were asked by legislators, "If we pass your bill, will you still send those birth announcements?" This doesn't mean that the women who came to the capitol didn't face barriers to getting their message across. In every state, consumers and midwives were critiqued for what they wore, for having crying or laughing children in meetings, and for being too "emotional."

I watched organizers in all of the states I observed provide tips for constituents—tips that would help them to become better citizens around a range of issues. One woman in South Dakota had "office hours" in her public library, where she sat for three hours a week and assisted constituents in communicating with their legislators and members of the press. She would advise them, "You should write it by hand. Tell them: I am your constituent, thanks for serving me/my state, please support the midwife bill." She would further direct them, "Send the letter to their homes," and mail them to all the members of the committees that would see the bill, as well as their particular legislator, whether they were on the committee or not. Each state organizer was certain that the best communication strategies came through personalized messages, legislator by legislator. At another information session, an activist for South Dakota Safe Childbirth Options (SDSCO) educated constituents on the legislative process, showing them links to the livestream of committee hearings and telling them "pages give [legislators] phone messages in real time." They urged their constituents to be activist in contacting their lawmakers, letting them know they were watching and listening. She later told me:

> Every year you learn—my first year, I learned that you can reserve rooms at the capitol in the evening, and host events. Six legislators and the new chair of the Republic Party showed up for the first thirty minutes of *The Business of Being Born*.[14]

Some of the education of constituents resulted in their own vitalization as political actors and candidates. In Missouri, physician Elizabeth Allemann filed to run against Chuck Graham; people in the state told me she did this mostly in an effort to get leverage with him on the issue of out-of-hospital birth. The husband of one Friends of Missouri Midwives member ran for the House, with lots of grassroots support from pro-midwifery advocates; he lost in the primary. And the full-time lobbyist for Friends of Iowa Midwives, Megan Day Suhr, ran for a seat in the Iowa House representing District 28, in 2011. She was unsuccessful but remains exceptionally active and influential in local Democratic Party politics. Even if they did not have strong homebirth advocates running for office, many state-level leaders felt, "Our new strategy could be to ask 'who are we going to go out and get elected? We have a lot of politically active people who will go out and work both sides of the aisle" to get pro-homebirth candidates elected.[15]

State advocacy leaders learned to use constituents strategically. One advocate told my research assistant we would "ask 100 people to do one thing [each]. . . . The consumers did a lot but it was hundreds of consumers doing one, or two, or three things."[16] Another told me that around election time she would say to people, "Even if you don't vote Democrat usually—vote for this guy—he is pro-homebirth."

Ophelia let me know that in Missouri, they would try to match the political ideology of the families with the senators with whom they were sent to talk, but sometimes they had to offer advice. She recalls having to remind constituents that homebirth is "both a pro-life and a pro-choice issue" and that if they find that they feel differently than their senator on abortion, "Please, just talk about homebirths." In other instances, she recalls, she would tell constituents, "Don't say women's rights with this senator. Focus on a family's right to have options." When I spoke at the SDSCO family weekend, organizers explicitly asked me not to use the word "choice" in my presentation on coercion in childbirth, as the idea of choice was too linked to abortion to be a productive way to frame their activism.[17]

In complex and fascinating ways, midwifery bills transcended party lines—in large part because midwives and advocates assiduously avoided the issue most likely to alienate supporters and legislators: abortion. In most states, as in South Dakota, "Very conservative legislators are on our side," as well as most moderate Democrats. But, as a South Dakota organizer noted, of the "very liberal legislators," not all are "on our side." This, she said, "really freaks me out—because pro-choice legislators are not pro-choice about birth."[18] Liberal legislators have tended to prefer medicalized care and expansion of access to the medical model. In Alabama, Michigan, and Missouri, advocates were told to absolutely steer clear of any abortion-related debate or conversation. As one activist in Michigan told me, they "simply had a rule that we didn't talk about abortion in Lansing. We all schooled ourselves not to say the word 'choice.' People didn't make choices; they decide, they have options." And Carol Leonard notes, whether pro-choice or anti-choice,

Midwives avoid the issue of abortion like the plague. No professional midwifery organization to date has adopted an official position on the abortion debate, preferring to ignore it in the hope that it will go away.[19]

Neither the American Civil Liberties Union through its Reproductive Freedom Project, nor Planned Parenthood would endorse pro-midwifery bills in any of the states with legislative efforts; for one pro-choice organizer in Michigan, "personally, [that] really stung," even as she realized that a Planned Parenthood endorsement "would have been the kiss of death." In Michigan, "the pro-life group is a single-issue group, so they also did not endorse the bill."[20] In Iowa, the main consumer organizers of the midwifery bill were themselves progressive city dwellers and were frequently frustrated by their legislators who were for various reasons opposed to out-of-hospital birth. As a conservative pro-life South Dakota consumer noted, with a bit of surprise, those in the middle were easier to reach sometimes, because "they have a different philosophy and view of birth."[21]

Beyond the abortion issue, there were other tensions within the state groups; in addition to normal personality conflicts, the groups' members disagreed on what to ask for within scope-of-practice agreements and on what strategies they should adopt. Sometimes, consumer interests differed from what midwives wanted, and neither group spoke with a clear, unified voice.

When legislation became a possibility, an important sticking point with midwives and consumers was what they would consider deal breakers in terms of scope of practice. Reluctant outside supporters of midwifery bills, like nurse midwives, often wanted those bills to contain restrictions on particular areas of practice. As one nurse midwife in Iowa told an assembled group as they planned for legislation, "ACNM won't mess with your scope of practice, but ACOG will, around the Big Three: VBACs, breeches, and multiples." She added that even though ACNM might not officially oppose a bill that included those capacities in their scope, they would tell legislators that they believed "Women in those situations are better served in hospital settings." These issues are controversial and need to be dealt with internally as well as externally. As a representative to The Big Push told the assembly in 2009, "In Missouri we are committed to achieving consensus in the living rooms, not in the legislature and not on the newspaper front page."[22] But she acknowledged that this consensus building is difficult. A midwife from

Michigan told my research assistant that many of the midwives in the state weren't happy with what they were doing.[23] A Michigan advocate told me separately, "Our group was not without contestation," and to stay cohesive "took a lot of peacemaking and love, as well as an acknowledgment that relationships are difficult. Midwives are so good at relationships, though." She took a similar message to the Birth Rights Bar Association's first meeting in Chicago 2017, closing her remarks that celebrated the passage of a pro-midwifery bill in the state by saying, "Our lobbyist told us that she can't believe we're still talking to each other."

There was also a built-in contradiction for many volunteers: Mobilized by the birth experience that many had recently had, those most likely to be engaged were women with young children at home—which can make it logistically hard to find the time and energy to do the work. Fortunately, as many leaders of pro-midwifery organizations note, that same mobilization moment of childbirth was also an exceptionally good motivator.

Most advocates for midwifery had a very personal connection to the cause. As a tireless South Dakota lead activist said, "I have eight daughters, and that is why this is important to me. I've had four beautiful homebirths, and I want them to have this option."[24] As one Michigan advocate told it, she became involved in the movement because of her experience with midwives, "just like any other consumer." She had had a homebirth in 2005, attended by a midwife, and "It seemed important to me to support her."[25] This was the case even though Michigan was, in a different advocate's words, "a clean slate," a place where, though not legal, midwives hadn't been prosecuted. Transports were fairly well received. Because of this, midwives felt they were safe. Rather than wait, though, advocates were encouraged by leaders of The Big Push to move forward with legislation.[26] As they recall, one of the leaders told them, "You have to set your own standards so they don't set them for you."[27]

Certainly, states with active prosecution against midwives had an easier time mobilizing consumers and midwives to seek legal status. The risk of prosecution is a strong motivator. Absent that perceived risk, consumer advocates sometimes had difficulty finding motivation for change. As an advocate for midwives in Michigan told a group assembled for the Birth Rights Bar Association, "Michigan wasn't prosecuting" when they began to advocate:

Which put us in a very bizarre situation—it put us in a difficult position. Midwives and families in Michigan felt safe—not like in Illinois or Indiana. Midwives in Michigan could practice above board so it was hard to motivate them for change.[28]

However, a midwife from another state where midwives did not have legal status, but were not actively prosecuted, spoke up to say that where she lives "[Consumers] can have a homebirth, I can go into the hospital [with a transfer], and I haven't had trouble yet. It's been pretty congenial. But the heat is coming." She went on to explain that she had heard there is a code, from the American Medical Association, that is used on charts by hospital staff for "inappropriate patients." The point of the code is that if you're not a good patient, if you're ungrateful or noncompliant, you can be billed more. Her concern? Given the experience that her colleagues in other states reported having with hospital staff who found ways to punish homebirth families who came in as transfers for emergency medical service, hospitals would code those families as noncompliant, and would make homebirth midwifery a more difficult proposition by letting word get out that the cost for emergency care after an attempted homebirth would be more than if a family had simply availed themselves of medical care. Whether or not the code exists as a reality isn't as important as the circulation of what counts as "knowledge" about coded patients—and the perception of risk that that knowledge constructs as a mobilizer for change.

So, advocates in Michigan got a freshman Republican representative to sponsor the bill. He had been born at home, and his wife had delivered their three children at home. Over the next four years and two concerted attempts, the bill died. In the year that they had success, the bill started in the Health Policy Committee, which was chaired by the spouse of a cardiac surgeon. The vice chair of the committee was a chiropractor, and they hoped he would be sympathetic, but it became clear the bill would not move through that committee. Their sponsor moved the bill to the Regulatory Committee and it passed through. "Miraculously," one of the organizers told us, "the opposition just didn't show up." That miracle, combined with the fact that "basically, activists were a bunch of capable people, used to getting things done," meant that the bill passed more quickly than anticipated.[29]

When the opposition did show up, the message that seemed to resonate most with legislators was the safety of homebirth and the increased safety of well-regulated midwives. As an organizer for SDSCO noted at a training session, "Their jobs as legislators is to protect the public, so we have to reassure them that this is safe."[30] People often assume that choosing a birth at home privileges the maternal experience of birth over the health of the baby, and it is important for midwifery advocates to explain how well-regulated out-of-hospital birth attendants, attending healthy and low-risk pregnancies, are just as safe (and even safer) than hospital birth.

At the statehouse, midwives and their advocates argued that legislation makes out-of-hospital birth safer in at least three key ways. First, licensed practice ensures some measure of standardization in terms of training and skill. Second, well-regulated out-of-hospital practice includes mechanisms for peer review, as well as for a consumer complaint process and investigatory oversight by a regulatory board. Third, legalization—even if only through decriminalization—enables midwives to feel safer in emergency situations to transport clients to hospitals and ensure continuity of care.

Midwives occasionally chafed at having to tell legislators about safety. At an Iowa organizational meeting, one midwife said that in her opinion, "Licensing doesn't make [homebirth] safer—but it does make it more accessible." She added ruefully, from her perspective, "Legislators need to hear us say it is safer, though."[31] Another participant at that meeting, a direct-entry midwife serving primarily religious communities, told the group, "People find me via word of mouth and don't care about my credentials. They want quality of care. I don't necessarily believe that legislating and regulating is to going to make for better care." A third participant, a midwifery apprentice, said she would seek the CPM credential if it were available to her; she agreed philosophically that mere legalization doesn't provide safety but argued persuasively that legal status, and regulatory governance, could instantiate in the midwifery community the part of the practice that she feels most impassioned about: informed consent of the client. For her, this consent happens through well-trained and regulated midwives providing education and options to those who will labor and deliver with them.

Even among those midwives and advocate who might have felt that legislation could make them safer, they didn't agree that legislators cared.

"Facts don't matter," an advocate from Idaho told a group gathered for a Big Push Knowledge Exchange. "Supportive legislators and a good lobbyist matter. Schmoozing helps—once they know you, you can chat with them, and educate them." She followed up by exhorting us to remember, "Legislators don't care about anything except getting re-elected."[32]

In all of these settings, the mobilization of citizen-consumers became tremendously important to remind legislators of the stakes of the bills they were considering. The notion of the pro-midwifery movement as a grassroots movement was key to their success in getting legislators' ears— especially when the new activists mobilized their particular skills and personalities, rather than trying to fit into a lobbyist model. Recalling a day around five years prior to the start of the legislative push, an organizer told me, "Ida [Darragh, head of NARM] asked me what I could do. I replied, I can feed people." Indeed, feeding people became a hallmark of much pro-midwifery organizing, from birth-themed Labor Day picnics and Legislative Cookie Day in Iowa to Advocacy Day in South Dakota, where SDSCO would reserve the Capitol Rotunda, "whether we had a bill or not," and "feed everyone." SDSCO members cooked and each year served "roast beef sandwiches on homemade buns, with veggies and bars."[33] In Ohio, advocates would host picnics in the rotunda on International Midwives Day; and in Ohio, South Dakota, Missouri, and Iowa, advocates would participate in M&M Days, bringing the colorful candy for legislators, in honor of "Moms & Midwives."[34] SDSCO organizers always told their consumer members, "Bring your kids," and "be the faces of those who can't be here." The events are notable for being "very family and homeschool friendly." I never attended a Lobby Day or event that wasn't full of children—and my fieldwork was in fact facilitated by having a nursling, and later a toddler, in my care.

The powerful visual semiotics of women and children gathering to lobby can't be ignored as an issue in reproductive health care. In the contemporary political moment, we've grown used to seeing photos of tables full of White men, gathered to restrict access to birth control and abortion. In pro-midwifery movements, we see tables full of food, surrounded by a diverse set of women, seeking access to a wide range of reproductive care and an expansion of possibilities about how, where, and with whom to birth.

THE OPPOSITION

At the first Birth Rights Bar Association meeting, one state-level advocate offered a pithy and precise set of reasons that it is so hard to pass a bill. Counting off on her fingers, she listed the problems quickly: "Medical associations, the medical monopoly, midwifery is a niche issue that is hard to get legislative traction with. And, it is easy to stop a bill—hard to pass one."[35] Activists were sometimes surprised, in the first years of legislative attempts, by the vociferous opposition their bills often faced and how easy it was to stop bills from progressing.

As a niche issue, impacting only a very small constituency, and in a way that midwifery advocates see as incredibly positive, initially it didn't make sense to them that the battle would be hard. They understood, of course, that, as was true in South Dakota, "We're having less than thirty homebirths a year—the majority of which are unattended. We don't have the numbers [to interest legislators]. And we don't have midwives [to make the case]."[36] But they underestimated the strength of the opposition.

Sometimes, legislators would come to the pro-midwifery bills with preconceived ideas about midwifery and home birth that made them loath to vote yes. In both Iowa and South Dakota, there were legislators with scary or tragic birth stories to support their belief that birth is safest in a hospital. In South Dakota, one activist told me, there is a "doctor who is a legislator who really got us in a bad space. He thinks midwives are great—in third world countries."[37]

There, as elsewhere, the main opposition to the bill came from, in the words of one organizer, "the medical community." Further, those most familiar with state legislators frequently noted that opposition typically came from those members of the House or Senate who either were themselves doctors or nurses or had a family member in the medical community. One legislator in South Dakota was married to a labor and delivery nurse who, in the words of an activist, was "rude to homebirth families and constituents." But, because that legislator is "very pro-life," the lobbyist believed that if constituents "talk about what is best for your baby," he might listen.[38] Also in South Dakota, the medical lobby had close ties to the governor during the last few years of the legislative push; and because the governor was unsupportive of legalizing CPMs, the feeling was that "the health department can't be in favor."[39]

In keeping with its formal policy stance that childbirth should occur "in properly licensed, accredited, equipped, and staffed obstetrical units," attended by "qualified and licensed personnel,"[40] the AMA has submitted amicus briefs in support of state medical associations seeking to continue the criminal status of lay midwifery in states like Missouri (during the state appeal of the legislation legalizing their practice).[41] ACOG has issued formal statements against homebirths for women attempting vaginal births after caesarean sections (VBACs) as well as vaginal deliveries for twins or breech births.[42] And the American Academy of Pediatrics has issued formal statements in consonance with ACOG's stance.[43]

As a result, several states have made it illegal for certified professional midwives to attend VBACs and require clients to write a formal right of refusal of care in order for their certified nurse midwife to attend them in a home VBAC. Doctors use the publications of their professional organizations to keep up-to-date; it makes sense that they would parrot ACOG and AMA language surrounding out-of-hospital care. The same is true of the American College of Nurse-Midwives (ACNM)—which is supportive of planned out-of-hospital birth but prefers it be attended by CNMs, rather than CPMs—and local ACNM chapters.[44] At the local level, when advocates would introduce bills to legalize CPMs, they found resistance from the local chapters of all of these groups. These positions have moderated somewhat in the past several years, with some of these professional organizations adopting a stance that privileges hospital birth but respects the autonomous decision making of women, regarding their choice of where to labor and deliver.

But until that moderation, state advocates reported high levels of anti-CPM activity among professional groups in their states. In North Carolina, for instance, one senator, who was also a medical doctor, "was against the bill for ten years" and made sure it never left committee. A speaker from North Carolina at a Big Push Knowledge Exchange session continued, "If you to go the ob-gyn society meetings in North Carolina, there will always be a presentation saying how proud they are of squashing the midwifery movement. They used to have a graphic of the ob-gyn hammer pounding on little people." In fact, this advocate told the group, "I have heard that at their annual conferences, they spend a half an hour or forty-five minutes just talking about us." Dr. Amy, an infamous anti-midwife blogger, was also actively campaigning against the midwives in the state, and from early 2000 to late 2008, the debate stalled. In 2008, North Carolina advocates introduced a bill that would mandate ob-gyns to sit down with CPMs and CNMs to "study" the issue. Advocates noted that in North Carolina, study bills are automatically filed, which was great except that then they were told that if the bill passed, it would include language requiring that midwives carry liability insurance. This move, advocates felt, had been engineered by the medical lobby, to be sure the bill was either defeated or impossible to implement.[45]

Some advocates told me that they were glad they came to the process innocent and naive, because it gave them the impetus to start something that, in many cases, became a decade-long fight, with unanticipated opponents. In her memoir of legalization processes in New Hampshire, Carol Leonard writes, "Because I've had no prior experience with the legislative process and have no idea what a circus this is about to become, I participate wholeheartedly."[46] As one midwifery advocate told me, "I felt so naive starting this process, and everyone said enjoy it while it lasts." Indeed, she found, after they introduced their bill, "Everybody and their dog crawled out from under the woodwork to oppose it." Even more frustrating, it was sometimes quite difficult for advocates to prepare for lobbying meetings and committee hearings, because the questions they received from those with opposing viewpoints often came "out of left field." In Michigan, one organizer told a gathering of the Birth Rights Bar Association, "People kept emphasizing things we didn't expect them to," and their opposition to the bill seemed, at times, "completely personality driven."[47]

A big part of any lobbying strategy is to seek neutral stances from those organizations that might otherwise be opposed. In Iowa, that included successful bids to get neutrality from Planned Parenthood of the Heartland, Iowa Nurses Association, Iowa Board of Nursing, Iowa Board of Insurers, Iowa Medical Society, Iowa Department of Public Health, and Iowa Bar Association. Strangely, some of the main opposition came from the Iowa osteopaths—and the opposition was rooted in the regulatory scheme, not a distaste for or distrust of out-of-hospital birth.[48]

Sometimes, education of the opposition became key. In Idaho, early on in the push for legal status for CPMs, the midwives were asked to give a presentation to the perinatology board on how they would like to see themselves be regulated. "They had billions of questions and were clueless," one advocate remembers. During the second year of the legislative effort (2009), the bill sponsor gathered a large group of stakeholders: Idaho Midwifery Council, Idaho Hospital Association, Idaho State Board of Pharmacy, Idaho State Board of Nursing, Idaho Academy of Family Physicians, Idaho Department of Health and Welfare, and midwives and legislators themselves. He hosted the meeting at the capitol, prior to the session starting, and Idaho Midwifery Council brought Ida Darragh, from NARM, to Boise for the meeting. She had breakfast with the legislators, then a meeting with physicians and the medical community. "After that," the Idaho rep to The Big Push told us, "Nothing came up again as a problem related to the CPM." She added, "We kept going back to the table with the Perinatal Project, and privately meeting with doctors." The chance to offer peer-to-peer education was one of the keys to getting a neutral position on the bill from the medical community.[49]

By 2016, it was widely understood that a bill incorporating US-MERA requirements would get a neutral stance, and perhaps even support, from the nurses in Iowa. One nurse-legislator acknowledged, "There has not historically been a lot of trust" between CNMs and CPMs in the state.[50] But, she told a group assembled for a strategy session in 2016, "As someone who has opposed this legislation for most of my professional life, the issue has been education." With the US-MERA agreement, she said, "That issue is resolved." US-MERA is often not enough to convince doctors, or hospital associations, however. In Iowa, though the nurses came on board, in 2020 the hospital association and doctors exerted enough influence, early, to kill the bill.

In fact, as a former lobbyist for Friends of Iowa Midwives noted in 2017, "The largest opposition has always been the Iowa Hospital Association, and that will not change." Indeed, hospital administrative staff and even nursing home administrators routinely spoke against pro-midwifery bills while they were heard in committee, and there was a sense that hospitals would take negative action against employees who supported out-of-hospital birth. In South Dakota, one constituent sent a handwritten letter to every legislator, chronicling the plight of her daughter, who worked for a local hospital. The daughter had chosen to have a homebirth attended by a CPM and then felt pressured by her employer to quit her job. One legislator was a nurse practitioner on the Health and Human Services Committee; she voted to have the bill go out of committee, even though she told pro-midwifery advocates that she was afraid such a vote would cost her a job. SDSCO organized a thank-you note campaign for her, and she received the notes with gratitude, and tears.[51] The key issue raised by medical professionals and associations is almost always safety of out-of-hospital birth. However, Stacey Tovino's review of the history of anti-midwifery legislation in California, Alabama, and Massachusetts calls these motivations into question; her research suggests that other factors, such as "the force of economic competition," may be the primary source of their opposition.[52]

It isn't only doctors, nurses, and hospital associations who lobby against the pro-legalization bills. In a move that confuses legislators, and consumers, every state has a handful of midwives who themselves are against regulation and legalization, and they show up to lobby against CPM bills. This happened in South Dakota and Iowa during the time I was engaged in research; it has certainly happened in other places. Sometimes, these midwives are homebirth CNMs, sometimes they are CPMs or CPM eligible, but seek stricter regulatory governance or stronger licensing qualifications. One such midwife in the vicinity of South Dakota was considered by organizers to be "a thorn in our side." According to organizers at The Big Push Summit, this midwife was "one of the main reasons why our bill didn't go through last year." She also "killed Wyoming's bill," because—years prior to the US-MERA agreement that eventually facilitated this—she wanted MEAC-accreditation for all CPMs. This midwife told legislators that there should be no direct-entry PEP pathway, and they listened.

More commonly, though, midwives against the bills are against licensure in general—they seek less regulation, rather than more. Even in states where compromise bills are struck—bills that would allow them exemptions on religious grounds or that would grant them grandmothered status as "traditional midwives"—they remain opposed. They are concerned that licensure for some of them, but not all, will leave them at risk of discretionary prosecution and stepped up enforcement. And, they critique the desire to be seen—recognized—and regulated by a state apparatus that they do not trust.

These midwives could often find common cause with legislators, many of whom would seize upon the presence of a regulatory board—its makeup and its funding—as problematic. On several occasions in the states I studied, opposition to regulating midwives had absolutely nothing to do with midwifery, as a practice. Rather, some state legislatures were made up of a majority of fiscally conservative Republicans who, as one Iowa activist noted, "won't pay for a regulatory board." Even though no other board in the state of Iowa is self-funded—that is, funded by the licensing fees paid by those regulated under it—Iowa legislators potentially in favor of the bill would want whatever board that regulated midwifery to fund itself.

In other states, legislators had hang-ups about regulating midwives because the legislators themselves were antiregulatory libertarians who were against any expansion of law, even expansion sought by those who would be governed under it.[53] Michigan, at the time advocates started seeking legislation, was "hell bent on deregulation,"[54] and the previous governor of Michigan had, for twelve years prior, "hated the idea of licensure—for any profession—period."[55] An advocate from that state ruefully told a group, "To even start the process, we're in the back of the line. So far back, we're in Ohio. On top of that, the state is broke and can't afford to regulate."[56] And, the political process itself makes an intervention difficult. In Michigan, the advocate told us, "We have term limits, and a two-year session. At the end of each session, almost two-thirds of the legislature is termed out,"[57] and any gains made by midwifery advocates in terms of educating and convincing legislators could easily be lost.

In Missouri, many legislators believe their state constitution requires that no words be added to the state code—so any bill that is passed must also strike words from other sections of the law, in order to avoid "over-legislating." In South Dakota, all regulatory boards have to be self-funded and self-staffed. The legislative obstacles in that state were "money and regulation," regarding the potential safety of out-of-hospital birth as a concern for legislators, an organizer said "not so much."[58]

These kinds of conversations absolutely have the potential to fracture coalitions and derail bills. In recent years, experienced activists and lawyers have advised those seeking bills to defer these hard questions to the rulemaking process. In a way, they argue, midwives and advocates should kick the can down the road in order to get legal status. They also point to the tenacity of South Dakota activists as a model for success. Indeed, the story of pro-midwifery legislation in South Dakota is an exemplar of everything I've raised in this chapter, regarding political mobilization for access to care.

SUCCESS IN SOUTH DAKOTA

South Dakota's effort for legal status was a twenty-five-year effort of a small group of dedicated activists, with Debbie Pease, their lobbyist since 2008, and her husband Quint at their core. Originally called South Dakota Safe Childbirth Options (SDSCO), and later renamed South Dakota Birth Matters (SDBM), this grassroots effort was dedicated to legalizing certified professional midwifery in the state. They hosted workshops on labor and delivery, maintained a lobbying presence in the state capital, produced websites and videos, and hosted potlucks and BBQs with candidates and legislators during the summers and fall that the legislature wasn't in session. I met many activists when I attended a two-day workshop held by SDSCO, in Custer, South Dakota—serving as a participant-observer and guest speaker—and attending several break-out sessions on topics as varied as shoulder dystocia during unassisted birth, holistic fertility control, and natural family planning.

The first step in legalizing out-of-hospital birth attendants in South Dakota was to legalize the presence of nurse midwives at homebirth, which happened in 2008. The bill that did so also decriminalized the presence of untrained family members attending homebirth. It did not, though, extend legal status to certified professional midwives or to midwives who had training but were not nurses. By 2010, three South Dakota CNMs were practicing out-of-hospital birth in the state, and there were reported to be another four who traveled in from Iowa and Wyoming.[59] Activists estimated that in 2011, there were "maybe five" nurse midwives living in the state and attending out-of-hospital birth. By 2016, that number had increased to around a dozen with state health department records showing thirteen nurse midwives to be licensed to attend out-of-hospital birth.

One of the problems women in South Dakota expressed was a lack of options if they wanted to have a VBAC. No hospitals in three of the smaller cities in the state (Vermillion, Madison, and Pierre) would allow a woman to even attempt a vaginal birth after caesarean—and CNMs were prohibited by ACNM from attending them at home.[60]

Part of the Custer conference was devoted to planning for the 2010 legislative session. Organizers had devised a strategy of floating two separate bills. Plan A, their lobbyist told a large group assembled for an information and strategy session, would be to seek "licensing, and an advisory board under board of nursing, with the same fees as those paid by nurses." This would take a two-thirds vote of the House and Senate in the state. Plan B would be a complex decriminalization bill that would take a simple majority; it was complex because the bill would allow midwives who were licensed out of state to practice legally in South Dakota and would contain a "repeal clause" or "sunset provision" that enabled revision in 2020. Further, based on her read of the legislators and hopes for the session, the lobbyist advised that the Plan A bill would start in the House, with the Health and Human Services Committee; the Plan B decriminalization bill would start in the Senate. She closed the informational part of the meeting by adding, "We hope the Department of Nursing will be neutral." Despite having what national NARM vice president Ida Darragh called "one of the most dynamic, committed organizing committees in the nation," the bill failed that year and did not pass in the several years subsequent. SDSCO activists remained committed—many of them citing their strong faith—not in the legislature, but in the Lord. When Ida praised her during a Big Push meeting, that lead organizer demurred, "If we get a bill passed, all glory to God."

The South Dakota organization strategically partnered with other groups in the state to shepherd a pro-breastfeeding bill through the state legislature in 2015, and it lobbied at each session on behalf of several other bills that were family and child related. Their work on the breastfeeding bill brought SDSCO to the attention of a local reporter in Aberdeen, South Dakota, who wrote a sympathetic story about out-of-hospital birth. The good press was important both for morale and for legitimacy.

In addition, SDSCO worked hard to understand the legislative opposition to their bill and to discern the places where their representatives might get hung up. A big issue was that some legislators wanted a requirement for liability insurance—a nonstarter for CPMs because it is difficult to access, expensive, and difficult to afford, and perceived to be largely unnecessary. In South Dakota at the time, CNMs weren't required to have liability insurance, though massage therapists were; SDSCO advocates needed to make the seemingly commonsense claim that midwives were more like CNMs than massage therapists. As Debbie Pease pointed out to me in 2016, "We've been doing a lot of work in the off season" educating legislators new to the process and have found a new sponsor, Representative Kris Langer, a real estate agent from a small town north of the largest city. Private college–educated, Langer had interned at a birth center during college and was sympathetic to the CPMs; she now served as the majority whip.

The bill that eventually passed in South Dakota was modeled on Wyoming legislation from 2010. It did not rely upon US-MERA competencies or accreditation, and it featured a self-funding mechanism for the board, as required by the state (and accomplished via crowdfunding). A key part of the bill was its vague language, stemming from an insistence that everyone agree "We get our bill, then we work on the rules," with a goal of "allowing everything to maximum scope of practice" and a particular concern that CPMs be able to access Pitocin and other necessary pharmaceuticals to make rural birth farther from emergency rooms safer.

This reliance on later rulemaking, rather than legislative specificity, was considered best practice for getting bills passed. For instance, in Michigan, advocates reportedly had a list of "non-negotiables" that they had agreed would result in them killing the bill if they came up. Several of the advocates I spoke with mentioned that this list existed—none of them would share what was on it—even after legalization and after rulemaking. Their philosophy was "don't include things [in the bill] that belonged in regulation," because rules can be changed.[61] CNMs in South Dakota "seemed to agree that CPMS should have the same rules they do," and were generally supportive of legislation. The nursing board itself didn't like provisions that CPMs could "provide or administer" necessary medicines and preferred language of "limited prescriptive power," which some worried would "confuse the legislators," but this was a negotiable point.

A key talking point for constituents, Pease stressed, was to reassure legislators that "There is *no* battle between CPMs and CNMs!"[62] She told a group of around twenty-two assembled for an evening of learning and letter-writing in winter 2015, "All the midwives got together and agreed," she stopped and smiled broadly, offering a self-deprecating laugh, "well, they agreed on what they could agree on."[63] The situation around CNMs was similar in Missouri, where nurse midwives were officially not in favor of a bill legalizing CPM practice. But, a Missouri advocate told me, "We never disagreed [with CNMs] in public. Never. We did our best to reach out to [individual nurse midwives] and have coffee and chat and [give them] the time to vent and then we asked them for help."[64]

Eventually, even though all of this planning and coalition building was a necessary backdrop, the success of the South Dakota bill (like the success in Missouri years earlier) ultimately hinged on a wildly contingent event. In South Dakota, HB1065, the bill to regulate CPMs, finally passed in 2017, a key organizer told me, "because Trump won." The new president brought with him a wave of anti-government sentiment contained within a group of legislators who wanted to promote radical individualism untethered to government control. They found that midwifery provided that for many families.

. . .

As midwives and their advocates mobilized to improve access to out-of-hospital care, they found themselves engaging in politics and activism in a range of ways—from lobbying, to letter writing, to cookie campaigns, to consumer education. They mobilized across party lines, strategically using law and politics to convince legislators of the safety and cost effectiveness of homebirth, creating a sense of urgency around a rather niche issue and building on other readily accessible discourses in their state political culture—including antiregulatory and libertarian rhetoric. They assiduously avoided terms and issues that could generate dissent within their coalition, and they relied on one of the traits essential to their professional success: relationship building.

In a way similar to other gendered movements—like mother-led movements against gun violence and drunk driving, the #metoo movement, and activism around sex work—midwives and their advocates use their positionality as women and mothers to their advantage; they also fight against stereotypes and normative assumptions about them, based on their gender and gender performance. While many contingencies and happy accidents contributed to the passage of bills in the jurisdictions where they were successful, it is also undoubtedly true that, absent consistent and persistent mobilization, midwives and their advocates would not have been able to use the windows of opportunity offered by a Trump presidency, a chance airline encounter, or the opposition simply staying home.

4 RIGHTS, RULES, AND REGULATION

> "It took us eight years to get a law in Michigan—but let me tell
> you, writing and passing a bill is a walk in the park, compared
> to rulemaking."
> —Deborah Fisch, Friends of Michigan Midwives advocate and lawyer
> and co-founder of Birth Rights Bar Association

IN AN UNANTICIPATED TWIST to the saga of political mobilization for legal status
in Missouri, local and national lawyers got to flex their state constitutional
law muscles, after the Missouri State Medical Association (MSMA) filed suit
against the bill legalizing CPMs in the state. The MSMA challenged the law
by saying that it violated the provisions of the Missouri Constitution, which
stipulates that state laws must be both a single subject and clearly titled. The
trial court struck the midwifery portion of the law as "violating original
purpose, single subject, and clear title requirements" of Article III, sections
21 and 23, of the Missouri Constitution, holding that the "single subject"
was "health insurance," and so the section legalizing midwifery via the term
"tocology" was neither germane to the subject nor part of the clear title.

Several years later, sitting in her living room, Ophelia rolls her eyes and
says, "The judge on that case? She was on the board of the hospital. Of course,
she ruled in favor of the medical association."

By this time, lawyer members of The Big Push list, such as long-time birth
justice activist Susan Jenkins, were involved in offering pro bono advice and
connecting the Missouri Midwives Association with law students and legal
clinics that focused on reproductive justice issues, to help coordinate the local
legal team's work. Ophelia tells me, "There are two law firms in Jefferson City
that do these kinds of things [state constitutional law practices]. The medical

folks hired one, we hired the other, for a $10,000 retainer." That lawyer coordinated with the state lawyers and reproductive rights specialists in defense of the law. Ophelia remembers her initial conversation with the lead local lawyer: "He said it [the total bill] would be around $30,000. It ended up being $120,000." Ophelia tells me, "We were emailing every week asking [people] for money. I was the one the attorneys would call when we were late [to pay our legal bills]." The Missouri Midwives Association held bake sales and took in one or two hundred individual donations each month; some of them were $500 and $5,000 checks, many were $2 and $5 payments for packages of cookies. One couple literally won the lottery and called to donate $25,000 in one go.

The Missouri Midwives Association continued to organize in other ways. In response to the press coverage after the bill signing, when "the media had a field day," Ophelia and others did a continual push to "generate good news stories" about midwives. Expecting that they would lose on appeal, they continued to push for a bill that would license and regulate. Ophelia tells me that it was "a hard year" and that many of the volunteers were "upset, overwhelmed, burned out." In fact, many consumers and midwives in Missouri didn't want to appeal the initial trial court's decision—they felt it was a waste of time, money, and energy. But Ophelia was steadfast, telling them, "*No*. We have to try the courts. Law will work better than politics."

The lead up to the Missouri Supreme Court took a year. The legal team mobilized to get amicus briefs filed. The state Supreme Court heard, on behalf of midwifery and the state law, from several national groups: Citizens for Midwifery; Midwives Alliance of North America; National Association of Certified Professional Midwives; National Our Bodies, Ourselves; and the National Birth Policy Coalition. The Missouri doctors had a brief from the American Medical Association. The oral arguments were, in Ophelia's memory, "pathetic." The state was rather reluctantly bringing the appeal, and the solicitor general was "unprepared."

And then, on June 24, 2008, it was over—in an anticlimactic but decisive fashion. In Ophelia's words, the Missouri State Medical Association's claims were "thrown out on a technicality." In a two to one decision, the Missouri State Supreme Court ruled in favor of the midwives—or, rather, determined that the litigants from the Missouri Medical Association lacked standing to bring the suit at all: They lacked standing to challenge the law that legalized midwifery in Missouri. Writing for the court, Judge Stephen Limbaugh rejected all of the claims for standing brought by the MSMA—from outright standing, to the third-party standing they sought by arguing that doctors would be "directly and adversely affected" by the legalization of midwives. The court dismissed this claim out-of-hand, saying that physicians in Missouri did not have a "legally protectable interest in the litigation" and therefore had no standing to sue. The physicians had also claimed that the potential for vicarious liability gave them standing, based on their belief that legal midwifery would cause there to be more medical emergencies related to homebirth, and it would substantially alter doctors' practices. This, too, the Supreme Court dismissed.

Finally, the medical association had claimed standing under *Planned Parenthood of Kansas and Missouri v Nixon* (2006), where abortion providers were successful in their claim for standing to challenge anti-abortion laws on behalf of patients. The court disagreed, writing that the MSMA lacked the third-party standing they claimed via their patients, as "patients who would be inclined to engage the services of certified midwives would have no interest in contesting the validity of the statute legalizing such service."[1] With a ruling that MSMA lacked standing to bring a case against the legalization of midwives, the Missouri Supreme Court didn't even need to reach the merits regarding the questions of single subject and clear title of the bill.

Ophelia tells me later—as did the former chief justice of the Missouri Supreme Court, in a separate conversation—that no one in the Missouri Midwives Association or Friends of Missouri Midwives realized at the time that they "had a friend on the court." But they did. The chief justice at the time was Judge Michael Wolff. Wolff had, in the 1980 and 90s, represented Cheryl Southworth and Sheila Nichting, two midwives subject to discretionary prosecution in his state. He remembered the cases well, when we talk several years later. And, of course he does. Southworth's case went to appeal on constitutional grounds, with Wolff as her attorney. Nichting's case was even more sensational: The birth center she had opened in Lake of the Ozarks had been raided by seven armed police officers just after the birth of a healthy baby; the police gathered sheets bloody from birth and afterbirth in garbage bags and hauled them away.[2] Wolff remembered that the police even took the placenta as "evidence of the crime of midwifery."

Later, the couple who had just delivered sued the county sheriff's office for $2 million for the distress caused them during the raid. They won a jury verdict, which the county appealed; the appeals court reinstated the verdict, agreeing with the family that the "armed, hostile, and arrogant" police search had gone "too far."[3]

Given his involvement as counsel on these cases, and his own personal understanding of midwifery and women's rights, Judge Wolff came to the Supreme Court bench well aware of the politics of midwifery in the state. And, Ophelia notes, he wasn't neutral—rather, he simply used his own expertise, as a justice and a lawyer, to "do the right thing," explaining midwifery to his colleagues, stressing the difference between the medical model and midwifery care, and joining the majority opinion.

And the Missouri Medical Association? Well, Ophelia says, "Losing really made the doctors mad. For two years they wouldn't even talk to us in the hall. They've not been civil to us since then." She shrugs, "It was a blow to their pride."

LEGAL MOBILIZATION FOR MIDWIFERY CARE

The coordination by reproductive rights lawyers and advocacy on behalf of Missouri midwives in the challenge over the constitutionality of their bill is very rare for those involved in legal mobilization for midwifery care. Far more often, lawyers are called upon to "clear the underbrush," to defend midwives against criminal prosecution and regulatory action and in so doing, to protect movement activists.[4] They also are called upon to litigate on behalf of victims of obstetric harm and violence and to help state advocates craft bill language and regulatory policy. Among those best situated to provide these services are lawyers associated with the Birth Rights Bar Association.

The closest thing going to a "cause lawyering" organization for birth rights advocates, the Birth Rights Bar Association is a national organization of lawyers, law students, and advocates dedicated to reproductive justice.[5]

[BRBA] promotes the rights of birthing people: physical liberty, bodily integrity, autonomy, privacy, due process, equal protection, religious liberty, and informed consent. In order to support birthing people, we also protect the right of midwives to practice their profession.[6]

BRBA's founders and governing board members include attorneys who work closely with the National Advocates for Pregnant Women and other rights-oriented organizations serving people who labor, deliver, and parent. Co-founder Indra Lusero told me that they went to law school after attending a Midwives Alliance of North America (MANA) conference in 2005 where folks lamented not having a "hot shot team of lawyers" who could help defend midwives. Lusero has endeavored to develop just such a team. Honorary BRBA board member Susan Jenkins has been a pioneer in pro-midwifery lawyering, serving as legal counsel for the American College of Nurse-Midwives (ACNM), the American Association of Birth Centers (AABC), and The Big Push for Midwives campaign. Jenkins was the recipient of the first ever Birth Warrior award granted by BRBA at the association's gathering in Chicago in 2017.

The association's printed materials and web page explain that "pregnant and birthing people" are routinely denied these rights, as are "midwives and other health professionals who care for pregnant and birthing families." Co-founder Deborah Fisch explained at the inaugural meeting in Chicago in 2018, "BRBA is really intended as direct representation, not so much consumer advocacy."[7] The BRBA gatherings and networks serve many purposes, and its work is easily legible as legal mobilization when its advocates call on law and legal systems for reform, for protection, and for acknowledgment of *rights* of birthing people. BRBA-affiliated attorneys file amicus briefs in cases directly impacting these rights, and they contribute as staff counsel for a range of cases including midwifery defense and as plaintiff's attorney in obstetric violence cases. BRBA attorneys do this work from the perspective of reproductive justice and expand that vision to include religious freedoms, gender equality, rights for transgender people, and the promotion of the professional scope of practice for midwives, all as ways to increase access to physiologic and dignified birth. They seldom go to trial, but do publish, and increasingly consult, on issues of the criminal prosecution of midwives. Their approach to legal translation for midwives centers on mitigating risk.

IN DEFENSE OF MIDWIVES: JUST DON'T GO TO JAIL

An early morning plenary session in a packed and energized hotel ballroom at the 2017 MANA national conference featured a tongue-in-cheek presentation inviting midwives to "play a game" *with the law*, against opponents of legalization. Presenters Indra Lusero and Deborah Fisch titled their session "Analyzing the Game" and equated midwifery practice under legal pluralism to the game of Monopoly.[8]

Lusero began the session by telling the hundreds of midwives assembled, "This is a game. We need to know the rules. We need to know who is playing and how to win. Otherwise, it won't be fun!" They introduced the players in this legal game: Midwives were on the board alongside parents, consumers, national pro-midwifery organizations, and legislators; these groups shared space with anti-CPM organizations such as the American College of Nurse-Midwives, the American Hospital Association, and the American College of Obstetricians and Gynecologists, as well as overzealous prosecutors.[9]

At the start of the presentation, Lusero noted, "Each player starts the game with different resources—and money isn't the only thing that impacts who wins the game."[10] Given their legal training and scholarly endeavors, I wouldn't be surprised if Indra and Deb have read both Galanter's "The 'Haves' Come Out Ahead" and Ewick and Silbey's *Common Place of Law*. As one lawyer who represents midwives told me, when I questioned her about the disciplinary move toward professionalization, "Well, we've all read Foucault."[11] As the session unfolded, with a hypothetical midwife moving around a Monopoly board and through several scenarios that put her at odds with regulatory and criminal law, midwives in the conference hall became restive. One stood up and exclaimed, "But some of what is happening in this example is illegal in my state!"[12] This, Fisch artfully pointed out, is exactly one of the points: Beyond hospitals having a monopoly on birth setting and culture, the plural legal landscape of midwifery makes it difficult to know what is legal and where, and it is incredibly easy to be afoul of the law, even in states where midwives have legal status.

As they interacted with the audience, Lusero and Fisch entertained other questions about unique situations they may face in the states where they practice. One midwife asked, "What if you have a regulatory authority action, and you need some time? How much time do you have to respond?" They cheekily answered, "As much time as the agency gives you." Then they added, "Agency actions are playing with procedure—use the process to your advantage." But, Fisch riffed, "Let's say you hear nothing from the agency for months—I bet you think it is safe to assume that the agency must have understood your perfectly reasonable account, and all is well." Everyone laughed. Lusero let the laughter die down and then told the crowd seriously, and clearly, "When an authority comes to you, no matter how convincing that authority is, you *must* tell them: 'My attorney really won't let me talk to anybody before I talk to them.'"[13]

Frequently throughout the session, in response to frustration about legal status and rules from audience members, Lusero and Fisch repeated a phrase that is familiar to those of us who teach and study legal mobilization: "Change takes time—law will change. But it takes time." It also, as their own careers as lawyers, activists, and consumers make clear, takes concerted mobilization across a range of styles and beliefs.

As the presentation began to wrap up, Lusero reminded the crowd, "Look, regulatory agencies have a range of punishments, and a private letter of admonishment is moderate compared to a suspension of license, or yanking your license. In most cases . . . "—and here they started campily playing to the crowd, cajoling them that in their practice, just like in Monopoly—"You will pass go! You will get $200!"

At that moment, someone in the hall yelled out, "Do you get out of jail free?" Lusero's response was absolutely serious, though said with a chuckle: "Just don't go to jail."[14]

Of course, Gina *did* go to jail—and Ophelia felt she could have—and defending midwives against criminal prosecution absolutely became an important part of the rallying cry behind legalization advocacy, as well as an important part of the story of midwifery told in any given locale. As we have seen, in the 1980s and 90s, as midwives began their renaissance in the United States, they were at heightened risk for prosecution, and that risk led them to defensively develop stronger national and local organization. The *Washington Post* reported in 2002 that in the 1990s more than 300 midwives were investigated, sanctioned, or prosecuted in the United States.[15] In Missouri this history helped eventual efforts at legalization. In other states, it simply drove midwives out, or underground.

In the early 2000s, a similar risk of prosecution reasserted itself—with similar consequences for organizing.[16] As Katherine Beckett and Bruce Hoffman rightly noted in 2005,

> [T]he threat of legal harassment has stimulated the expansion and organization of alternative birthing communities; the establishment of local,

regional, and national ties between these groups; and, later, the emergence of national and international organizations dedicated to the protection of birthing alternatives and midwifery.[17]

The threat and reality of the criminal prosecution of midwives also offered a more traditional and readily recognizable form of cause lawyering to those advocates who were inclined to use their professional training in defense of those midwives.

In Ohio, when a midwife there was charged with practicing medicine without a license in the early 2000s, the national Big Push movement was born. In Pennsylvania in 2005, a state where non-nurse midwifery is technically legal but unregulated, the state has fined Diane Goslin $11,000 for attending an Amish homebirth as an unlicensed midwife and, after the death of the baby she delivered, ordered her to stop practicing immediately. The representative from the State Board of Nursing told the press, "Her violations of the law are grave because her conduct puts women and their newborn infants at risk."[18]

In 2006, *The New York Times*'s Adam Liptak cited law professor Stacey Tovino, who told him that prosecution almost always starts with a tragedy.[19] He reported on the prosecution of Indiana midwife Jennifer Williams, which took place after she attended to the birth of Oliver Meredith, who died. Melanie Moore, mother of six, and an Iowa midwife for fourteen years at the time of her prosecution, has CPM certification that the state does not recognize. In April 2007 she was charged with practicing medicine without a license, a class D felony. She faced up to five years in prison and/or $7,500 in fines if found guilty.[20] Also in 2007, another Iowa midwife, Kathy Deol, was charged by the Iowa Board of Nursing with "incompetency . . . or willful or repeated failure to practice within the scope of current licensure or level of preparation."[21] Deol was a registered nurse who admitted that she attended out-of-hospital birth but claimed that she did so in her capacity as a lay midwife, because the state refused to license CPMs.

Of course, legal status doesn't always make practice safer. In Missouri, Ophelia tells me, right after legalization, "There were prosecuting attorneys . . . who were going to be more active" and made those plans for prosecution and stepped-up enforcement known to the community. There were three different counties, in particular, where midwives feared aggressive prosecution. But, she tells me, "We went to the AG's office and talked him out of it."

In perfectly legal Simi Valley, California, Marcia McCulley was arrested in 2007 by officers with guns drawn, charged with practicing medicine without a license. She was a nurse practitioner and licensed midwife, but both of those licenses had been suspended by the relevant boards when they learned she was attending out-of-hospital births for moms seeking VBAC. Though the district attorney for the state dropped all charges against her, the administrative findings cost her $68,000 in restitution of the legal fees incurred by the medical boards investigating her, and her practice in southern California was destroyed by the negative publicity. Selective prosecutions and investigations have continued, with arrests in Colorado, Massachusetts, Arizona, and Pennsylvania causing concern at MANA meetings in 2015, 2016, and 2017.

Then, at the very close of 2019, another arrest rocked the national midwifery community. Elizabeth Catlin, a certified professional midwife who had long openly served Mennonite and other rural communities of upstate New York—though New York does not authorize the practice of CPMs—was brought into custody twice in late 2018, reportedly after a doctor new to the region took issue with her practice. Police originally let Catlin know that she was under arrest for "pretending to be a midwife."[22] The New York district attorney eventually charged Catlin with 95 felony counts, including one count of criminally negligent homicide.[23] If convicted on all counts, Catlin faces up to 473 years in prison; this is the most vigorous prosecution of a midwife in contemporary times.

All of these arrests—and, further, the threat of arrests—have significant impacts on the midwives subject to them and to practices in the region. They also have significant chilling impacts on midwifery care across the country—as CPMs and direct-entry midwives who practice out-of-hospital birth wonder if they are next. They will certainly remember Lusero's exhortation, "Just don't go to jail."

At meetings of the BRBA and MANA, midwives and advocates have a unique forum to discuss prosecution—how to avoid it and how to live through it. Clearly, failed homebirths and bad outcomes, as well as hospital transfers, all trigger investigation and make a midwife vulnerable to prosecution.[24] As one midwife told my research assistant, "The unnecessary death of just one baby in a whole state has a really big impact," both in terms of morale among families and midwives and in terms of the state's interest in and surveillance of midwifery practices.[25] In fact, Illinois—the home of the two inaugural BRBA meetings—is a state that had "pretty much shut everyone down through prosecutions."[26] Not always, though. Valerie, a midwife in a state where her practice is illegal, told activists gathered at the Birth Rights Bar Association that she has been working forty-plus years to legalize direct entry midwives, while continuing to attend births. "I got cease and desist orders in the late 90s. My response was to keep doing it."[27]

OBSTETRIC VIOLENCE TORT LITIGATION

Another form of activist lawyering associated with midwifery advocacy takes place when lawyers represent women in tort and malpractice suits alleging obstetric harm and violence from their in-hospital care providers. Attention to obstetric violence has grown recently, in part because of excellent feminist legal scholarship on the topic[28] and in part because, in their own practices, midwives use hospital birth stories and qualitative data to understand obstetric violence as a motivator for consumer demands.

Ndeya—a birthworker and graduate student—who has collected 100 birth stories of women of color in the Bay Area—told the audience at the BirthKeepers Summit during a plenary on obstetric harm, "You shouldn't have to fear violence" when you give birth, but that, unfortunately, many women do. Arishka, who also addressed the group, said she entered midwifery because "I swore I would never treat women the way I had been treated" during pregnancy, labor, and birth. And Sushila told a packed auditorium that her experience of birth—being strapped down and given a forced episiotomy—made her decide to become a midwife. She purposely did not go into nurse midwifery, where she felt the medical model would be replicated, but instead began a direct-entry apprenticeship where she felt she could play a role in reclaiming both women's knowing, and women's ways of knowing.[29]

Kathi Valeii, the author and activist behind Birth Anarchy, presented a breakout session at the BirthKeepers Summit on birth violence:

Women are subjected to forced vaginal exams in spite of their verbal protests; they have episiotomies and amniocentesis done against their expressed will; they have medications placed without awareness or consent;

they are tethered, physically held down, and verbally bitch slapped into compliance.

Unlike acts of sexual assault that take place in the known realms of a domestic situation or random acts of senseless violence, women who are subjected to obstetrical violations on a hospital table under a spotlight during birth often do not feel like they have a voice. Not only is she silenced during the experience, but she is told to calm down if she chooses to mention it afterward.

A woman who feels her assault was rape and uses the term finds herself ridiculed—told that her use of the word negates the experience of one who's experienced "true" rape. But what other word is there for someone whose sexual organs are exposed, whose legs are physically pried open, who is subjected to forced penetration over and over amidst her screaming and pleading for it to stop? And what makes one version of rape real and another not, anyway?

Valeii told those at her workshop session, "We have to stop blaming women for the circumstances of their births—just like we have to stop blaming women for sexual assault."[30] Rather, she and others argue, we must blame the way industrialized birth proceeds and those practices within the medical model that fail to treat birth as a natural and normal event. Sheila Kitzinger, in her oft-cited history of midwifery in contemporary societies, agrees that obstetric violence is akin to rape—and, she argues, it is not as much the pain that mothers feel and mourn, as the lack of respect, consultation, and consent.[31]

Elizabeth Kukura notes, "There has been no comprehensive study of obstetric violence in the United States, and no estimate of its prevalence exists in the research. . . . [but the] lack of research on mistreatment in childbirth does not mean the problem is nonexistent. . . . Instead, it reflects the extent to which it has been obscured from public awareness."[32] In response to calls from lawyers and mothers for increased attention to coercion, force, and abuse during childbirth, activists and researchers have begun collecting and disseminating stories of obstetric harm.

Recently, the website Birth Monopoly has amplified their collaboration with two different projects: "Exposing the Silence" and the "Listening to Mothers." Birth Monopoly defines obstetric violence as "the normalized mistreatment of women and birthing people in the childbirth setting. It is an attempt to control a woman's body and decisions, violating her autonomy and dignity." The website offers examples of obstetric violence—including when "an episiotomy is cut without consent," when doctors "ignore a laboring person's question," and when hospital personnel "speak only to the white doula instead of the black patient."[33] The site offers legal advice as well as resources for healing.

Although tort law "in its current form is an inadequate tool for addressing the problem of obstetric violence,"[34] it is a tool that could still be usefully developed. The lawyers affiliated with Birth Rights Bar Association, who often overlap with lawyers for the National Advocates for Pregnant Women, work hard to represent people harmed in birth and strive to change the legal language by bringing tort and malpractice actions against hospitals and doctors for obstetric violence.

One form of this harm is a forced C-section, which is theorized by women's lawyers (and the Eleventh Circuit) to be a violation of their due process rights.[35] *The Guardian* reported in 2017 that, "In 2003, researchers surveyed the maternal-fetal medicine directors at 42 hospitals [in the US] and learned of nine cases in which a hospital forced a pregnant woman to undergo treatment using a court order."[36] The National Advocates for Pregnant Women has documented thirty cases of forced C-section via court order between 1973 and 2005.[37] An untold number of women have been forced to undergo these treatments without a court order, some under threat by their doctors of being charged with child abuse or endangerment.[38] The 2016 case brought on behalf of Rinat Dray highlights the policies internal to private hospitals that permit this coercion.

Dray, an Orthodox Jewish woman, refused a doctor-recommended C-section for the birth of her third child. She had had two C-sections previously, and the complications from those surgeries had negatively impacted her ability to bond with those children and mother them. Dray's religious affiliation is important to note here—not because the medical intervention was a further violation of her religious rights but because, as an Orthodox woman, she hoped to have many children. As she had delivered via C-section twice previously, she knew that a vaginal birth for her third would be the best way to avoid future C-sections and that a third C-section would guarantee her next deliveries would also be surgical. She wanted a chance to avoid another surgery and asked for more time during her laboring period.

Medical charts indicate that the doctor was cognizant of her desire to labor longer and that Dray was conscious and capable of decision making. The doctor disagreed with Dray and overrode her decision.

The hospital's policy, which permits and even instructs doctors to override pregnant people's wishes if they differ from medical opinion about what is best for the fetus, goes against guidance by both the American Academy of Pediatrics (AAP) and the American College of Obstetricians and Gynecologists (ACOG). Both AAP and ACOG "condemn procedures performed without a mother's consent for the benefit of her fetus."[39] An ACOG Committee on Ethics policy statement reads, "Pregnancy is not an exception to the principle that a decisionally capable patient has the right to refuse treatment, even treatment needed to maintain life." And, a joint statement from ACOG and the AAP reads, "Even the strongest evidence for fetal benefit would not be sufficient ethically to ever override a pregnant woman's decision to forgo fetal treatment."

Dray's lawyers argued that what Staten Island University Hospital had done was both against the law and unethical. Wendy Chavkin and Farah Diaz-Tello, lawyers for National Advocates for Pregnant Women, argued:

> Obtaining consent from a competent patient is not only an ethical obligation in medicine, but also a legal one. With very few exceptions, the law vests the final decision-making authority in patients. Performance of a medical intervention, even a lifesaving one, against the patient's wishes is a battery; failure to adequately inform the patient of risks and benefits with the intervention constitutes negligence.[40]

Notably, as NAPW and BRBA lawyers point out, no other class of person can be required to undergo medical treatment in order to save another's life. Only pregnant and laboring people are limited in their decision-making capacity in this way.

The forced operation caused damage to Dray's bladder; the refusal to honor her bodily autonomy caused damage to her dignity. Though she had vigorous representation in her claim against the doctor and the hospital, Dray did not win her lawsuit.[41] The courts, referencing New York State's ban on abortion at twenty-four weeks in support of its opinion, held that Dray could refuse treatment that would help her but could not refuse treatment on behalf of the fetus, as it was over twenty-four weeks gestational age.[42]

Such use of anti-abortion measures is not unheard of to coerce laboring women into surgery; in Utah, in 2004, Melissa Rowland was charged with homicide after she delayed having a C-section, and one of her twins was stillborn. She pled guilty to a lesser charge of child endangerment.

Glamour magazine and several other mainstream media outlets have taken up the issue of forced C-section and have profiled Dray and other birthing people who were forced to undergo unwanted and often unnecessary interventions.[43] The language these women use to describe their experiences is striking: Dray and others recall "begging" and "pleading" with physicians; they have limited memory of the surgeries by which their children were born, only that they "cried throughout it all," and they felt disempowered, unheard, and denied their own advocacy. Many developed postpartum depression, had difficulties breastfeeding and bonding, and developed PTSD from the trauma of the forced surgery.

The amicus brief filed by the Birth Rights Bar Association along with four other organizations offered narratives from other women harmed through coercive and forceful means during labor and delivery, as a way of contextualizing what happened to Dray within a larger set of social and institutional factors. They document one woman in New York who was "forcibly twisted from her position on her hands and knees onto her back for no medical reason, just as her baby's head was emerging," and another, in Arizona who said, "When I asked why I needed a C-section they started to threaten me. The nurse said in a very strict tone that I needed to cooperate, otherwise I could have my baby taken away. She pointed out that I was a young mother." The threat to call child welfare offices was often cited as a reason mothers "consented" to various procedures, and a reason why they did not pursue litigation or redress after them.[44]

A mother in Texas said that when she challenged the obstetrician who wanted to induce her labor, his assistant

> told us that he was very upset with me and I wasn't to leave until saw him or they'd have to call CPS. . . . When he finally did arrive . . . he verbally abused me, and my husband—yelling at the top of his lungs about what a horribly selfish and dangerous parent I was. He said if I didn't go through with the induction today that he would do everything in his power to make sure CPS would take my children.[45]

In an academic journal article published in 2013, NAPW lawyers Lynne Paltrow and Jeanne Flavin document more than 400 arrests or forced interventions on pregnant women in the United States between 1973 and 2005. This illustrates the propensity of doctors, hospitals, and the state to coerce or force behaviors that women may not see as in their own best interest.[46]

One of the founders of the Birth Monopoly website, Cristen Pascucci, was instrumental in supporting Caroline and J. T. Malatesta when they sued their care provider in Alabama. In the aftermath, Caroline wrote the birth story of her son Jack for the site. She wanted to labor on her hands and knees, she remembers, but the nurses refused to allow it, and physically held her down, while she was pushing. She writes:

> The nurses held me down and pressed my baby's head into my vagina to delay delivery as he was trying to come out. It literally was torture. I screamed, "Stop!" to the nurses, but no one listened. The medical records summed up my reaction to the physical force quite well: "Unfortunately, the patient was not able to [act] in a controlled manner. She was pretty much all over the bed." My doula ran in around this time. I looked at her in desperation and pled, "Help me!" but she could not. This went on for six minutes—me struggling, the nurses physically holding baby Jack in my body—when the doctor arrived. The nurse let go of baby Jack's head, and he was born immediately into the doctor's hands. I vividly remember the moment his head popped out. My right foot was planted firmly on the bed, elevating my hips as I tried to get off my back one last time, and a nurse was pushing my left leg awkwardly and asymmetrically toward my chest, causing me horrible pain.[47]

Malatesta suffered nerve injury as a result of the birth, as well as emotional trauma.[48] Four years later, she still had debilitating chronic pain and had been diagnosed with PTSD. A stay-at-home mom of five, Malatesta's labor and delivery dramatically and negatively changed her life, and the life of her family. After a two-week trial, an Alabama jury awarded the Malatestas $16 million—agreeing with them and their attorneys that the hospital staff visited obstetric violence upon her during the labor and delivery.

At the time Malatesta labored and delivered in Alabama, the state was ranked the seventh worst state for C-sections in the United States. With a rate of 35.3 percent, it was considered one of the worst states to have a baby, second only to Mississippi.[49] CPMs were illegal and the movement to legalize them had suffered innumerable setbacks. Amazingly, though—and as a direct result of the successful tort action, the publicity it generated, and decades-long activism of the Alabama Birth Coalition—in 2017, Governor Kay Ivey signed HB315, legalizing CPMs. The night before the law was passed, with just hours before the session ended, moms, midwives, and advocates threatened a sit-in at the capitol to bring the bill to a vote.[50]

In her statement upon signing, Ivey said:

> After thoughtful and deliberate consideration, I signed the midwifery bill because it gives mothers more options to choose how to deliver their baby, while simultaneously ensuring that those midwives who practice in Alabama are qualified to do so.
>
> . . . HB315 strikes the appropriate balance of removing regulations to allow midwives to practice, while also making sure offered services are safe for and in the best interests of mothers and children.51

The Alabama Board of Midwifery issued its first licenses for CPMs on January 18, 2019. Decades after lay midwifery was criminalized in the state in 1976, Alabama now has three CPMs practicing openly.

The issue of obstetric violence is a difficult one to read and speak about—but it is central to the shifting consumer demands for midwifery, it is central to midwives' own reasons for entering their profession, and it is central to some of the lawsuits that have contributed to legal status in states that have previously been intractable on change. Tort litigation against hospitals and doctors on grounds of obstetric violence is also a clear area of legal mobilization for birth justice lawyers.

REGULATORY GOVERNANCE AND RULEMAKING

After the political maneuvering necessary to getting legislation written and passed, advocates were often surprised to find that it felt like their struggle toward licensure was just beginning. National organizations assisted in the rulemaking conversation by providing both moral support and expertise. For instance, the multidisciplinary and multiperspective researchers associated with the Homebirth Summit followed a painstaking process of consensus-building, across nine vision statements and nine task forces, wherein "everyone in the room had to agree on everything." The regulatory policy task force determined that three aspects of the regulatory environment are the most crucial to the success of midwifery in any given state: prescriptive authority, autonomy of practice, and type of board for governance. Their guidance provides a useful template for state regulations.

Even so, the outcomes of rulemaking vary tremendously from state to state. Differences abound around composition of the regulatory board, scope of practice, insurance requirements, eligibility for reimbursement, autonomous practice, and review of regulations. And, though midwives and advocates do not lack for models from around the country to consult for guidance, the language is often obfuscatory, alienating, and confusing—requiring, in some instances, both legal and medical translation.[52] The effort is also worth it, though: Well-written regulations, midwives and researchers agree, can positively impact, "on a generational level, the quality of care."[53]

Because it is easier to pass a bill that doesn't have details regarding practice—and because passing bills that are vague usually means that constituents and midwives end up with better practice recommendations for safe out-of-hospital birth—most state advocates seek bills that simply legalize and regulate, while deferring the work of rulemaking to after enactment. National advocates advise groups to write bills "using boilerplate language for other professionals in your state, and just put CPM in there" or to take boilerplate language from other states' CPM legalization bills and "insert your state."[54]

This makes tremendous sense to get a bill passed, and to get midwifery regulated appropriately. But, as a Michigan attorney told us, "It took us eight years to get a law in Michigan—and let me tell you, writing and passing a bill is a walk in the park, compared to rulemaking."[55] At this point in the process, though the rulemaking was accomplished by a committee that didn't include attorneys (at least not in their capacity as attorneys), legal expertise around regulatory policymaking was useful to have. Both legislative and administrative processes "necessitate insider baseball," but the former necessitated political savvy and interpersonal relationship building, the latter required knowledge of other states' regulatory bodies, combined with a deep understanding of the best practices for out-of-hospital birth attendants.[56] A presenter at a MANA session explained that while the political process was winner-take-all and zero sum, at its best "Rulemaking on regulations is consensus-based and evidence-based."[57] Rulemaking combines both legal and midwifery expertise.

Before the state can adopt rules for midwives and adequately regulate them, it must authorize a committee to make decisions. And even that decision is controversial. How many midwives will be on the committee? How many consumers? How many ob-gyns, labor and delivery nurses, and nurse-midwives? Should organizations who opposed the licensure bill have a seat at the table for rulemaking? Sometimes legislation outlines the composition of the study committee for rulemaking, oftentimes it does not. After the number and types of board members are decided, the question of specificity comes up. Which ob-gyn should serve? Which midwife? Which consumer?

To even get to the table can be exhausting.

Most midwives and advocates agree that the best board is one that is made up of people familiar with out-of-hospital birth, and certainly not made up of people hostile to the practice. Because a primary role of the governing board is to field and investigate complaints that are brought to it, it is essential that the board be comprised of people who understand midwifery care and are not unreflectively hostile to out-of-hospital birth. Though midwives and their advocates did not emphasize the importance of an investigatory component, it was clearly an essential part of the push for legal status. As Ida Darragh, vice president of NARM, told the group gathered at The Big Push, "In an illegal state you can't figure out who is a good midwife or not. And everyone suffers from rumors. Licensure [and a process of complaint management] make it procedurally clear how to investigate."[58] For many reasons, good governing boards also increase consumer confidence.

Some states seek to regulate midwives under boards of "healing arts" or "alternative medicine," which often include chiropractors and herbalists/naturopaths. Some want them regulated under the same bodies as massage therapists, dieticians, and aestheticians. In New Jersey, midwifery is regulated under the state's Board of Medicine, and many members of the board are reportedly hostile to homebirth. Midwives almost always prefer an independent board, based within the Department of Health, dedicated to midwifery and out-of-hospital birth and recognizing the distinct profession of midwifery. In some cases, legislators hoping to "kill a bill" will propose an unworkable board makeup, hoping the effort at legalization will stall or die. This happened in New Hampshire on the way to a legalization vote. Carol Leonard writes:

To my horror, when I finally see a copy of our bill, it isn't anything like our original draft. Now, midwifery has been placed under the Board of Medicine (not the Department of Health and Human Services). And to make matters worse, the proposed Board of Advisors who makes the decisions pertaining to midwifery practice consists entirely of *physicians*. There isn't a bloody midwife in the bunch! I am horrified. This bill is a joke. It will simply legislate midwives out of existence.[59]

Leonard and the other New Hampshire midwives had been working with Representative Eugene Daniell, a man in his eighties who sponsored the homebirth bill because, in his words, he'd "be damned if anyone is going to tell him where he can or cannot be born or where he can or cannot die." When he saw the language of the bill, he looked puzzled and said, "Isn't this Board like throwing the fox into the hen house? Why do these boys always feel the need to tell the girls what to do?" He tabled the bill to rework it, and New Hampshire's midwifery bill passed the next year, following emotional testimony from a mom who, after her baby died, said she would still absolutely use midwives again.[60]

In Iowa, the 2012 bill would have had midwifery regulated by a board comprised primarily of Iowa Midwifery Association members. Later iterations of bills in that state would have it regulated by seven board members—three CPMs, an ob-gyn or family physician with homebirth experience, a certified nurse midwife with homebirth experience, and two consumers. This is very similar to schemes in many states—some add a pediatrician—and many are considered "stacked" with those who already agree with out-of-hospital birth and have experience with it.[61]

The conversation in every state rulemaking or legislative action relating to legalization and regulation also includes a discussion of licensing fees to support the regulatory board. Though it is historically rare, in this era of constrained budget and a professed love of small government, states are increasingly asking new regulatory bodies to be, or to become within a set period of time, self-funding. One state, for example, has set the fee at $450 per license, with a $200 fee to renew. The fees will reduce to $75 to renew, once the board is self-sustaining through licensing fees—which, given the scarcity of midwives in the state, will be several years, if not decades. The same state made an exception for Amish midwives, who do not need to pay a fee in order to be licensed, which will further slow the board from being self-sustaining.[62]

Fee structuring is difficult, as a representative from Florida told a group of advocates. "We're [seemingly] expensive because rather than calculating the cost of regulation across all professions, they give you a piece of a pie. On the nursing cost spread, it [nursing] costs the state about 25 bucks; but midwives fees are about 500 bucks and that still leaves [the board] running a deficit of a couple hundred thousand dollars." She noted, "In times of economic hardship the cost of regulating midwives comes up" as a problem for the state.[63]

The ideal situation is a state-funded regulatory board made up of people who understand and are not hostile to out-of-hospital birth attended by a CPM, with reasonable licensing fees and provisions that strengthen peer review. Absolutely ideal is seldom fully possible.

Once the governing board makeup has been determined, rulemaking efforts often turn toward defining scope of practice and prescriptive authority. In order to be safe providers of health care, midwives must be able to carry specific medical equipment and administer specific medications. Midwives do not usually seek prescriptive authority but do often argue that in order for their care to be safe, they need to be able to "obtain and administer" several items. These include Pitocin, which is used to augment labor in hospital settings, and is also essential for stopping maternal hemorrhage after birth; oxygen (for moms and babies); analgesics to enable their ability to stitch tears without pain; antibiotics; erythromycin ointment to prevent neonatal conjunctivitis; and vitamin K to prevent a rare but dangerous bleeding disorder in infants.[64]

In some states, there are no problems with this list. In Iowa, for example, the former lobbyist for the midwives told us, "The formulary has never been an issue here—legislators are okay with it, pharmacists are fine with it." She added, "Heck, they used to think midwives carried [drugs] anyway."[65] I recall conversations with Iowa legislators who happily analogized, for me, the kit a midwife would bring to a birth to the kit a veterinarian would bring to a farm, when assisting a stalled heifer, mare, or ewe in labor. In other states, though, the formulary is highly controversial—especially surrounding Pitocin, which legislators worry will be used as an abortifacient. Sometimes, regulatory policy forces midwives who practice legally to carry things that are illegal—like oxygen and Pitocin—in order to better serve their clients.

Another significant issue within the regulatory governance that surrounds midwifery relates to the scope-of-practice debate—which types of pregnancies and births will automatically be "risked out" of out-of-hospital care. "When physicians come to the table, there will be scope of practice negotiations."[66] Physicians and midwives disagree on the viability of out-of-hospital birth for three conditions in particular: VBAC, breech, and multiples. Midwives often remind legislators that a C-section is major abdominal surgery. Good candidates for VBAC—those who have the right kind of stitch, who are prescreened, and who are working with a skilled practitioner—have a very good chance of avoiding that surgery and experiencing physiologic birth.

In many cases, the safety of practices involved in midwives' attendance at particular births with breech presentations or for a particular mom wanting to experience VBAC is subsumed by a blanket statement against such practices made by professional organizations like ACOG.

Sometimes, statutory authority and rulemaking combine to create strange limitations on practice. In Florida in 2009, for example, the state's attorney interpreted the statute authorizing the state's twenty-seven birth centers to constitute a ban on the practice of VBACs in those locales—but the CPM legalization statute and rulemaking allows VBAC at home. Because Florida has an astronomically high C-section rate, 56 percent overall with 72 percent in one hospital in Miami alone, a sizable number of women and their pregnancies are impacted by this confusing interpretation.

One of the most important—and sometimes quite difficult to achieve—aspects of midwifery care under state regulations is the guarantee of autonomous practice: the guarantee that a midwife's practice is not predicated on a supervisory relationship or collaborative agreement with a physician. Not only is it difficult for midwives to find supervising doctors, but research by medical school faculty has shown that such supervision may well be unnecessary. In fact, in studies of nurse midwifery, it is well established that there is a

> positive association between state-level policies that support autonomous
> [nurse] midwifery practice and a larger midwifery workforce as well as
> more midwife-attended deliveries. States with regulations allowing au-
> tonomous practice had approximately double the supply of midwives per

1,000 births. . . . [W]omen giving birth in states with autonomous mid-wifery practice had a nearly 60% greater chance of having a CNM as the delivery attendant.[67]

Even more important, there are "correlations between autonomous practice and better birth outcomes" for CNMs.[68] Advocates for CPMs believe the same would be and is true of their practice—and evidence on integration of care, collated and distributed by the Birth Place Lab, indicates they are likely correct.

Aside from these larger issues of board composition, formulary, scope of practice, and collaborative agreement, there are also dozens of smaller administrative considerations to be made during rulemaking. For the most part, national organizations like MANA and The Big Push advocate for outcomes in rulemaking that will put licensed midwives into compliance with ICM and MANA standards. This requires changes, sometimes, that previous legislative sessions and governing bodies did not view as important because professional standards change. The insertion of sunset review provisions enables states to go back to fill these gaps, though sunset review is occasionally stressful for midwives and advocates.

As one Pusher from Florida told the assembled group at the Knowledge Exchange Session in 2009,

> I am, unfortunately, the president of our organization. Florida is pretty quiet—but we have an expectation of having a sunset review in the near future, which sent us into a mini panic a year and a half ago. We keep harassing the sunset review committee, and all we can get out of them is that review will happen by 2014. You get a year's notice, and everything that falls within DPH is due to occur by 2014. When the pro-midwife Florida law was dissolved last time, it happened in sunset. So, we're trying to get our ducks in a row in terms of fundraising and robust organization and looking at ways to combat what we expect to come out of sunset.[69]

In Oregon in 2012, for example, a sunset review of existing regulatory governance led to the recommendation that birth certificates should "capture the intended place of birth and intended attendant" so that use of midwives would be reflected in the data gathered by the state.[70] This change in the Oregon law brought the state, which is thought to have generally good regulations for practice, back to national standard as set by MANA. Such specificity on birth certificates enables better data gathering, which in turn will inform best practices.

Indeed, the role of regulatory bodies in facilitating evidence-based practice was often lauded by pro-legalization advocates. As one Iowa advocate noted, "If midwives were regulated, it would be easier to track data through the Iowa Department of Public Health." Her colleague added, "This would facilitate evidence-based care."[71]

California and Washington have legally protected and privileged peer-review processes, as a benefit "conferred through the professional association," another nod to international standards of practice.[72] And, in Maine, midwives laud the regulatory process that led them to allow reciprocity—such that when licensed CPMs from out of state move to Maine, they are legal to practice; this eases the transition to practicing in the state and removes barriers to access.

Finally, midwives benefit (and so do consumers) when they are able to be reimbursed via Medicaid and private insurance for their services. Sometimes, the question of reimbursement comes up during rulemaking; other times, it comes up as part of health care conversations held elsewhere in the state government apparatus. And, though there is a clear benefit to consumers to have coverage, it isn't always an uncontroversial ask. For instance, a midwife named Beverly told me that in Missouri, there was the sense prior to legalization that "St. Louis [midwives and consumers] really want Medicaid—rural midwives don't." Further, some advocates believe that "City midwives are more professional and would rather be more mainstream" so they wouldn't be riled by rules on the way to reimbursement, whereas more renegade rural midwives would chafe at excess reporting requirements that come with Medicaid reimbursement.

In Florida, 50 to 55 percent of women are covered by Medicaid for pregnancy and delivery. Florida midwife advocates report that while the reimbursement rate is "sucky" at around "30 percent less than ob's get," the state does reimburse quickly and easily. Insurance companies are also required to cover homebirth services at the same reimbursement rate as the state, though midwives there report that the reimbursement process for private insurers is slow.[73]

All of these considerations add up to what one speaker at the Birth Rights Bar Association described as a "byzantine process"; she found that it was "harder to write the rules than write the bill." Fortunately, though, it is also a process that—because the law has been passed and the state is invested in it—is "weighted heavily towards success."[74]

. . .

Legal mobilization for midwifery takes several forms and infrequently includes the kinds of cause or activist lawyering common to rights-based strategies. Occasionally, lawyers mobilize to defend midwives who are being prosecuted, or to provide representation for women seeking redress against obstetric harm. More frequently, legal mobilization on behalf of midwives takes the form of legal translation in pursuit of regulatory governance: Lawyers explain rulemaking and help advocates navigate an often exhausting and sometimes bewildering set of processes to establish good policies to govern midwifery. Legal mobilization for midwives is about rights, certainly—but it is also, importantly and more frequently, about rules and regulations.

5 CATCHING BABIES AND CATCHING HELL
Constitutive Interactions in the Limits and Shadow of the Law

"I catch babies, and I catch hell."
—Susanne, a midwife in California

I BEGAN MY RESEARCH on this project while living in a perfectly legal state. In California in 2005, CPMs were licensed and regulated—and had been since 1993 and the passage of the California Licensed Midwives Practice Act. Midwives in the state were able to advertise for clients, receive Medi-Cal and insurance reimbursement, and be mostly open in their practice. It was not difficult to find CPMs to attend homebirth in California, and I had no problem finding interview subjects. There were listings of midwives in the yellow pages, online, at birth centers, at birthing classes, at the yoga studios where I practiced, and at the natural food groceries where I shopped. My friends had used midwives, and even the nurse practitioner at my HMO could have given me a referral or two, if I had only known to ask. Many of the moms I knew had had out-of-hospital birth attended by midwives; it seemed a cultural norm.

One day, though, a friend told me that her midwife (who had attended the births of both of her sons and was also the family's licensed chiropractor and homeopath) had closed the birthing part of her practice.[1] The physician with whom she had had a longstanding relationship told her he could no longer afford to carry her on his insurance plan. Indeed, Stacey Tovino notes that, after 1993 and the legalization of lay midwifery in California, "Many medical malpractice carriers discontinued coverage of, or dramatically increased premiums for, those physicians who supervised midwives."[2] And, though California law does *not* require certified professional midwives to carry malpractice insurance, the regulations do require midwives to disclose their uninsured status.[3] As well, in order to rent office space, many landlords require the renter to be "appropriately" insured. My friend's midwife could not afford to purchase her own insurance for a coverage amount that made sense for her practice. So, rather than risk operating in violation of the law (without a supervisor) or without insurance coverage, this midwife abandoned that part of her practice.[4]

I learned quickly that the disclosure requirement and demands of landlords motivated some other midwives to seek coverage. Patti, whom I interviewed over a long breakfast at a Denny's in a strip mall in Orange County, had recently purchased malpractice insurance when I spoke with her. "I just got it," she tells me. For $2,600—just shy of what she would charge one client for prenatal care and birth—she could afford a year's coverage of up to $50,000 liability. She scoffs, "It's nothing. It was a total waste of my trip, of my time." She continues:

> And the only reason I got it was because the office I was working out of required me to have medical malpractice, so I found a place that sold it. . . . I had to go to Utah to get it. 'Cause California doesn't *have* it. . . . The only place I could find it is in Utah. . . . Anyway, this insurance company was a smaller insurance company, and the rule in Utah was you could go there to procure your insurance, but they couldn't come to you. Could not do it over the phone; you had to do it in person.

It sounded so illicit, this buying of insurance. When I ask her how she had even found the company that covered her, Patti says, "friend of a friend." Then she continues, "So anyway, it turns out I could only afford about $50,000 [in coverage]. Which won't cover anything." She reiterates, "I mean, it is a waste of time. [The practice I collaborate with] they want [us to have] a million dollars. Well a million dollars is going to be like $30,000 or $40,000 a year." She shrugs,

> I've been practicing for fifteen years, never been sued. . . . And most midwifes don't have it. So, like I said, the only reason [to get it is] because you need it, you need it to rent office space. So, that's why I got it. It was just jumping through hoops to close loopholes.

In this case, the law was clear—Patti wasn't required to have insurance coverage; but she couldn't rent office space without it.

The requirement that midwives have collaborative agreements with physicians had a similar impact on practice in southern California. When I met with Angie, I asked her to explain the relationship she, as a midwife, had with the doctor with whom she worked. The transcription from that portion of the interview reads like this:

[SILENCE THEN LAUGHTER]
RENÉE: You don't work with a doctor?
ANGIE: Nobody can find doctor backup.
RENÉE: Which is required . . . ?
ANGIE: Well, according to the law . . .
[SILENCE]
ANGIE: Please turn the tape off.

Those midwives in California who were unwilling or unable to get in-surance coverage, and unwilling to shoulder the perceived liability risk, or were unable or unwilling to get a physician to "supervise" their practices, and were afraid of the consequences, closed down their practices. This didn't mean that homebirth ended. Nancy, a mother in Los Angeles County, upon hearing that her midwife had closed her practice out of fear of lawsuit and inability to afford coverage, told a group of women assembled for a La Leche League meeting in spring of 2005, "Women in the South Bay are going to start taking things into their own hands."[5] She meant, as I soon found out, that women unable to find lay or direct-entry midwives for their homebirths were going to form networks to teach each other how to give birth at home, unassisted—just like before CPM licensure.

APPRENTICE RELATIONSHIPS

Of course, I was also beginning this research at a time and in a place where all of those issues had been brought to the fore by tragic circumstances. The Hollywood Birth Center had just been closed down, after a bad outcome in a birth attended by an apprentice midwife operating without a preceptor present. Given this, the apprenticeship question in particular was on the minds of many regulators and midwives in California at least, and it was evident from press reports that the status of the law was anything but clear.

In fact, neither the 1993 law legalizing lay midwives, nor the 2000 amendment to the law outlining NARM credentialing, discussed the apprenticeship issue. This isn't an incredibly odd omission,[6] given that CPMs often gain their knowledge and experience primarily through apprenticeship relationships, and NARM's credentialing explicitly recognized apprenticeship models as part of the PEP route to the CPM. Midwives assumed the practice of apprenticeship and knowledge transfer in that way was valid under the language of the law. Some regulators and most midwives interpreted the lack of wording about apprenticing in the California law as a tacit acknowledgment and endorsement of centuries of midwifery-training practice and NARM rules. Others, though, interpreted the lack of wording to mean that California midwives all needed to go through some sort of formal didactic educational process in order to obtain licensure and certification.

California lawmakers moved to rectify the confusion with clarifying legislation in 2005. That legislation allowed apprenticeship relationships, but also placed constraints on the role apprentices could play in birth. In 2006, though, even after legislative clarification, several California midwives cited the ambiguity in the law, and the prosecution of the apprentice and the preceptor at the Hollywood Birth Center, as strains on their practices. When I spoke with Patti, she told me:

> There's a big deal about apprentices right now. . . . Okay, the whole idea behind lay midwifery or traditional midwifery is that you learn it in the field. Yes, you're gonna take neonatal resuscitation or you might take IV therapy or you know, you might take an ob crisis class at a hospital or . . . even a fetal monitoring class. You do take some classes, and you read lots of books. But the main learning mechanism is learning with another midwife and learning on the scene. And part of it, too, is using, I feel, using your own intuition, because you know, I think you know as a human being what another person would need. . . .
>
> So, for a while there, there was a big brouhaha about midwives taking apprentices and how it's practicing medicine without a license. You're encouraging—you're aiding and abetting practicing without a license. . . . Which . . . it's criminal. For me; it would be criminal . . .

Even though she interprets it as a criminal act to take on apprentices, she does so, both to enable her to manage a growing practice and because, she says, "This is a tradition we've been trying to preserve." She and other lay midwives acknowledge that they are attempting to preserve this tradition in the face of competing professional interests:

> But a lot of the medical profession, sometimes even other midwives, they will say, "Well, let's make us more professional. Let's go to school. Let's not do it the old way. Let's do it the new way." Well, that's fine for them. If they want to go to school and get their little degree, and their ego feels better about going to college, great. But, you know, there have been women for the last, I don't know how many thousands of years, that were midwives that couldn't write, couldn't read. And yet they knew the herbs, they knew the dosages and all that.

This implicit endorsement of nonprofessional knowledge is a direct challenge to the medical model of birth. It also challenges the move toward licensure and professionalism that is evident nationwide in the pro-midwife movement. Notably, Patti articulated it to me a full decade before the US-MERA compromise was struck. As Kim Osterholzer put it in her memoir, "Taking an apprentice tends to be a costly, exhausting, risky endeavor for a midwife, which is why so many gifted midwives choose to eschew it. It is, however, a necessary endeavor" to the transmission of knowledge.[7]

INSURANCE

Questions related to insurance are frequently paramount in the minds of midwives as they practice. Will they be required to have liability insurance? Malpractice insurance? If so, will they be able to find it? Will the doctors with whom they work, in states where such relationships are mandated, be able to be insured? And, will midwives be able to be reimbursed by insurance companies for the care and services they provide their clients?

It is rare for people in close relationships with each other to sue each other.[8] And, studies of medical malpractice and liability suits show that patients "cite poor communication and lack of trust as reasons they choose to sue."[9] The care provided by midwives to the families they serve very infrequently culminates in any kind of legal claim that would trigger insurance payouts for malpractice or liability. Of course, when that care *does* trigger a suit, it is usually for a death or substantial harm to an infant, and $50,000 in coverage won't suffice.

Insurers recognize this, and in a MANA session on purchasing insurance coverage, presenters from insurance companies told the midwives that there is a higher likelihood of litigation when families "feel providers are disrespectful, communicate poorly, fail to listen, or try to hide their fault." To the extent that midwives make a habit of communicating "honestly and with empathy," and are in close relationship with their clients, they tend not to be sued. Further, they noted, "most malpractice claimants seek answers, not money"—and midwives are well-equipped to provide the answers that families need, enabling them to avoid litigation.[10]

Indeed, in that session, the first question—which came only three minutes into the panelists' opening remarks—was not about avoiding harms due to litigation but rather about whether insurance coverage would help midwives who are subject to regulatory action. The questioner wasn't concerned about her practice being negatively impacted by claims filed by parents, or lawsuits on their behalf; the questioner was, logically, more concerned with state action or hospital action that would interrupt her provision of care. As a different midwife explained from the floor, "I've never had a bad outcome. But, my local hospital has made multiple complaints against my license." One complaint alleged that she provided inadequate pain management, another was for "delay of care" during a time when she and her client sat in the ER waiting to be seen. She is more concerned about actions coming from those moments, and seeks insurance against them, than she is about lawsuit. Acknowledging that this was often the case for midwives, nevertheless the two presenters said it would be extremely unusual for insurance companies to provide protection against regulatory action.[11]

The second question—again, an early interruption from the floor—asked how much midwives should report to their insurance company regarding their practice, or how detailed their recordkeeping should be. Upon being told that "over-reporting" was always "the best way to go" because the insurer would see the midwife as "pro-active," midwives in the room scoffed, believing that over-reporting to the companies would trigger action against them, and assuming that "the risk of being dropped or rates going up" comes with reporting too many details or too many adverse outcomes. And, midwives in the room expressed their agreement with one midwife's stated belief, born of experience and stories, that "any report can lead to state action."[12]

The midwives in the room grew even more restive when the panelists explained the norm for rate setting among insurers, noting "Our rates are determined by the litigiousness of the area you're practicing in" rather than the general non-litigiousness of homebirth clients in relationships with midwives. The midwives expressed even more dissatisfaction when the insurers noted the extremely low rate of pay-outs in the claims they had seen and processed. Anne, the insurance company representative, noted that of the eighty-five claims against midwives her company had processed, only twelve (around 5%) had resulted in pay-outs. Many of those, the midwives were advised, came about due to lack of documentation that contributed to the sense that the midwives would have poor credibility in the event of a jury trial and potentially increased perception of their negligence. The panelists were aware of only one "big ticket" claim that resulted in a major, million-dollar pay-out from their company—it was a case where the insurer told the group, "The midwives really did screw up."[13]

One midwife spoke again from the floor: "As a solo practitioner, I can't afford $6,000 a year to insure myself against something that isn't going to happen." At this point, a midwife interrupted happily, telling the group, "I'm so excited. I texted my husband just now. We didn't think we could get liability insurance in California. We can! And, we can afford it!" She was a bit of an outlier, though—another, also from California, upon hearing that failure to consult with or refer to an ob-gyn was also a reason for pay-outs, expressed her frustration that she couldn't find an ob-gyn with whom she felt safe consulting or referring. The underwriter responded, "It has been reported that 25 percent of mothers don't receive ultrasound when attempting a VBAC," he looked aghast. "As an underwriter that keeps me up at night." His point was lost on the midwife though, who felt he had not heard her. She again stood and told him, "There is only one ob in my part of the state who will do a VBAC ultrasound consult, and it will cost $350. Only one."

What's more, another midwife chimed in, "As an unlicensed midwife in a state that refuses to make me legal, I can't get a consult, and I can't even purchase an insurance policy if I wanted one!" Another stood up and said, "I live in an alegal state. I could give reports all day long. But I have no collaboration. No support."[14] And, no insurance.

As Indra Lusero describes the situation, "In many places, professional liability insurance is not available to home birth midwives." And, when such coverage is available, it is "inconsistent, unstable, and incomplete." But, "Without insurance a single incident could put an uncovered midwife out of business."[15] The panelists didn't have much comfort for the midwives who pointed to these problems. One of them looked at the group at one point and shrugged rather helplessly, telling them, "That's just how the system works," before acknowledging that the medical profession has "an overblown sense of liability," to the detriment of birth attendants working outside of the dominant paradigm.

In addition to concern about midwives having proper insurance coverage, legislators in states with pending pro-midwifery bills would frequently raise a question that doctors and hospital associations bring to them: the question of insurance for vicarious liability. If, legislators wondered, a midwife's client is transported to the ER, and something goes wrong but it is the midwife's fault, will doctors and the hospital be liable to suit? This isn't how medical liability usually works, but legislators and doctors seem to need constant education on that issue, and there are almost always unnecessary attempts to insert language into pro-midwifery bills that would indemnify doctors against vicarious liability.

One researcher and advocate from Massachusetts shared with the Birth Rights Bar Association that her perception was that the role of lawyers during bill drafting was to clarify these questions for legislators, and that they frequently raised questions about insuring for vicarious liability, "even though," she looked understandably annoyed, "it isn't even a thing."[16] As Lusero told a group at MANA, "If someone is not in charge of your practice, they cannot be held liable for your actions or inaction. The problem with vicarious liability is perception, only." They then recommended that everyone read Susan Jenkins's article "The Myth of Vicarious Liability" and provide it in summary form to legislators who raised vicarious liability during committee hearings.[17]

Another—very different, but quite important—set of questions relating to insurance center on questions of payment. Will insurance companies reimburse clients for the services offered by midwives? Even though home-birth costs much less than hospital birth and ob-gyn provided prenatal care, many women who might seek out-of-hospital birth attended by a CPM are unable to afford these services without insurance coverage, especially when compared to the lower out-of-pocket cost of an insurance-reimbursed hospital birth. Further, midwives have reason to wonder if insurance companies will process payments in a way that comports with state law. At MANA, Lusero fielded a comment from a certified professional midwife who told the group that sometimes the insurance company puts the wrong credential on her check, calling her a "CNM" on one check, a "CPM" on another. They told the CPM, "Do. Not. Cash. The Check. It is insurance fraud if you do, even if it is a mistake on their part."[18]

Finally, if insurers will reimburse for out-of-hospital birth, will they do so in a timely and efficient manner—something that can be particularly important for the small, low-volume midwifery practice? In the documentary *The Business of Being Born*, viewers watch one frustrating scene where the operators of a birth center in the Bronx spend what looks like hours on the phone with the insurers, verifying code, seeking payment. These Black women, serving Black women, had to "beg"—as one of the midwives says to the insurance representative on the other end of the line—"to be paid." As Lusero puts it in analyzing the complex problems surrounding insurance coverage,

> [All of this] impacts whether health insurance will cover home birth midwifery care, which keeps the pool of clients small. . . .
>
> [Therefore] most actuarial data does not include good information about home birth. . . . This is another part of the self-perpetuating system that diminishes the viability of home birth midwifery. The data is not available because the practice is small, the practice is small because it is viewed as risky; the lack of data makes the practice seem risky, which keeps the practice small. It's a loop of bad information leading to bad results.[19]

All of these issues surrounding insurance bring to mind, concretely, Jonathan Simon's analysis of the ideological effects of actuarial practice. As a form of knowledge itself, actuarial knowledge is distinct from the individual behavioral focus of disciplinarity; actuarial knowledge attempts to alter entire physical and social structure. Such practices and knowledge create their own common sense and ideology, as well as the structures within which practices are possible (and not). Simon wrote,

> [I]ndividuals . . . are increasingly understood as locations in actuarial tables of variations. This shift from moral agent to actuarial subject marks a change in the way power is exercised on individuals by the state and other

large organizations. . . . [P]ower . . . now seeks to predict behavior and situate subjects according to the risks they pose.[20]

Midwives are subject to the power of, and limits of, actuarial data about their own practices.

SUPERVISING PHYSICIANS

Of the states where it is legal for direct-entry and certified professional midwives to attend homebirth, only four—California, New Jersey, New York, and Delaware—have required written collaborative-practice agreements between the midwives and doctors.[21] Midwives, doctors, and regulatory officials in these states widely acknowledge the problems with these agreements.[22] Primary among the problems is the fact that physicians are increasingly unwilling to enter into supervisory relationships with midwives because of pressure from ACOG and the AMA, as well as their hospitals, practice groups, and insurance companies.

When I asked one midwife in California to list for me the legal and political issues facing midwives in her state, she began with the problem of the supervising physician. Tova told me:

Well it's . . . it's very difficult. Written in the law is that we have to have a supervising physician, but they cannot legally write their names saying they're supervising us because of their insurance. And their insurance will drop them if they're involved with a homebirth. So, therefore we're all practicing without a supervising position.

That was the choice Tova made: to continue practicing, without supervision.

Indeed, as amicus *briefs* in the Dray case explain to the court, collaborative agreement requirements expect midwives "to obtain agreements from obstetricians—their competitors." This is like "requiring Costco to get permission from Walmart to open a new store."[23]

Requirements for supervising physicians not only inhibit midwives' ability to legally attend these births, but they also propose to give the supervising physician a much broader, indeed truly supervisory, role in the pregnancy and birth. These requirements are an unwelcome interpretation of the relationships for many midwives and their clients, in that they reinforce the hegemonic idea that the only safe place for birth is the hospital, an idea challenged by all planned out-of-hospital births. And, such requirements infringe on the autonomy of their practice, a condition that has been proved to improve nurse-midwifery care,[24] from which we can extrapolate to improved care by a CPM as well. Lawyers for the Birth Rights Bar Association argue that the evidence shows autonomous practice to be an essential aspect of quality midwifery care.[25]

Doctors, labor and delivery nurses, and some nurse midwives see birth as a medical event; they view the pregnant and laboring woman as a "patient," in need of medical care, supervision, and perhaps intervention.[26] Usually, women seeking out-of-hospital births attended by CPMs do so because they want to remove natural birth from the medical model: They seek an intervention-free birth and view such a birth as a normal and natural occurrence. They and their care providers view the supervisory-physician requirement as an unnecessary intervention of the medical model into normal, healthy birth.

Additionally, even those midwives who agree to follow the law in states where supervisory agreements are required find it very difficult to actually comply with legal demands. It is financially prohibitive for doctors in private practice to buy the malpractice and liability coverage necessary to carry a midwife on their plan, in compliance with their practice standards, and hospitals routinely refuse such insurance coverage to doctors as providers wishing to have these relationships. The inability of doctors to get coverage leads to their refusal to participate in supervisory relationships; often this refusal is a reluctant end to a longstanding and mutually beneficial relationship.

So, midwives either go out of business or practice in flagrant disobedience of the law. Michele Munz, a reporter for the *St. Louis Post-Dispatch*, covered the fight for decriminalization in Missouri. Of the supervisory relationship requirement, she wrote, "In California and Delaware, midwives flout the rule because so few doctors will work with them." And she quoted a representative for the California Medical Board, stating, "We are aware that everyone is in a quandary on that point."[27]

We must wonder what the impact is, for perceptions of law's legitimacy, when "everyone" is aware that the law is nearly impossible to comply with. As Hadar Aviram notes in her treatment of animal liberation activists, "People might . . . accept or reject perceptions of their own illegality and construct their perspectives about legality, legitimacy, and the relationship between morality and the law."[28] In this case, because the law is difficult to enforce, midwives engage in widespread disobedience, which is met by selective prosecution. Many midwives understand and experience this combination as prohibitive of their practice. Yet, like animal liberation activists, "Despite their deep critiques of the law . . . [midwives also] see law as an essential ally in the fight."[29]

TRANSPORT ARRANGEMENTS

Given doctors' professional stance against homebirth, it is not surprising that potentially one of the most stressful parts of a midwife's practice involves the emergency transfer of laboring women to a hospital setting. Tova, a midwife from southern California, told me that some transports are "smooth, smooth, smooth" and are undertaken because of nonemergency conditions, like an extremely long labor ("failure to progress" in the medical model). In Tova's estimation, part of her success in smooth transfers is the positive personal relationship she forges with doctors and hospital staff:

> You know, we have a backup doctor in place; I make a call. I say, "Here's what's going on," and they say, "Great" . . . but you know . . . that's a large part of, of being able to transport in the current political climate. You know, it's being, it's having the people skills to deal with it . . .

However, Tova acknowledges the fear that accompanies even these nonemergency transports to "friendly" hospitals:

> I think it's really important [to have people skills and relationships], because even if there's nothing wrong technically, I mean even if I'm only transporting because the mom wants an epidural—I mean, unlikely, but it happens—maybe she's tired; she wants an epidural. Just because there is that supervision wording in the law, I can be arrested, 'cause I'm practicing without supervision, I'm practicing illegally.

At this point in our conversation, I ask Tova—mostly joking—"So, do you have a lawyer on retainer?" I am surprised when she points to her (unauthorized) apprentice who is also a practicing attorney, and they both laugh. The lawyer/apprentice Pamela clarifies: "Well it's not that I do midwifery law, but I . . . I would step in."

When I ask Patti if she feels a threat of prosecution during hospital transport, or is worried about things going, as she put it, "sideways," Patti is even more explicit in her discussion of the perils of such a situation. She starts her answer with a deep sigh and a long pause, then continues:

> There's different pockets of . . . of . . . areas where I feel a threat. If I have to transport to Orange County, I feel a threat. I'm very scared to take a woman into Orange County, any hospital . . . any of them; because they will . . . they call the police. And they write a report and they . . . they report it to the state.

At one of their plenary sessions during the MANA conference, Deborah Fisch and Indra Lusero spoke at length about risk of state action, and they agreed that transport heightens risk. They covered material meant to educate midwives about the risks of their practice and the ways to mitigate those risks. One of their PowerPoint slides, displayed to an audience of at least 200 midwives asked: "When are you at risk?" The answer, by the end of the session, felt like "always."[30]

Certainly, midwives know that their practice can be at risk if they are not practicing in a legal state. But midwives practicing in legal states also face risk. These occur if they have had any contact with the criminal justice system or any of the regulatory agencies governing their practice, or if they work in places while also facing hostility of doctors or midwife-on-midwife strife. Risk comes to midwives after bad outcomes: the injury or death of a baby or mom or trauma to the mother, the baby, or other family member. Bad outcomes, Fisch and Lusero stressed, can also be a matter of perception—a birth that didn't go as a mom had hoped, even if the result was short of trauma, injury, or death. Bad outcomes of any kind are risky. Any time a client has to be transported for hospital care, risk is present. Risk, they told the group, is also present when midwives and clients disagree about care—particularly when a midwife effectuates a hospital transfer in a life-saving measure, against the wishes of the birthing woman and/or their partner.[31]

The circumstances of a client's life can also contribute to risk—especially those circumstances that do not cause them to be risked out of homebirth but do contribute to risk for the midwife. Among those life circumstances that add to a midwife's risk are intimate partner violence, a history of mental illness or mental health concerns, a history of Child Protective Services involvement, drug use, and the immigration status of the client or members of her family. Lusero noted, "Involving the law in one thing tends to bring the law into other areas." As Priya Morganstern, an attorney with the Birth Rights Bar Association, told the advocates assembled in Chicago in 2017, "I urge you not to feel like you need to serve everyone who wants to have a homebirth. I'm sorry but you need to think of yourself, your family, your community, and the movement." In other words, some of the women who would most benefit from an empowering woman-centered birth and quality prenatal care are those who are riskiest for a midwife to attend. Lusero acknowledged this, with regret, but told midwives gathered at MANA, "I urge you to take on the defense of your profession as your duty."

Knowing that this "call to duty" would be grating, Lusero acknowledged that most would still make decisions about client care that were in the best interest of the pregnant person. They reminded those gathered, "It's good to have a lawyer in your corner." And their take-away advice to the crowd, displayed on its own slide, was met with much laughter. Do what you must, they said, but, please: "Avoid risk."

The joke is, of course, that risk cannot be avoided. Given that, Lusero and Fisch stressed, midwives must

> Know your rights, trust your gut, know your limitations, get to know the players, line up powerful friends, identify a lawyer in advance, have a plan, maintain records in real time, keep secure paper and digital backups, keep copies of your records off-site, and prepare: put aside money for lost income, and a retainer for a lawyer. Invest in your legal safety.

They went further, each of these exhortations bullet-pointed on a slide:

- Do not say anything until you talk to an attorney
- Do not let anyone into your house unless it is a police officer with a warrant
- Do not try to be helpful to investigators
- Admit nothing!

And the limited good news? "If this is a criminal matter, you have constitutional rights."

Fisch and Lusero listed resources for midwives who found themselves afoul of the law. They recommended that midwives reach out to the ACLU, the BRBA, their state professional organization, national midwifery organizations, elected officials ("they know the law on the ground"), and the attorney they should already have at the ready, preferably someone local: "You want a lawyer from your area, one who knows all the judges." Lusero left them with this advice: "Remember this sentence: I'm sorry my attorney won't let me talk to you until I speak with her."[32]

In this presentation and others, risks associated with midwifery practice are clearly seen to be assuaged by the law. In fact, they figure knowing about law as empowering in the same way that knowing about pregnancy and birth is empowering. This is undoubtedly true—and having a lawyer in your corner is excellent advice for midwives.

But sometimes the problem a midwife faces isn't a legal one. Indeed, the distinction between what is legal and illegal becomes unimportant in the process of practice. Variability of law is *part* of the shadow it casts, part of its power. Legal status is related to, but not determinative of, a problem of social disapprobation. Absent changed social norms and medical approval, this is a problem where, as Tova explained to me about transport situations, *"The law will not protect you."*

LIMITS OF LAW

If failed or poor implementation of law leaves midwives operating within the shadow of law to their detriment, the limits of the law are also clear in the way that they form obstacles to chill their practice. Even in states where their practices are legal, midwives continue to face harassment and unprofessional behaviors from medical and state actors, when they facilitate home-to-hospital transfers in emergency situations. But, it is insufficient to show that legal institutions fail to function as they claim. It is crucial, when we notice that failure, to examine and interrogate the very ideals and principles that law claims for itself. As Susan Silbey writes, "The standards that legal institutions announce, even as they fail to realize them completely, are part of how legal institutions create their own power and authority."[33] Even as marginalized individuals are failed by and even victimized by the law, they continue to believe that it can be of benefit to them.[34]

As I sat down with Patti, she put it this way: "I catch babies, and I catch hell." Every midwife I have interviewed, and every homebirth parent I have spoken to, has at least one story about "catching hell" from doctors, relatives, nurses, and friends for their choice of an alternative birth experience. At times this catching hell takes the form of direct state intervention; home-birth advocates at the Birth Rights Bar Association meeting told stories of public health officials and child welfare agents doing home visits with unfounded allegations of abuse and neglect, once the homebirth is recorded officially, or of falsified concerns about the mental health of the mother, regarding her decision to birth at home. Sometimes it takes the form of pharmacists who hassle clients when they bring prescriptions written by their midwives. Other times women simply know that medical profession-als, friends, and family members meet their birth choices with suspicion.[35] Midwives and their clients note that homebirth in the United States is simply seen as odd, different, and crazy.

Many women told me that longstanding friendships had been strained by their decisions regarding the births of their children, and their friends' reaction to such decisions. When my friend told me so many years ago, "You know, birth isn't an extreme sport," I knew, as I shared with her my desire to have an unmedicated birth, that she was mocking me. She was judging the decision I had made regarding my own bodily autonomy. I certainly didn't feel like I could share our plans with her anymore. I am not alone. Internet sites devoted to birth and homebirth abound with stories from women whose in-laws, parents, friends, and co-workers are shocked and repelled by their decisions regarding their births. People may gently mock unmedicated hospital births, but they are often vociferously opposed to homebirth.

People who had, or had attempted, homebirths reported to me during participant-observation that they had not told their "normal" or "main-stream" friends about their choice to give birth at home; many of them had not told mothers-in-law, parents, or siblings of their decision to give birth at home with a midwife. They told me they didn't want to be looked down upon, seen as strange, or interfered with in their decision. They also may have had prenatal care with a physician, whom they did not inform of their plans, for fear of patronizing, contentious, and harshly judgmental conversations.

This fear is not unfounded, nor is it limited to the arena of child-birth. Feminists' studies of the medical profession have repeatedly shown that medical textbooks, medical school classrooms, and doctor–patient relationships are fraught with power relations that disadvantage female pa-tients. Sexism, and demeaning and sexist assumptions, are rampant in these texts and interactions.[36] Women, they find, are often constructed as hys-terical hypochondriacs and are told to be submissive to medical authority.

The judgment is worse when laboring people are unexpectedly brought into the hospital system. Midwives may be treated rudely or be coerced into watching their clients receive substandard care. And, sometimes, catching hell means that a woman will be subject to derogation, and even obstet-ric violence, because she came into a hospital after a planned homebirth. Midwives tell me that women feel "punished" by doctors and nurses for pursuing homebirth.

In these everyday practices of meaning making, emergency situations are used to reinforce the norm of hospital birth and the primacy of the medical profession, while midwives and homebirth families are marginalized and rendered legally suspect and out of the mainstream. And, unfortunately, the law does not readily solve the problem of potential harassment of CPMs and laboring mothers that arises during hospital transfers. Patti tells me about a friend and client of hers who had previously had several successful births at home, but who ran into trouble with her most recent birth and decided she needed an epidural to get through the labor. Patti tells me:

> So ["Vickie"] goes to the hospital at one or two in the morning. I get there about two, and she's already got her epidural. . . . So anyway, she's very comfortable, and the little nurse comes in and says, "You know, doctor said to check you often. . . . " Well, my friend is kind of a loud mouth; I want to put it like that. She's very bold and told them, "Oh yeah, I had two homebirths and I'm only here for the epidural and we'd prefer to be left alone." Uh uh, that nursing staff did not like that. So, anyway, I'm noticing that, you know, sometimes with an epidural you, you feel pushy, you can still feel pushy; sometimes you can't. Well, we are noticing that things are changing. And I said, "Vickie, are you pushing?" She says, "I don't know."
>
> And I lift up the sheet and the baby's coming. So what do I do? I go out in the hall, and I kinda wave down the nurse and I said, "The baby's coming." So—and as a midwife I cannot practice in a hospital, right?
>
> Okay, so [that nurse] comes in and the head nurse comes in and the nurse with the baby warmer comes in. They stay against the wall. And the one

nurse says, "Oh, you want a homebirth? Have a homebirth then. . . . "
My client is delivering her baby and of course as a midwife, you want to
[help]. . . . I looked her in the eye. I said, "Vickie, reach down and pick up
your baby. [Patti makes her voice sound like Vickie's] "Oh I can't. I can't."
I told her, "Yes you can. You can."

Something told me, the Holy Spirit told me, "Do not touch that baby."
She picked it up and here this baby is against this gown and she tried to
pull up her gown to cover it and she's yelling for a blanket and they're all
just standing there.

Patti is so angry, over breakfast, as she remembers this story that she trem-
bles with emotion at the memory. She says to me, incredulous, "You talk
about malpractice; breach of confidence, breach of care?" The story isn't
over, though. Patti goes on:

The nurse that had the baby warmer handed somebody a blanket to put
over the baby and handed [Vickie] a bulb syringe so she could suction
her own baby. . . . So then the doctor comes in and starts yelling at Vickie
because she was like secretly planning a homebirth. Every time she started
to say something, he cut her off because he had already heard the story
from the nurses that "she didn't tell us that she was in labor" or she was,
you know, pushing. Well if they're watching their monitors . . . they should
know if she's pushing. I was the one that had to go out and get them.

Patti believes that the nursing staff was not only punishing Vickie and making a point, but they were trying to entrap her into practicing midwifery
in a setting beyond her scope of practice. She tells me, "They were waiting
for me to do that." And, as further proof of what she perceives to be their
intended deceit, she says, "Later they came in with the birth certificate and
they wanted me to sign it. And I said, "No, I'm not signing it."

Telling me this reminded Patti of another time, "same hospital, different
client, different doctor." She brought her client in for "failure to progress,"
after a labor that was going too long for Patti's comfort:

They put her up in the bed, in the stirrups, and she's pushing. And this
doctor comes in, and he, this doctor knew me. . . . It is a very small hospital. And um, she [the client] says, you know, "I don't want an episiotomy."
And he's like, "Well I'm a doctor, I'll decide."

And she said, "I do not want an episiotomy."

He took his two fingers . . . and we're all [right there]. . . . I'm standing against the back wall, my assistant is next to me, and our eyes are about to bug out. He literally ripped her open. . . .

She got punished; [she got] punished for [trying to have] a homebirth.

As horrifying as this story is, I heard things like this all the time during my fieldwork—from women who had planned homebirths that ended in transfer, as well as from women who had planned hospital births that included violent interactions with medical professionals. I remember telling this story to a friend, who is a pediatrician. He said that the doctor had behaved horribly, of course; but he also let me know that when a family he provided care for came in, after an attempted homebirth that resulted in a transfer and emergency C-section, he visited the mom in her hospital room and "really gave her hell" for even attempting to labor and deliver outside of the hospital.[37]

This kind of treatment of women and their midwives from doctors and nurses isn't part of the technical legal and regulatory apparatus surrounding the practice of midwifery. But it is clearly a significant stress on such practices, and it contributes to midwives' and families' view of the law surrounding midwifery care. As Lusero writes, "Being able to practice legally doesn't protect midwives from bias against midwifery."[38] And it doesn't protect their clients.

Many midwives—Patti included—understand that this tenuousness is, at core, about gender. Before answering her own rhetorical question, she asks me, "Why can't we just have our babies at home, you know? It's not a bad thing to do. . . . " She shrugs, then gestures emphatically. The problem is, she says, homebirth is seen as "a threat to the community." She continues, "Anytime you do something different that goes against the grain, people don't like it, you know? When women started wearing pants and bobbing their hair, when men started wearing ponytails, people got all upset." By tying out-of-hospital birth to seemingly trivial gender role disruptions like wearing pants or ponytails, Patti demonstrates that she clearly understands the often-irrational fear people have when women and men disrupt gender hegemonies—and the reaction is all the more violent and irrational when they disrupt (newly) traditional and hegemonic understandings of the role and place of women in birth.

Social and cultural disapprobation—even when not experienced in ways as severe as Patti's clients endured—certainly does trickle into other areas: the doctor–midwife relationship; the insurance company's coverage (or not) of procedures; prohibitive needs for insurance coverage written into bills by legislators who are embroiled in dominant ideologies of birth and risk; and tremendous oversight from state regulatory bodies, not all of which are composed of people with experience in out-of-hospital settings. All of this ultimately affects the availability of homebirth attended by a midwife. Dominant ideologies about birth that give primacy to ideas about risk, the necessity of medical intervention, and the role and interest of the state in women's reproductive choices serve to make homebirth de facto illegal, or at the very least incredibly difficult to obtain, and clearly not the "normal" choice—even in legal states.

Midwives and their advocates who seek professional status and legislation are clear: Changing the law regarding the availability of midwifery care might be a necessary first step, but it is not sufficient. They have long known, anecdotally, that midwives operating in legal states still face extreme constraints on their practice and often operate in a culture of fear similar to those practicing in illegal and unregulated states.

Recently, however, researchers have found ways to measure the negative impact of these constraints on midwives' practices. At the 2011 Homebirth Summit, researchers discussed their growing understanding that formal markers of regulation were inadequate to the task of knowing what needed to be present for care to go well. Using publicly available data, they came to understand that "confounding factors" interrupt quality of care. As a group, they decided to gather data from regulatory experts on the ground, to see "how rules go into practice"—in law and society language, to measure the potential gap between what the rules say and how they are implemented— and, more importantly, to measure the impact of that gap on provision of services.[39]

Growing from this work by Homebirth Summit members, Saraswathi Vedam convened an additional group of scholars to work on mapping the integration of care in every state onto the outcomes of the birth, while making unique demographic data available and searchable via a website associated with a published scholarly article.[40] I was a member of that research group for eighteen months and learned much about the ways that legal status might help integration of care, but doesn't guarantee it, as well as how such integration helps achieve better outcomes for moms and babies.

The takeaway from the mapping project is clear: Legal status for midwives is important, but it is not the only way to get well-integrated, seamless, care. Because midwives' success in law and politics may not translate to professional legitimacy, or to cultural acceptance of alternative birth practices, midwives must also fight to change cultures of birth in order to better integrate care.

LEGAL CONSCIOUSNESS IN THE SHADOW OF THE LIMITS OF THE LAW

Even when it is shown to be limited in its capacity for transformational change, Susan Silbey notes, "Law help[s] shape and constitute cultural norms and expectations. It [is] also an instrumental tool available for skillful users."[41] Nor should law be understood "solely in terms of what is law in the books or what is observed as behavioral or organizational processes. It is the relationship," Silbey writes, "between the threads that constitutes institutional durability."[42] Law is durable because midwives and their advocates understand it to be—and because it exerts itself in multiple ways.

As Patricia Ewick and Silbey's study of legal consciousness demonstrates, some attitudes toward law posit individuals as "with the law," some as "before the law" and subject to its whim, and others as "against the law," seeking to avoid its gaze.[43] Those who mobilize law—who seek rights or access—can be understood to hold beliefs about its capacity that are, at the very least, instrumental. Ophelia tells me that she had realized early on, "It's all a big game." Reflecting on the advocacy that she has led toward legalization, she says, "Yep. A big game. And we told our supporters in the state to play it." Certainly, midwives and their advocates expressed views of the law and the legal system as "necessary evils," to be used "strategically," as well as something "to be avoided," and as "impossible to change."[44] These views of law and its varying capacities played a role in how midwives and their advocates decided to use it (and not). So, too, do circumstances dictate how legal mobilization would unfold—and for the most part, legal mobilization on behalf of midwives is *not* courtroom advocacy and rights seeking.

Midwives and advocates engage with law and politics in a very self-aware way, and simultaneously articulate a range of perspectives on law and the legal system and their relationship to it. Legal mobilization scholars know and express this; they find that individuals within marginalized groups often knowingly compromise while pursuing legal mobilization, and they view law as a strategic resource to be used instrumentally for the advancement of movement goals.[45] Further, these studies often show that actors understand that such mobilization holds both opportunities and constraints,[46] and they may knowingly accept normalization and domestication of their claims in order to achieve victory.[47] Yet what I found incredibly interesting about the mobilization done on behalf of professional status is that, in most states, "Lawyering wasn't important for licensure."[48]

Legal mobilization done on behalf of midwives and consumers was often explicitly *not* about gaining legal status. Rather, it became important in the criminal defense of midwives, in tort litigation over obstetric violence claims, in the moments of regulatory rulemaking, and—yes—in defense of the Missouri law, as it faced a state constitutional challenge. A crucial thread running through all of this lawyering was the ability and willingness of the birth justice bar to translate legal language for midwives.[49] Lawyers helped midwives and advocates understand technicalities during rulemaking and the meaning of subpoenas, bylaws, and court doctrine. One advocate in Massachusetts noted that, "Lawmakers share a legal language and can communicate"[50] with each other—so lawyers who drafted memos and communications were really helpful.

At MANA and the BRBA meetings, Indra Lusero, Deb Fisch, and others offered crucial legal education and translation for midwives and advocates. I saw example after example of this legal translation at national meetings of all sorts. During one MANA session, for example, Lusero reminded attendees who were nurse midwives and beginning to offer a home practice, or those who held both CNM and CPM credentials, "As you transition from hospital practice you can lose your hospital privileges. . . . Privileges are hospital *bylaws*, not *law laws*."[51]

During a different session at a different meeting, Lusero and Fisch posed this hypothetical to the crowd: "Let's say [you're a midwife and] you've been called upon to talk about something you heard in peer review. . . . What are the rules about what you have to answer? Well," they told the crowd, "if you're subpoenaed, you have to [answer]. If not, you can decline. And [some states have] protected peer review [even against subpoena]."[52]

In my early research on midwives, I was surprised to find that even when they are operating in states where their practice is perfectly legal and explicitly regulated, CPMs continue to face regulatory circumstances that cause them to define parts of their practice as illegal and to experience their practices as precarious. The most onerous issues they reported include: the requirement of a supervising physician; the necessity of procuring insurance; the ban on proctoring or having apprentices; the fear of selective prosecution initiated by any one of the plethora of regulatory bodies to which they are answerable; and the practical need for a workable transfer relationship, made difficult by social and professional disapprobation of their practice. Lusero writes:

> Once regulated, the risk of [midwifery] practice depends on these fac-
> tors, which vary from state to state: how easy it is to lose your practice,
> how much power the medical field has in the administrative/regulatory
> scheme, how enfranchised consumers are, how safe midwives feel.[53]

These concerns—and their variability—combine to make CPMs in even legal states feel embattled. Their stories— shared at MANA, BirthKeepers, the BRBA, The Big Push, and via message boards and other social media—also serve to heighten the perception of risk regarding regulatory law among midwives who are not yet organized to seek legal status. Such risk consciousness is also part of midwives' and advocates' legal consciousness.

As activists within and scholars of the civil rights, disability rights, and gender equity movements would surely agree, legalization of a practice and legal status of an identity do not necessarily bring legitimation and cultural acceptance. Nor does the articulation of rights mean those rights will be granted. The gap between promise and implementation has been well documented.[54] Like many law and society scholars, I have long been interested in this gap between law as it is written and intended, and law as it is practiced and implemented—what I have here and elsewhere called the "limits of law."[55]

Scholarship in this area has proposed that reliance on law for social change proves futile for most social movements, and researchers have investigated flawed and failed implementation in the lower courts,[56] as well discretionary policymaking at the "street level" in bureaucratic and agency implementation,[57] and state implementation of federal reform legislation.[58] And, studies focused specifically on the civil rights movement in particular have attempted to deeply understand the limits and opportunities posed by strategies focusing on litigation as legal mobilization.[59] Crucially, several studies have made clear that the implementation of reforms, whether judicially mandated or achieved through legislative action, can be stymied in multiple ways by "powerful local interests"[60] and by those who either willfully disobey, or are ignorant of, the reforms—especially when those reforms are meant to challenge dominant cultural norms regarding women and others seeking equality through rights.[61]

My interviews with midwives in varying regulatory regimes indicate that they experience the gap between law and practice, and that disjuncture negatively impacts their professional lives. In the face of these findings, which reflect the consensus of extensive sociolegal literature regarding legal implementation—that implementation is often flawed and at times fails outright to achieve its goals—we may turn to legal consciousness in an attempt to make sense of the continued use of law and legal strategies by those hoping to create transformational change. Why, indeed, do individuals and groups continue to use legal mobilization as a tool for social change, even in the face of evidence that implementation is flawed and contingent, and success often relative and transitory?

Joshua Wilson's studies of anti-abortion advocates' legal mobilization theorizes that the legal consciousness of these actors is an essential component of their continued use of law, as well as their extralegal activism.[62] This literature, and the literature on legal implementation, offer a way to understand the failure of pro-midwifery legislation and decriminalization to positively impact the practice of homebirth midwifery. Midwives are seeking *transformational laws*—laws meant to radically alter how institutions operate—and transformational laws require more than policy language to accomplish their goals.[63] They require deep cultural change and political action, in concert with legal mobilization. Absent significant cultural and social shifts, transformative legislation does not come with an enforcement guarantee, nor the ability to enable action on newly granted rights or modes of access.

· · ·

My research, as presented in this book, has assumed that midwives and their advocates are embedded in contexts that shape their consciousness of law, and may have the impact of reifying the importance of law in their daily lives and practice. Among these contexts are late capitalism in neoliberalism with its shifting emphases from rights consciousness to consumerism, attention to racial privilege (and lack of racial privilege), gender identity, and the politicization of beliefs in regulatory and state power. I have been interested to tease out the role of daily life,[64] in the form of midwives' articulation of their professional practices, in the creation of legal consciousness—a consciousness that stems in part from the way laws are implemented, and contributes to legal mobilization, as a matter of how activists and midwives understand legal culture.[65] My interest in the legal consciousness and mobilization of midwives and pro-midwifery advocates developed in this chapter has also been grounded in understanding that legal status does not transform culture—at least not alone, and not quickly. As Linda Krieger reminds us, "Traditional norms and institutions do not vanish overnight . . . norm competition does not end with the enactment of a transformative legal regime."[66] The result of a merely instrumentalist focus on legalization might well be that many midwives will operate in legal states, with legal status, yet remain, or at least consider themselves to be, at risk for serious regulatory oversight, prosecutorial discretion, and social disapprobation.

Transformation of cultural norms around any issue is particularly difficult, of course, to achieve. This is true for midwifery advocates in large part because humans—lawyers, judges, regulatory officials, doctors, nurses, clients, friends, and mothers-in-law—are all engaged in the process of institutionalizing particular ideas and ideologies about birth. While law might in fact allow for out-of-hospital birth attended by a midwife, the everyday practices of people and interactions of folks do much to create hospitable, or inhospitable, environments for a legally available option. As Krieger's research on the implementation of the Americans with Disabilities Act shows, transformative law is most often mobilized by social outsiders against social insiders, who "are often better able than their outsider opponents to exploit the law's soft spots . . . and restrict the law's application."[67] Doctors within hospital settings, and regulators for the boards of health and nursing to which midwives must answer, are insiders able to reinforce dominant culture's norms, even in the face of a legal midwifery practice. Midwives and their advocates know this, which is why they spend considerable energy working to change birth culture in their locales.

6 DEEP TRANSFORMATIONS, DEEP CONTRADICTIONS

Changing Birth Culture One Movie, One Picnic, One . . .
Tiny Little Epistemological Shift at a Time

> "I'm so far right, I'm left."
> —Anne, a CPM in California, in 2006

ON MAY 1, 2015, the first ever BirthKeepers Summit convened in California, at Berkeley City College.[1] More than 450 midwives, doulas, and their advocates and allies attended three days of panels, interactive workshops, keynote addresses, and direct action. From the opening ceremony—which featured time for intention setting, the placing of an altar, a chant, a "song prayer," and a keynote panel—to the closing direct action at the meetings of the American College of Obstetricians and Gynecologists (ACOG)—the BirthKeepers Summit was a distant relative of other midwifery conferences I have attended. But, it was, indeed, a relative.

The summit was titled "MotherBaby/MotherEarth," invoking an environmental ethic of feminist care. Many birthkeepers held science gently, in the same hands that practice traditional women's ways of knowing. The same midwife who invokes Gaia and gives her laboring mother herbs also talks about evidence-based care and the neurological and immunological benefits of delayed cord clamping. She knows the best practices to mitigate transmission of STDs to the baby—both herbal and pharmaceutical.

Indeed, one of the most eagerly anticipated and well-attended events at BirthKeepers Summit was a talk by a male medical professional: Dr. Michel Odent. Odent, a French obstetrician, gave a presentation on birth, science, and evolution that valorized women and birthing, as well as a history of the genetic evolution of hormonal structures. He called for "multilingualism" in birthing, saying, "Today in order to be useful, you must be bilingual. You must combine the language of the heart with scientific language. Otherwise you will be useless."

Odent argued that by disrupting the process of birth—via technologies like bright lights and synthetic hormones, surgical interventions, quick cord cutting, and reduced bonding after birth—we are changing our evolutionary biology and "circumventing natural selection."[2] He argued that we will eventually see the extinction of oxytocin—the "love hormone"—from our system, because of the way synthetic hormones are used to induce, stall, and manage labor. He worried about the impact on melatonin, when birth takes place in bright rooms, and reported having witnessed a decrease in neonatal activity that he attributed to the brightness of birthing chambers. Ultimately, Odent claimed that our industrial birth practices are harming mothers and babies, and with that I have no argument.

Odent shared the stage with birthing pioneer Suzanne Arms and with Katsi Cook, an Indigenous environmental and woman-centered activist who argued that "the social and cultural body needs care" with attention to "ecosystemic interconnection." Panelists argued that our culture has "an imbalance, where mind/science has gained prominence" in birth, over the body—and to detrimental effect. They pointed to the "scientific hubris" of these interventions; Arms admonished the crowd, "Just because we can do something [in labor and delivery] doesn't mean we should."[3]

In highlighting the contributions of women of color and Indigenous midwives, as well as acknowledging and including queer and transgender communities, the summit celebrated and struggled with multiplicity; there was no coherent, consistent picture of birth experiences. Just as at The Big Push gathering six years previously, but perhaps more markedly, visions of reproductive justice were not uncontested, and at times midwives and advocates were in tension with each other, especially as White women struggled to be anti-racist allies, and younger women made claims about feminism and birth that seemed to slight those who had been in the movements longer.

Running through the entire BirthKeepers Summit was a critique of capitalism, colonialism, and imperialism. These themes were manifest in the structural underpinnings of the program: who was invited to speak and how they were introduced; the support of local artisans and community partners; the lack of a printed program; the semiotics and visual rhetoric of the space and its decorations. In opening and closing ceremonies, priestesses called in the Four Directions and thanked the ancestors. There were Pagan, Celtic, Buddhist, and American Indian rituals—including a smudging of the space, a gong for timekeeping and purification, an altar with water to collect energy that would later be dispersed, a ritual for claiming stories and another for asking questions. By claiming sacred space, conference organizers also insisted on the sacral qualities of birth itself.

At the start of the summit, primary organizer Molly Arthur emphasized the complex nature of a project of finding joy in these processes and relationships of birth and death. We are, she said, "all related; all kindred." At the same time, though, we have differences, which are to be "respected" through an emphasis on a commitment to "equity, compassion, and justice" and with an eye toward the quality of life of future generations of humans and nonhuman animals. Arthur quoted bell hooks, who asks us to move stories "from the margin to the center," and as such to reclaim and re-story women's lives.[4]

Indeed, several of the breakout sessions at the BirthKeepers Summit were presentations that reclaimed women's histories and experiences and moved them from margin to center. These oved beyond what have become standard retellings of the history and herstory of midwifery, including stories of granny midwives, of African American women, of Indigenous midwives, and of immigrant midwives.

Many of the speakers offered their own testimony and analysis as part of "decolonizing" knowledge, birth, and medical practice, as well as the histories of those subjects. As Rickie Solinger's historical survey of motherhood and reproductive politics so clearly demonstrates, the ability to "make a family" in the United States is marked by race and class privilege; "family" has long been a privilege for Whites in the middle class. Speakers at Birth-Keepers disrupted hegemonic assumptions about motherhood and family and claimed a wider space for those identities and configurations.

Alongside presentations that widened the cultural understandings of mothering, the BirthKeepers Summit offered an expanded role for midwives to include not just birth—but death. Several women described themselves as midwives and doulas who offer "a full spectrum of care," including midwifing women through their abortions, miscarriages, and stillbirths. An Indian American reproductive justice advocate called her work "life keeping" and "loss keeping" and articulated her approach as "holding space for life's transitions." One birthworker and abortion provider told the group, "There are not two groups of women: those who have babies (the good women) and those who have abortion (the bad women)."

This widening of scope—an acknowledgment that some midwives serve people seeking abortion and an insistence on reproductive autonomy—was not uncontested. At one point, a woman addressed the audience from a microphone at the side of the conference hall. She called herself pro-life and asked if she would find solidarity and welcome in the room. While interventions from the audience around issues of Whiteness, feminism, and essentialism were met with cheers and standing ovations, this person's question was met with hisses, boos, and an invitation that she sit down. As we've seen, the politics of choice can be contentious in the pro-midwifery community, but this intolerance was unusual.

The BirthKeepers Summit included a rich tapestry of voices from outside of the mainstream of American feminism. Presenters included founders and members of the reproductive justice movement in the United States. Loretta Ross, one of the founders of SisterSong, continually and productively challenged White mainstream feminist panelists to broaden their understanding of reproductive justice, feminism(s), and antiracist work. Her breakout sessions on antiracist work were well attended, and her contributions from the floor, during several panels on feminism and birth, were spirited—and met with raucous cheers and standing ovations from women of color and allies in the audience.

One of the most stunning moments was when Ross intervened in a panel on feminism and birth. In evident frustration, Ross said from the floor, "Please do not dismiss all the work that got us here. *I am deeply saddened that you think this is the first time that birth is being addressed by feminism.*" She later interrupted again, asking the speakers, "Can you put 'White' feminism in front of that? *Please.* Black women, and Indigenous women have been fighting for birth rights for four hundred fucking years." In her later presentation, where she took the stage to outline what reproductive justice is, Ross told the crowd, "I can make a distinction between problematic allies, who I have a lot of, and certified enemies, who I have more of." She stood silently for a minute, nodding slowly, then added: "Standing in solidarity, sisters, doesn't mean standing in front."[5]

How, I came to wonder, do these re-visionings of race, gender, reproduction, and justice get communicated in small-town Iowa, South Dakota,
and Missouri—as well as in St. Louis, Kansas City, Des Moines, and Sioux
Falls? How does culture around birth, and those who attend it, change?

COMMUNITY BUILDING, CONSUMER EDUCATION,
AND GROWING A CLIENTELE

Early in my fieldwork, attending The Big Push Summit, I wrote in my fieldnotes, "It must be hard to build a consumer movement when you're suspicious of your consumers!"[6] Even in 2017, finding a midwife in some locales was—as I was told during an interview with Ophelia, a midwife who
had practiced without benefit of legal status—"a reverse referral system."
Midwives in these situations were reasonably suspicious of the people who
called for their services and needed them to be vetted by other midwives or
friends before accepting them as clients. They were frequently concerned,
given rumors of activity they heard from other midwives, that clients were
sent to them as part of a sting operation by the state.

Many times, I heard midwives tell these women, "I'm sorry, midwives are
illegal here, and I can't give you names and numbers . . . but [someone else]
might know someone." There were plenty of potential clients, one midwife
told me, who were probably perfectly "legit," but "I would only tell them, I
might know someone. . . . " And then she would check them out as much as
she could before deciding if she should help them out. Sometimes, midwives
would send out "red alerts" on people seeking care who just didn't seem
legitimate or were people no one in the state seemed to know.[7]

The lack of easy-to-find midwifery care didn't stop people from giving birth at home; and it didn't stop them from finding midwives. "Birthy
people" find each other, even in illegal states. As Ophelia told me, by the
time they hired her, "All of my clients were well aware that I was practicing
illegally" and had gotten to her through word of mouth. In Iowa, in 2016,
midwives themselves estimated that there were ten CPMs in the state who
were not regulated and maybe five direct-entry midwives practicing there.
About those numbers, one doula demurred, "Some underground midwives
are harder to find." Yet, because the records of the Iowa Department of
Public Health indicate that around 500 women in Iowa give birth at home,
every year, we know *someone* is attending to them.[8] Tapping into that hidden

consumer base—and providing education to them, their friends, and other potential clients—was a key activity for those mobilized on behalf of midwives. Finding them—and building community around them—was often a pleasurable part of an activist's work.

Ophelia told me that three main organizers in Missouri spent considerable time finding people "in every pocket of the state." Sometimes, they would simply drive to a new town and "start with the health food store," putting signs up on bulletin boards and inviting participation. They would also cull those bulletin boards for leads on others who might be interested in the cause of midwifery: "I'd see a person who was talking about some other issue and google them and call them up. If they felt that way about vaccines . . . " Ophelia trails off, smiling. If, she means, they were against vaccines, they were probably in favor of homebirth.

For the people who were on their mailing list, Missouri organizers sent weekly updates via email, filling everyone in on what was going on at the statehouse and in the Supreme Court, as well as educating them about alternative birth locales and practices. Ophelia told me that she made sure the newsletters were "gossipy, interesting, warm." She smiled and noted, "People liked reading them. . . . By the time we were fundraising for the Supreme Court fight, we had 800 people on our mailing list."

In fact, there were many overlapping communities to tap into in all of the states with active legislative efforts. La Leche Leagues and pro-breastfeeding organizations were full of moms who had made counter-cultural choices about feeding their babies. Attachment parenting groups were full of families that had at least considered alternative birth settings. Holistic health fairs offered another set of potential consumers and community members. And, organizations that focused on helping women heal emotionally from birth trauma and C-section were similarly fertile ground for organizing. "Birthy people" hung out together everywhere—from these organizations to the yoga studio, health food store, and chiropractor down the street.

In Iowa, that community has gathered explicitly every year on Labor Day, for picnics in parks in a rotating set of cities. These are family affairs—complete with belly dancers, drum circles, and Iowa pork—and are a chance for friends from different parts of the state to catch up. I adopted my Newfoundland, Clementine, after hearing about a pup who needed a home, during the Raccoon River Labor Day picnic in 2008. We also host speakers and films. A new doula in town, to raise awareness of her practice, hosted a screening of *Why Not Home?* And when Cosette Boone (a CNM) opened her eco-friendly, gorgeously redesigned birth center space in the Sherman Hill neighborhood of Des Moines, Iowa, she hosted rotating tours for community members, birth folks, and philanthropic donors to the project.

The birth community in central Iowa supports apprentices seeking financial assistance for didactic learning; it supports midwives when their husbands die or when their children need help; it provides a space of learning and safety for young and unpartnered mothers—where doulas offer free services to those women in need through the Young Women's Resource Center.

In sum, in Iowa I witnessed and participated in community created by and through advocates. I am confident that the same is true in Missouri, South Dakota, and every other state with active legislative efforts and active midwives.

DIRECT ACTION

Sometimes, local birth communities engage in direct action meant to either facilitate out-of-hospital birth in hostile environments or protest the lack of options. By "direct action" I mean a range of social movement activism that is separate from the lobbying and letter-writing typical of advocacy.

Direct action takes several forms within pro-midwifery movements. In South Dakota, members of the organization Safe Childbirth Options hosted workshops for rural and ranching families on emergency care for unattended births; at these workshops a trusted medical doctor ("Esther") taught husbands and other family members how to help women through birth when problems like shoulder dystocia and placental abruption occur. Members of that group had birth kits that they would share with families. Esther offered her private phone number to those families and would frequently coach them, by phone, when they ran into trouble or needed advice during an unattended birth. She told me that they just needed "more rebel midwives" in the state, to help carry the load of the two who practiced, at the time, under cease and desist orders. She also told me that she wasn't incredibly concerned about the families that birthed unassisted, making a distinction (as most South Dakotans do) between "West River" ranching families and "East River" city folks.[9] In an interview with me, Esther says:

You know, the West River women, I hear them preparing for their births, saying, "Hey, you got that video. I need to watch that video." They're swapping books. They're swapping videos. They just talk to each other. They're encouraging each other. And they have unassisted births. And um, and they do a darn good job of it.

I mean, just for the, the cases that I'm aware of, I haven't heard of the complications.

Whereas . . . when you look at what has been the catastrophes in homebirths in [East River] South Dakota, if you start dissecting those down, you end up at some point saying, "Oh my gosh, what where they doing at home?" Just about anybody that wants to have somebody help them with a homebirth is not a good candidate for homebirth. . . . The people that I actually trust to have a really normal physiologic birth, an orgasmic birth, um, they're not wanting any help anyway.

In addition to helping families when they birth "off grid," Esther engaged in pro-midwifery advocacy at the statehouse, speaking in favor of legislation to legalize and regulate CPM practice.

In several cities across the country, I learned of midwives and doulas who organized to serve as birth attendants for those who desperately needed help: homeless, incarcerated, and detained individuals. Some, reportedly, also served to provide first trimester abortion services to women in need. In New York, which the Guttmacher Institute considers to be "very supportive" of the right to abortion, radical nurse midwives joined forces to open Buffalo's Womenservices and the Birthing Center—a single building for both abortion and birth. This kind of full spectrum care, even in states where it is legal to procure these services, constitutes direct action in its insistence on providing women access to the results of their autonomous decision making.

And, in Iowa, I knew of midwives who worked to help women who couldn't otherwise access midwifery services, in a political climate that put them at risk of state involvement if they came to the attention of welfare-related authorities. I recall a text message I received from an attorney in another state, seeking a midwife for a woman near me. For several reasons, the expectant mom was interested in avoiding hospital care: She had not had prenatal care, she was using marijuana, and her partner was in the country without documentation. The lawyer reached out to me, I reached out to a midwife, who reached out to a midwife, who found her a doula, who was willing to drive her to a third midwife's practice for her appointments.

On the national stage, midwives and their advocates have waged a long-term fight for gender-inclusive language, and they have succeeded in getting the Midwives Alliance of North America (MANA) to change the wording of the Core Competencies of Midwives. They accomplished this controversial change through threats of boycott, through consciousness raising, and through sustained dialogue centered in justice seeking. And, at the close of the BirthKeepers Summit in both 2016 and 2017, midwives and advocates engaged in what political scientists and sociologists would easily recognize as more traditional direct action: locating and timing those meetings so those assembled could protest at the national gatherings of the American College of Obstetricians and Gynecologists, with dozens of midwives leafletting, marching, chanting, and singing outside the hotels.

MOVIES, MARKETING, AND MEDIA

One popular and effective ways to build community, while educating consumers, is for a birth organization to host a film screening. They have many to choose from—documentaries that show histories of childbirth in the United States, films that offer a cross-cultural and global perspective, close-up looks at the contemporary US context. Almost all of them feature at least one birth—sometimes the first birth a viewer has ever seen, almost always the first out-of-hospital birth they've witnessed.

Advocates believe that showing out-of-hospital birth in all of its myriad varieties is an effective way to show families their options. My personal experiences, as a viewer—as a professor who shows these films in my Reproductive Law and Politics class—and as a participant-observer at several screenings—shows me that watching these births changes our mindset about what birth can become; learning the history of midwifery in the United States is a powerful way to move people to support CPMs.

The first time I viewed one of these films was in 2004, when I attended a day-long yoga class for expectant parents in Los Angeles. After a rigorous workout, my husband and I joined dozens of couples sitting on mats for a talk that covered topics related to natural birth and birth support, including the role of orgasm in stimulating stalled labor and the use of hypnosis or techniques of mindfulness to manage the pain of contractions. After a lunch of curried mung beans and brown rice, we all settled in on sheepskin mats to take naps. Over cookies and chai tea, upon waking we watched a film that captured different types of births: hypnobirthing, orgasmic birth, and mindful birthing, as well as footage of women giving birth in the Aegean Sea, attended by a midwife and several dolphins. I will admit, it was an *incredibly* Los Angeles experience.

The second film I saw was quite different—*All My Babies: A Midwife's Own Story*. The 1953 film offers a history of Black midwives in the Deep South in the 1910s and 20s and their interactions with the nurse midwives who traveled from the north to improve infant and maternal mortality rates and to offer education to the granny midwives. Screened at The Big Push Summit in 2009, this documentary takes the perspective that regulation and certification have roots in paternalism and that such regulation/certification could have detrimental impacts on traditional practice and access to care. It also offers a nice corrective to what often becomes a filmic romance: In slavery and Jim Crow, out-of-hospital birth wasn't an ode to women's desire for a "natural birth experience"; it was a necessity. *All My Babies* was also screened at MANA meetings in later years, with large audiences in attendance.

By far the most influential film produced in the last twenty years on the topic of homebirth is *The Business of Being Born*. After its successful release in 2008, producers Abby Epstein and Ricki Lake partnered on a television mini-series in 2011 that has had a tremendous impact on the birth community. Moreover, the original documentary became the template for countless other films about birth—in hospital and out of hospital.

These movies all include references to safety, interviews with doctors to validate that safety, interviews with doctors who make it clear that they disdain out-of-hospital birth, and interviews with moms and partners talking about their decision to seek homebirth. Each film highlights the statistics around birth, discusses risk factors and decision making, and shows the reasons why a hospital birth might be unnecessary or undesirable. Where the more recent *Why Not Home?* was produced by a nurse practitioner and tends toward earnestness, *The Business of Being Born* intersperses Monty Python clips with interviews of annoyed doctors, film of peaceful water births alongside those of women's comedic labor groans and sailor-style swearing, and scenes of moms and toddlers at play in Central Park, juxtaposed with midtown traffic.

In these movies there are always scenes of calm, peaceful out-of-hospital births; always at least one water birth; and always scenes of a mom in a difficult labor that ends with her empowerment while she catches her baby. There is almost always, also, a transfer: One birth in each of the major films about contemporary homebirth midwifery ends with an emergency that results in the mom being transported to the hospital, where she labors comfortably with an epidural or has a C-section, and a healthy baby. These scenes serve to reinforce the common knowledge among midwives and advocates that very few births need to take place in a hospital, but that when they do, midwives are qualified to identify a need to transport, and hospitals are there for emergencies. In this way, even the emergency births and births requiring interventions are reassuring to parents considering birthing at home. As a midwife profiled in *Why Not Home?* said of her client Michelle's transfer, "Placenta previa is a solid reason to not have a homebirth."

While one function of these films is to highlight the normalcy of people who choose to birth at home, another is to show their uniqueness and to appeal to viewers' social class and sense of community in outside-the-norm parenting practices. In much the same way that celebrity pregnancy functions,[10] homebirth advocates are aware that films about out-of-hospital birth help to market midwifery services to elite consumers. As Barbara Katz Rothman told the audience at MANA, "Forget the moral aspect here. Money doesn't trickle down, fashion does." She argued that if midwives can "make something happen around the elite end," the popularity of homebirth will increase. She concluded, "Some of you have to go after the top. Someone needs to go after the super fancy rich people . . . form a committee and rotate it through."[11]

Indeed, *The Business of Being Born* offers a rather glamorous look at out-of-hospital birth accompanied by a CPM in New York City. The mothers are all healthy, fit, calm, and physically beautiful. They might not be your typical homebirth mom, but then—who is? At fundraising screenings of *Business of Being Born* and *Why Not Home?* I witnessed well-heeled and fashion-forward homebirthers rubbing elbows with bonneted Mennonite women, sitting near witches who were sharing popcorn and swapping stories with Evangelical women in Christ-centered marriages. A deep desire to support their midwives motivated them to form community—and the movies gave them both a template, and an excuse, to bridge otherwise insurmountable divides.

RIGHTEOUS AND RESISTANT

As we saw in previous chapters, not everyone who supports midwives is in favor of legislation and regulation. In my fieldwork in Iowa, South Dakota, and Missouri, I came across many midwives who articulated a desire to continue to practice, without benefit of regulation—and they would scoff at the word "benefit." These women will show up to protest at state lobby days for midwives and will tell their legislators to vote no on pro-midwifery bills; in states where they do have access to licensure, they will avoid the regulatory gaze of the state, at all costs. And, in my fieldwork at national meetings of midwives and their advocates, I witnessed midwives and their advocates struggling with what it means to have a more radical vision for birth and for women and families' rights, as against the idea that they require regulation, state sanction, or as one midwife said to me with a bit of a sneer, "state permission." Indeed, not all midwives and advocates desire a relationship to the state, and instead critique the desire for regulation of their work with pregnant and laboring women.

These women do not fall into an easy left–right political dichotomy but instead operate in a space where birth is the primary point of reference for their politics; left and right dichotomies (and voting as a primary mover of democratic practices) are less important. In fact, left and right bleed into each other. And, many of those who articulate an anti-regulatory/anti-state politics *also* work for legislation and regulation, and understand the need for it in the service of the public good. These midwives are well aware of the tension in their position.

Some of those articulating this tension are Indigenous midwives and women of color midwives, operating within a reproductive justice framework, and anarchic and eco-feminist midwives of all racial identifications, who would like to deny the power of the state to medicalize, legalize, and regulate pregnancy, labor, and delivery. Others are midwives serving fundamentalist or otherwise closed religious communities, operating within a religious liberties framework that seeks to deny the power of the state to regulate access to care that falls within their standards of modesty, understandings of gender roles, and—in particular—their view of the family and parents' rights.

When articulating their relationship to their clients and to the state, these midwives may stress the religious nature of their practice above other factors. Some midwives refer to their profession as "a calling," much like the ministry, and explain their work through words of faith and piety. In her memoir, for example, Kim Osterholzer tells her readers, "I knew without a doubt that God created me to be a midwife among the Amish."[12] Even if they don't use the language of being called, many midwives stress the important role that they play in marginalized religious communities—providing services to Amish women, Orthodox Jewish and Christian women, Christian Scientists, members of the Church of Latter-Day Saints, Jehovah's Witnesses, Quiverfull communities, and some Muslim women where cultural imperatives for modesty could prevent them from seeking male medical attention.

Many, but not all, of these religiously conservative midwives also endorse homeschooling, selective or anti-vaccination practices, and a pro-life agenda. They very much believe that their stance is one that protects families, including women, from unwelcome government intervention. These birth attendants also, perhaps incongruously, stress women's roles in preparing themselves—through education and other means—to take charge of this aspect of their reproductive lives. During her apprenticeship, Osterholzer (a born-again Christian who herself refuses antibiotics and other traditional medical care) tells readers:

> I was admonished midwifery is not about us midwives. It's about the families we serve and their hopes and dreams. It's about inspiring confidence and autonomy, and about education and encouragement and empowerment; never about accolades, never about reward, never about shining, never about rescuing—never, ever about delivering.
>
> I was advised midwifery is also about having a clear head and solid footing. It's about being ready to love and respect, to accept and serve folks as they come.[13]

Esther, the family practice doctor living in South Dakota, begins our conversation by expressing pleasure that I was familiar with the book *Taking Charge of Your Fertility*. She also expresses her disappointment that most people haven't heard of the author (Toni Weschler) or the book. Some women, she says, wait until some plastic strip that they pee on tells them if they're pregnant. They have no idea. Like they completely weren't present when that spirit entered the room. So for people who are not aware, I really struggle [when] they say, "Oh, we want the natural birth."

I think that we were designed to [birth] on our own or with our husband. You know, that it's an intimate thing. It's not designed to need a big intervention. And so, there's that design. But obeying that design doesn't start at the time labor starts. Obeying the design starts every day that you eat, every day that you exercise, every day that you're in the sun, every day that you go to bed on time. The whole obedience to design is all of that.

So, then . . . [when women are not prepared] there's so much of a loss of their rights, you know?

Without my prompting, Esther transitions our conversation directly toward the law. She asks herself, "And so when I look at it, it's like okay, what do I want the law to say?" She answers, clearly,

I want the law to say you can do what you think is right, you know? The woman is intelligent enough to decide who she needs and what she needs. She's intelligent enough to decide who's qualified and who is not and we'll just respect that.

Esther declines my invitation to extend our conversation into abortion, telling me that the real question is to be sure every child is created consciously and that questions about abortion aren't the right questions to ask. Rather, she wants us to focus on asking what gets in the way of women's control over their fertility, their ability to consent, and their bodies. "I mean, when you say, 'Oh, I'm gonna be pro-choice, or pro-life? It's like you want to pick the worse of two dumb answers."

Before moving on, I follow up with Esther about her stance on legalization, as I knew she had been a very effective speaker in favor of the bills whenever they went before committee. I ask if she felt that legalization was a "justice issue," as one of the West River moms had told me was the purpose of her engagement in the movement. After a very long pause, Esther answers:

I don't know. The more I think about it, I think that licensing midwives just is gonna totally corrupt what midwifery is supposed to be. . . . By the time you put all that licensing and all that regulation . . . then all you've got is people trying to fill out paperwork, trying to make it look like they're doing as good as the hospital while they're at home. And they're not any longer doing that part of midwifery that initially attracted me.

I ask her if she felt like she was in the position of supporting a bill that did something she didn't actually find beneficial. She looks relieved that I see her dilemma and tells me:

> Yes. I kinda keep running around with that one because we worked so hard to get licensing but if they don't get that licensing then, then most women . . . [she chuckled] I mean there's a few wild women out here in the [Black] Hills that can read a book and their husband can read a book and they can watch a couple videotapes and they can, between the two of them, push a baby out and have a great time, okay?
>
> But most of the people haven't had that kind of preparation—haven't had that kind of learning to think like that. So, for those people, if they're going to ever move in that direction, they're going to need [a midwife].

This is similar to what Ophelia told me was her viewpoint on licensure and regulation. Ophelia said, "I guess I have a more libertarian viewpoint," and then told me that she didn't think the government should regulate how people parented or where they gave birth. "It was definitely my early motivation," she said, "that people have the right to choose whatever they're going to do, that families and women have the right to choose where they will labor and who will attend them." She summarized her views, "I don't think it's the government's business to step in and infringe on people's rights in this area."

But, she said, sadly, "I don't think parents are getting full information [from their midwives], and so they are not able to give full consent." Some midwives, in Ophelia's estimation, are not ethical, well trained, or responsible. So, she told me, she had come around to the need to licensure. But, she despaired, "I don't know that there is any good way to regulate midwives and still let parents have rights."

I had, years earlier, asked Brenda, another Missouri midwife—one with a high-end practice in the St. Louis suburbs—what her ideal law would look. I told Brenda, "Some midwives say, 'Just get the government out of it altogether." She chuckled and affirmed, "That would be my preference." Then she elaborated:

Educated people educate themselves. They know what they want. . . .
They have the right to have whoever they want to have there where, I
mean, if they just want their granny to do it for 'em, they should have that
right to do that, and I just think it's sad that they don't.

Before I could interject, Brenda went farther:

And yet we have an abortion law. I mean, it, it just, it's so conflicting in
my mind. It's okay to kill a baby, but it's not okay to birth a baby? It's, it
just doesn't fit in my mind. I just can't put the two things together, but . . .
[and here she indicated the apprentice midwife she was preceptor to, who
was sitting at her side and obviously in disagreement] I come from a different place than she does on that, too. But we still work together well.

All of these women, across more than a decade of fieldwork and ranging
over more than a thousand miles geographically, also affirmed to me that
each—for political and religious reasons—homeschooled and avoided vaccination. Like Gina, the South Dakota midwife who prayed for guidance after
receiving her cease and desist letter, they also all felt that their "rebellious"
stances derived from a sense of ethical or religious duty. Thinking of work
by Kay Levine and Virginia Mellema, who discuss the legal consciousness
of those who see themselves as rebellious,[14] I remember asking Brenda, "Do
you have a sense of yourself as some sort of outlaw, underground, illegal
person? Did you before you started what you're doing? I mean, are you a
rebel in normal life?" Her answer:

Absolutely. I'm a rebel. I've been a rebel all my life. I was homeschooling
before it was legal to homeschool in Missouri. I homeschooled for thirteen years. Because I just had a sense of, you know, what is right.

Following up, I wanted to know, "If what you think is right is in conflict
with law, it's more right?" Again, she answered strongly and affirmatively.
Our interview continued:

BRENDA: Absolutely. It's more right to follow, for me it's more right to follow God's law than it is to follow the law of the state, 'cause that's who my
ultimate boss is.
RENÉE::And if there was a law saying you couldn't, you still would?
BRENDA:Yes, exactly.

Before I could even ask Esther, the family practice doctor, she let me know her stance on these issues as well—interrupting her own autobiography to tell me, "Oh, we homeschool, and no, my kids are not vaccinated."

We have a cultural view of parents who homeschool and don't get their children vaccinated as both backwards and anti-science. But, in fact, as Eula Biss writes in her wonderful set of essays on vaccination, unvaccinated kids tend to be White, middle class, and born to educated mothers—the kinds of children born to Esther and Brenda, for sure. It is their view of the person vis-à-vis the collective that makes them decide not to vaccinate—not their lack of education or even a lack of belief in science. "For some of the mothers I know, a refusal to vaccinate falls under a broader resistance to capitalism,"[15] Biss writes, and "refusing immunity is a form of civil disobedience." It is also a refusal to participate in "a public" that they do not trust nor want to engage.

And, crucially, this refusal is neither left, nor right—neither simply conservative, nor progressive. This was brought home to me early in my process of learning about midwifery advocates, during an interview in 2006 with Marie who worked as a legal, licensed midwife in south Los Angeles County and Orange County. We were nearly two hours into our conversation, and our talk had turned to issues of regulation, licensure, surveillance, and politics. Marie told me:

> Pretty soon we're gonna have tattoos and chips in our ears. That's the way I look at it. They're already putting chips in dogs, I mean . . .
>
> So maybe you can still go off grid, a little, with your birth. So many women aren't registering their births. They are not vaccinating.
>
> And that's like, you can be so far left, you're right.
>
> Somebody asked me, "Well what are you? Liberal? You're probably a liberal, aren't you?"
>
> I told them, "Don't group me into being a Democrat or a Republican because I'm not either one." I said, "You know what? I'm so far right, I'm left."

Marie is, in fact, a beneficiary of a licensing law that helps her practice—a beneficiary of state power. But she remains hostile to it, and suspicious of it. Some of her suspicions would resonate with a very different group of people—those involved in the movement for reproductive justice, who know that institutionalized racism, and its particularized expressions, transcend party lines and are often expressed via state power.

REPRODUCTIVE JUSTICE

"Reproductive justice" is a term coined by Black women activists and scholars in 1994 in response to the ways that White women constructed a feminist agenda that appeared to exclude significant concerns in its focus on abortion. The organizational home of the movement, SisterSong Women of Color Reproductive Justice Collective, defines the goals of the movement in this way: "The human right to maintain personal bodily autonomy, have children, not have children, and parent the children we have in safe and sustainable communities." Movement co-founder Loretta Ross and her co-author Rickie Solinger concisely articulate the tenets of the reproductive justice movement in a primer on the field published in 2017:

1. The right *not* to have a child
2. The right to *have* a child
3. The right to *parent* children in safe and healthy environments[16]

They elaborate that they define those rights—and the population to whom they apply—expansively. A reproductive justice stance advocates for the sexual autonomy and gender freedom of every human being and holds that "Safe and dignified fertility management, childbirth, and parenting together constitute a fundamental *human right*."[17]

In a speech at the first ever Birth Rights Bar Association conference in Chicago in April 2018, author Khiara Bridges noted that reproductive justice includes the right to safety in childbirth, the right to ending health disparities that disproportionately impact postpartum women of color and their children, and the right to have dignity in health care. Scholars and advocates of reproductive justice tie their movement to the work done by Black Lives Matter activists, to women working with the Black Mamas Matter Alliance, *and* to the Indigenous-led #NoDAPL resistance movement against the Dakota Access Pipeline. These people, primarily women—primarily women of color and primarily Black women—articulate reproductive justice to be the panoply of rights to bodily autonomy and safety that should be accorded *all* humans, with an emphasis on the moments that those bodies might—or might not—reproduce, birth, and parent.[18]

Rooted in an understanding of the history of reproduction in the United States as racist, classist, ableist, and misogynist, scholar-activists working within a reproductive justice frame draw attention to "the history of white supremacy operating in a capitalist system [that] penetrates and misshapes the present."[19] As such, reproductive justice (RJ) draws attention to, and describes, contemporary contexts of reproductive decision making and constraint. RJ offers critiques of capitalism, and critiques of the way that nations have built themselves on the backs of, and with the bodies of, women of color.

Reproductive justice, as a frame, reminds us of (or educates us about) forced reproduction in slavery, of the sterilization of native women and Hispanic women, and of the loss of Indigenous and enslaved midwifery traditions. It also reminds us of (or educates us about) the constraints on reproduction for White women living in poverty, or without "benefit" of a husband, and the ways that White, propertied women have been both co-erced and incentivized to reproduce. Reproductive justice reminds us (and educates us) that the bodies women of color and poor women were used in obstetrics wards and teaching hospitals without their consent; and that history "clarifies the need for protection from coerced sex and reproduction and also from coerced suppression or termination of fertility."[20]

As Solinger explains in her book *Pregnancy and Power*,

> [W]omen-of-color organizations have been clear about the dramatic limits of the mainstream pro-choice/pro-abortion rights agenda. . . . [C]hoice has masked the equal importance of *access* to reproductive health services and the *right* to these services and has obscured the link between all forms of oppression. . . .
>
> Members of all of the relatively new women-of-color groups fighting for reproductive justice have faced and fought reproductive indignities. These women have all worked to end fertility-related oppression.21

And, Solinger notes, all women define the stakes of reproductive justice differently, given their different racial and ethnic identities and histories.

Reproductive justice, then, offers an alternative but also complemen-tary framing to the project of professionalization of midwives. Into a con-versation where rights discourse has been rather assiduously avoided, RJ advocates articulate a panoply of human rights to bodily autonomy and safety. Midwives are poised to become conduits for achieving some measures of reproductive justice through multiple means—not the least of which is the provision of culturally sensitive services to clients and through the avoidance of birth trauma, obstetric violence, and disparate bad outcomes for women of color in communities nationwide.

As Bridges notes, in her ethnography of the construction of race through interactions of pregnant women with staff at a large New York City teaching hospital,

> A poor pregnant woman may experience the disempowering and de-pendency-producing efforts of a medically managed pregnancy as yet another demonstration of her powerlessness within society. Indeed, pre-natal care so delivered may be understood as a disciplinary mechanism that educates poor, pregnant women about their status within society and the behavior expected of those who occupy that station.[22]

And, Bridges most recent work—as well as reporting by Linda Villarosa at the *New York Times*, has shown clearly that holding higher socioeconomic status does not help Black women achieve better care. Quite simply, legacies of racism, internalized bias on the part of doctors, and the daily stress of living in a society that actively devalues them all put women of color at higher risk in labor and delivery.

The widely publicized case of tennis champion Serena Williams offers an excellent example of the ways that economic class cannot triumph over neg-ative impacts of race and gender. The story quickly became popular culture folklore: Shortly after the birth of her daughter Alexis Olympia Ohanian Jr. (called Olympia by Serena), Serena suffered a near-death experience. In an interview she gave to Rob Haskell for *Vogue* magazine, she discussed her postpartum experience in detail:

> Olympia was born by emergency C-section after her heart rate dove dan-gerously low during contractions. The surgery went off without a hitch; [father] Alexis cut the cord, and the wailing newborn fell silent the mo-ment she was laid on her mother's chest. "That was an amazing feeling," Serena remembers. "And then everything went bad."
>
> The next day, while recovering in the hospital, Serena suddenly felt short of breath. Because of her history of blood clots, and because she was off her daily anticoagulant regimen due to the recent surgery, she immediately assumed she was having another pulmonary embolism. (Serena lives in fear of blood clots.) . . . She . . . told the nearest nurse,

between gasps, that she needed a CT scan with contrast and IV heparin (a blood thinner) right away. The nurse thought her pain medicine might be making her confused. But Serena insisted, and soon enough a doctor was performing an ultrasound of her legs. "I was like, a Doppler? I told you, I need a CT scan and a heparin drip," she remembers telling the team. The ultrasound revealed nothing, so they sent her for the CT, and sure enough, several small blood clots had settled in her lungs. Minutes later she was on the drip.[23]

Months later, *New York Times Magazine* editor Linda Villarosa interpreted the chain of events this way, "Though she had a history of this disorder and was gasping for breath, . . . medical personnel initially ignored her concerns. Though Williams should have been able to count on the most attentive health care in the world, her medical team seems to have been unprepared to monitor her for complications after her cesarean, including blood clots, one of the most common side effects" of that form of delivery.[24]

What's more, Villarosa writes, "Even after she received treatment, her problems continued; coughing, triggered by the embolism, caused her C-section wound to rupture. When she returned to surgery physicians discovered a large hematoma, or collection of blood, in her abdomen, which required more surgery."[25] Williams was hospitalized for six weeks. A week before the *Vogue* interview, Williams—one of the strongest athletes on the planet—had "walked the length of a neighborhood block for the first time since returning from the hospital."[26]

Williams disclosed the problems with her care on Facebook, Instagram, and in the *Vogue* article, and people took notice. The *New York Times Magazine* devoted front-page coverage on April 11, 2019, to Villarosa's stunningly stark article about the maternal health disparities for women of color in the United States. Villarosa explained what researchers are coming to realize: "the disparity in death rates" for laboring and postpartum Black women in America, which is three times the rate of White women. This is not due to genetics but rather is due to "the lived experience of being a black woman in America."[27]

Indeed, Black mothers and Black babies have disproportionately bad outcomes related to birth than people of other races living in the United States. What's more, these disparities have a perplexing history—in that they are not getting better with time or technology. Villarosa studied public health data and found that in 1850, the infant mortality rate for Blacks was 340 per 1,000; the White rate was 217 fetal deaths per 1,000 live births. From 1915 to 1990, the "number of babies of all races who died in the first year of life dropped by over 90 percent," but "that national decline in infant mortality has since slowed." Chillingly, "Black infants in America are now more than twice as likely to die as white infants," which amounts to more than 4,000 Black babies lost each year.[28] Black infant mortality is bound up with the crisis of death and trauma inflicted on Black mothers, who are three to four times as likely to die as a result of pregnancy-related complications than their White counterparts.[29]

Scholarship and public health data make clear that this *is* about race. Higher educational attainment and wealth do not mitigate the impacts of living as a Black woman in this country. As Serena Williams experienced, Black women report that their own understandings of their bodies are discounted by medical professionals. Studies show that Black women are even offered lower doses of pain medication, compared to their White counterparts, and they experience higher rates of preterm birth, consistent with their self-reporting of experiences of racism in their daily lives.[30]

Rickie Solinger argues that the medical profession and doctors have long "taken a central role in constructing women's reproductive capacity as the site where her womanhood is defined or defiled."[31] In her book about the profession's roots in the slave system, Deirdre Cooper Owens includes a story about her own experiences with ob-gyns, as a middle-class professional Black woman. She writes, "Academics might have declared that race was a social construct, but doctors seemed to treat my blackness as biological."[32] Indeed, when her fertility doctor dilated her cervix—twice—without offering her pain medicine, Owens knows:

> I am a direct heir of James Marion Sim's medical legacy, and I reject critiques that demonize black and women scholars as unobjective when we dare to make personal connections with the historical actors we study, especially if they were enslaved.[33]

Along with the notion that Black women are hypersexual, Black women's bodies have been envisioned as unreliable, their reporting of symptoms has been suspect, and their babies have been seen as the result of hyper-fertility. Black women have often been told to simply work to avoid pregnancy altogether—or to be hyper-responsible while pregnant. Indeed, Villarosa, who now directs the journalism program at City College of New York, was the health editor at *Essence* in the 1980s and 90s. In her article for the *New York Times Magazine*, she reflected on her time at *Essence*:

> [The magazine] covered the issue of infant mortality by encouraging our largely middle-class black female readers to avoid unwanted pregnancy and by reminding them to pay attention to their health habits during pregnancy. . . . [W]e also promoted a kind of each-one-teach-one mentality: encourage teenagers in your orbit to just say no to sex and educate all the "sisters" in your life (read: your less-educated and less-privileged friends and family) about the importance of prenatal care and healthful habits during pregnancy.[34]

This approach—pregnancy avoidance and maternal responsibilization—is certainly insufficient to the challenge of maternal health disparities caused by structural inequality.[35]

Yet is an approach that stays en vogue. It even briefly dominated the headlines coming out of the annual meeting of the American College of Obstetricians and Gynecologists in the spring of 2018. At that meeting, which featured a focus on maternal death, a speaker who was otherwise concerned with racial justice as a starting point offered a slide that enraged advocates. On it, a cartoon condom, compete with a happy face, told doctors that to lower the maternal mortality rate and end racial disparities, they should help women avoid unwanted or unintended pregnancies. Contraception, the slide said, was the best way to avoid bad outcomes of childbirth.

Immediately, reproductive justice advocates protested. Midwives, doctors, doulas, and mothers from all walks of life tweeted angrily at ACOG's account using the hashtag #BirthJustice, organized phone campaigns, and bombarded the organization's Facebook pages. ACOG soon apologized and clarified the organization's official view: The best way to prevent maternal mortality is to address care that grows from systemic racism and causes disparate bad outcomes for women of color in the United States. The incident, though, reinforced a negative view of the way that doctors and hospitals interact with women of color.

Researchers from the Black Women Birthing Justice Collective found that, when they can access midwifery and doula care, Black women feel respected. "None of our participants who worked with a midwife/doula team reported feeling disempowered or very disempowered, compared to 31 percent of those who were attended by a physician/nurse team."[36] However, accessing midwifery care is not easy for women of color in most communities—in part because of community norms about hospital birth as best and homebirth as "White." As one of their research participants, "Kaelah" told Julia Oparah and her coauthors, "I wanted to have a home birth and everybody I talked to—all black women—said you are *so* white. You can't."[37] She ended up having a vaginal birth, in an Oakland-area hospital. Analyzing Kaelah's narrative, they write,

> The view that the alternative to the dominant medical model of birth is "crunchy, granola" and limited to white women was reiterated throughout our research. Participants who were not connected to black home-birth networks often struggled to believe that it was something of relevance to black women, a perception reinforced by the virtual absence of black women in films about natural and homebirth.[38]

And yet, Oparah and colleagues write about their research participants—all Black women living in northern California: "As they moved through their pregnancies, a surprising 27 percent of our participants hoped to have a homebirth. Ultimately, 20 percent of our participants gave birth at home."[39] They continue:

> Nationwide, 0.6 percent of all births occur in the home (31,500 in 2010), and one quarter of the are unplanned. Clearly, our research recruited a disproportionate number of black mothers who were intentional about birthing at home, probably because these women are more likely to be part of informal networks related to birth activism and to be interested in sharing their birth stories. At the same time, our research demonstrates that there is a significant and overlooked black home birth community in California . . . [40]

They conclude that "peer networks, family birth stories, and political convictions" in response to the medicalization of childbirth and the persecution of community midwives, "influenced participants who desired a homebirth," as did the availability of care provided by women of color.[41]

The provision of care that values a woman's dignity, as required now under reproductive justice principles adopted by New York City's Bureau of Maternal, Infant, and Reproductive Health,[42] will impact more than a mother's sense of self-worth and identity; it will impact, midwives and others hope, the tremendously bad outcomes women of color of all socioeconomic classes face in hospital birth. Bridges reports, "Black women die from causes linked to pregnancy and childbirth *at more than three times the rate of white women.*"[43] In New York City at the time of her fieldwork, the maternal mortality rate for Black women was more than five times that of White women.[44] Oparah and colleagues powerfully state, "In a country where simply being black is a risk factor in pregnancy outcomes, maybe the way to improve outcomes is to truly listen to what black women say they need, recognizing they are the experts in and of their own lives."[45]

While their practices have long enabled holistic birth services to a range of clients—and have centered exactly on the expertise of women in their own lives, bodies, and births—midwives are recently and increasingly adopting a reproductive justice frame to explain their scope of practice and care. They do this individually, in marketing materials and conversation; and they do this through their professional organizations' meetings and at other national gatherings of providers and consumers. Midwives and their organizations adopt reproductive justice frames to talk about their existing clientele and to expand access to women of color and poor women; they also adopt this frame when telling the history of midwifery and while working together to imagine its future.

Jennie Joseph, who operates a birth center and midwifery school in Winter Park, Florida, is legendary in the field of midwifery. Joseph, a Black woman from the United Kingdom, runs her practice on principles of "commonsense birth," with open access hours to facilitate care and a philosophy that emphasizes quality care "for all." Her technique, trademarked as The JJ Way®, is reputed to provide incredible outcomes and to serve higher risk women in a particularly useful way. And, as those who spoke about her at The Big Push meeting in 2009 noted in reverent tones, Joseph "is tracking her statistics."[46] Nationwide, midwives work together using Joseph's model to serve incarcerated women, homeless and housing insecure women, and women living in homes that shelter them from intimate partner violence.

A focus on indigeneity in the Americas has been figured as another way to reclaim the history of midwives, while drawing attention to racial and class inequities in birth. As Bronwen Preece notes, "The more than devastating effects of European colonization severely impacted the practice of Indigenous midwifery."[47] Further, the continued need for Indigenous women in remote areas to travel to hospitals in urban areas is an indication, for Preece, of neocolonialism and the ongoing impact of settler colonialism on indigenous families. At The Big Push, advocates were already seeking a "postcolonial vision" of what births could be and screening videos about aboriginal and Indigenous practices of birth, alongside the documentaries about granny midwives and *The Business of Being Born*.

In 2015, the MANA conference in Santa Fe, New Mexico, hosted a pre-conference workshop that was only for Indigenous midwives; thirty women attended—among them fourteen CNMs and a handful of CPMs. In her report out about that workshop to the general MANA conference attendees, Marinah Farrell, then-president of MANA, said, "The changing face of midwifery is about reclaiming activism. Our traditional midwives are now young. They are reclaiming the profession for themselves and taking it back to their communities." She noted that this new activism brought with it a "new urgency to talk about human rights, social justice, and reclaiming dignity," along with the growing certainty that midwives need to articulate their "right to practice midwifery anywhere we want."[48]

SERVING PEOPLE WHO LABOR AND DELIVER

Very recently, a politics of professionalization has collided with a politics of justice. The gendering of birth as "female" felt commonsense, and pursuing elite clients seemed necessary to survive. But, as activists sought both justice and visibility for an expanded clientele for midwives, they began to use the terms "people who labor and deliver" and "people who give birth," rather than the modifier "women."

I was not present for the leadership level conversations at the Midwives Alliance of North America that led, in 2014, to the revolutionary change to gender-inclusive language within the Core Competencies of Midwives. I was present, though, for the continued contestation over the use of gender-inclusive language and the continued, important affirmations of "a client's absolute right to self-determination and bodily autonomy" provided via care that is "culturally safe, autonomous, and community based."[49]

Of the many interventions from the floor at the BirthKeepers Summit, one stood out for its insistence on this absolute right to self-determination. An audience member reminded the group, and the organizers, "This has been a woman-centered conversation." The person went on, "But women aren't the only people who give birth. Transpeople give birth. Agender people give birth." Pausing to allow the crowd to cheer, they concluded, "We need to recognize that."[50] This reminder provided from the audience, met with tremendous applause, is important—especially because the inclusion of transgender people in the politics of midwifery can be a sticking point, when binaries of feminine and masculine are still widely accepted as essential.

At the MANA meeting following the 2014 decision, organizers brought in a justice-focused comic and mediator to help midwives process the change. Unaware of what I was about to witness, I sat in the evening session with eighty to ninety midwives and advocates and watched a verbal altercation escalate into a shoving match, as midwives advocating for "woman-centered care" and midwives advocating for "gender-inclusive care" continued to rehash the decision. At the core of the woman-centered claims is a deep fear that, if we lose the specificity of "women" in language around birthing, we will lose the gender justice core of midwifery. As one midwife tearfully shouted, "I serve women! Women. Because we are treated horribly in birth—because we are women." Another amplified, "Birth is where women can claim our power—don't erase us, and our power, with this language that doesn't even include us."[51]

In the aftermath of this 2015 MANA meeting—and again in 2016, 2017, and 2018—the debate continued. MANA's web page provides a concise history of the changes and the controversy. On the "advocacy" page, the site reads, in part:

> In December 2014, the Midwives Alliance Core Competencies were revised using gender-inclusive language in order to better reflect the diversity of midwives and the clients they serve. The Core Competencies establish the essential knowledge, clinical skills and critical thinking necessary for entry-level practice for direct-entry midwifery in the United States. They provide the basis for the CPM. . . .

Concerns that gender inclusive language could potentially harm women led to an open letter to MANA in August 2015 from "Woman-Centered Midwifery" asking that the revisions be reversed. MANA responded:

> Whereas pregnancy, birth and breastfeeding are unique to the female sex, there are those who seek midwifery care who do not gender identify as women. Considering the national initiatives challenging health care professionals to provide gender neutral services and gender inclusive health care materials, we committed to a document reflective of these national trends and consistent with our values. In the process of crafting these revisions to our Core Competencies, many of the midwives involved found ourselves undergoing a paradigm shift and realized that many of these issues and practices apply more broadly to include other family members. Changing to gender neutral language reaffirms the midwives' goal with relationship to the whole family system. Inclusive language helps us all learn to be more aware, sensitive and humble to the needs of each family system and the devastating effects of marginalization. No individual wants to be singled out or identified as "different" or less worthy. As long as a single client is excluded from the midwifery community, all clients are potentially vulnerable to discriminatory treatment.

On social media, the debate continued—with many prominent members of the midwifery community making strong and compassionate statements in favor of the shift in language. One midwife posted to Facebook:

> Sending love and light to the members of MANA who have just been through a really hard contraction trying to figure out how to be more inclusive, while still preserving their commitment to women and birth. Midwives in the US have been poorly treated by medicine, law enforcement, legislators and worried mothers-in-law for decades. And they do important, hard work. The work of making sure that we have a maternity care system that works for everyone regardless of anatomy, gender identity, race, ethnicity, nation of birth, religion, . . . is no small thing.[52]

Another posted an open letter that reaffirmed:

> It is really quite simple. Not everyone who gives birth is a "woman." Using gender-inclusive language is an act of love and care to let trans and gender

non-conforming folks know that they are also welcome at the table and can access the personalized, gentle, and respectful care midwives offer. Not one person I know who is pushing for this inclusivity wants to erase women or our struggles for personhood and lives free of harassment or violence. Not one person pushing for this change is not aware of the ways women and birth have been continuously abused and pathologized in our U.S. culture. We just ALSO ask for understanding of the existence and struggles of trans and gender non-conforming people. This is a YES/AND situation not an EITHER/OR situation and there is room for everyone.

If your fierce love for women and your desire to provide them with respectful care brought you to midwifery, I praise you. You can continue to fully honor your experience of women and womanhood and also love, value, and include people with other experiences.

If it is important to you to continue to specifically honor the experience of women and mothers in your speech, you can simply use other words like "people" and "parent" alongside "women" and "mother" to include all people. I personally often switch back and forth between saying "woman" and "person" as I am speaking about birth.

No one is going to force you to use gender-inclusive language. You get to choose because you speak for yourself alone. But our national midwifery and birth organizations speak for us all and they have a responsibility to make these changes so that all people are welcome at the table.53

As the national organization that sets the standards for midwifery care and provides the authoritative language regarding Core Competencies and the Midwives Model of Care (which is, on the website, termed "woman-centered"), the language that MANA uses is indeed important. So are the alliances the organization makes with groups advocating and supporting change, and the welcoming environment created for all people at MANA meetings.

The advocacy section of the MANA website closes with an excerpt from a letter to the midwifery community written by Birth for Everybody, an organization that strives continues to support and educate about the need for trans-inclusion in MANA documents, culture, and language. That letter—signed by more than 1,500 individuals—clearly ties the movement for gender equity and inclusion to the principles of care and dignity embodied by midwifery more generally. It reads, in part:

We honor and uphold the right to self-determination and bodily autonomy for all people. We believe that as midwives, our purpose is to support parents and babies throughout the childbearing year, taking into account the unique physiological, psychological, and social well-being and needs of each client. It is our work to provide individualized education and counseling, as well as client-centered prenatal, intrapartum, and postpartum care. We understand the importance of providing compassionate, holistic, and culturally sensitive midwifery care, and we strive towards making the Midwives Model of Care™ accessible for every person and family who seeks it, regardless of race, ethnicity, religion, ability, sexual orientation, gender identity or gender expression. We acknowledge the disproportionate effects of transphobia on those with other marginalized identities such as being a person of color, low-income or disabled. Many racial health disparities that concern midwives and impact our communities are experienced in greater numbers by people who are both Black and transgender. These lives especially are in need of the kind of respectful, compassionate, and individualized care midwives can offer. We assert that we can honor the power of the female body and at the same time extend this reverence to all people who are pregnant and giving birth, and that to do so is in full alignment with the heart of midwifery.

This letter—along with the seismic shifts around gender identity and gender inclusion taking place within MANA and other midwifery communities—makes an organic and authentic move: It places the birthing person at the center of any care decision and at the center of any analytic meant to understand it. This insistence on the particularity of each person's lived experience, grounded in an ethic of autonomy and dignity, is a way by which midwives use their knowledge, in line with the birthing person's knowledge, to achieve good process and outcomes. Midwives are always mindful of these tensions; and they argue that this overt reclamation of a particularistic, body-centered way of knowing enables shifts to trans-inclusion, gender expression equity, and authentic care for *all* clients, without necessitating a midwife to redefine her values or beliefs.

EXPANDING THE MARGINS OF REPRODUCTIVE CARE

The transition to a reproductive justice frame is not universal within midwifery circles—*nor should it be*. In fact, it would be an act of White appropriation and privilege for midwifery—an overwhelmingly White profession in the United States with an overwhelmingly White clientele—to simply, blithely adopt as its own the work that reproductive justice has done, and is doing. Reproductive justice "demands that all pregnant people have an equal opportunity to make and exercise decisions about their care, including out-of-hospital birth"[54]—but reproductive justice is not limited to that. Rather, midwives can acknowledge that their practice is a critical—but incomplete—part of reproductive justice,[55] and White midwives can be accomplices in the work of racial justice.

As well, conscientious midwives are committing to creating spaces of welcome and mutual education, to determine how best to provide culturally appropriate care in recognition of the dignity of the laboring and delivering people they serve. Because 70 percent of the clients that midwives *already* serve are vulnerable by virtue of age, education, race, or socioeconomic status,[56] almost anywhere midwives expand their client base, they are expanding access to out-of-hospital care, and care beyond the medical model, to women who desperately want and need it.

. . .

In *The Balance Gap*, Sarah Cote Hampson investigates the conditions under which women access family leave policies in their workplace. Adopting William Haltom and Michael McCann's schema, she explores institutions, individuals, and ideologies as they converge to form legal consciousness, asking "How do individuals come to use the language of the law to interpret their situations?"[57] Like most scholars of legal mobilization and consciousness, Hampson answers that these assertions of legal language take the form of rights claims and rights talk. However, her work also shows that we need not require claimants to speak a language of rights in order to understand that they are articulating legal consciousness; Hampson clearly states that she is interested in "the interactions that individuals have with the law in their everyday lives . . . [and] how individuals think about the law and in tracking the mutually constitutive relationship between legal action and legal consciousness."[58]

Fundamentally, scholars who study the connection between legal consciousness and legal mobilization are interested in questions of how people use legal concepts, legal terminology, and other kinds of connections with the law in their everyday lives. Though Hampson's emphasis, and the emphasis of most of the literature, is on "when and how [people's use of legal terminology] matters for rights claiming,"[59] legal consciousness and legal mobilization need not be about rights; midwifery mobilization shows quite clearly that mobilization for transformational change need not engage in rights claiming, and must include cultural and normative transformation.

Indeed, as is appropriate and necessary, midwifery advocates are working on several projects simultaneously—adopting legal strategies, political strategies, and cultural strategies. Raymond DeVries and Rebeca Barroso argue that the most promise for midwives lies in strategies that "strengthen the structural position of midwives and work to create supporting cultural ideas."[60] This may seem to require that birth activists shift from a focus on law and enter what Idit Kostiner calls a "cultural schema."[61] In this schema, activists

> mostly see the law as being marginal to activism. They do not view law as an important tool for social justice, nor do they see it as the "enemy" of social justice. Rather social justice in the cultural schema seems to be beyond the reach of law, as operating in a different realm of existence.[62]

But, though Kostiner seems to take activism within cultural and legal schemas to be mutually exclusive, I understand them to be mutually constitutive. When activists are in a legal space and schema, they adopt language targeted toward legislative, regulatory, and legal actors; when they are in a cultural schema, they take direct action (even direct action that puts them at odds with law),[63] use social media, traditional media, and film. In a cultural schema, they throw parties and picnics; they engage in deep and meaningful conversation with each other; they use language that law perhaps can't hear.

CONCLUSION

Attending to Birth in Sociolegal Scholarship: Embodied, Interdisciplinary, and Authoritative Knowledge

> "You're bringing everyone under the regulatory umbrella—
> you could say it is disciplinary."
> —Participant in Midwives Alliance of North America
> roundtable session on US-MERA

I AM A WORKING-CLASS KID from small-town South Dakota. I have always had a job—from working at the age of five as a pin setter and machine cleaner at the bowling alley my mom owned, to earning a dollar an hour shoveling snow for our entire block. During high school, I worked the early shift at our local bakery; from five to seven each morning, I filled donuts, sliced the bread, washed the giant mixing tubs, and arranged the morning's pastries, then rushed to make it to school for first period band practice.

My high school was small—my 1990 graduating class of fifty-three students remains the largest ever graduated. We had no Advanced Placement courses, no language study except German, and our guidance counselor had never had a student take the SAT. My mission, as a teenager, was to find a way to leave. Because I had opinions, and wasn't reticent to share them, my teachers told me I could be a lawyer. They didn't mean it as a compliment. Only a handful of us left the region after high school graduation: One of my closest friends went to the Coast Guard Academy, and I went to Bard College on a full-ride scholarship. There, my professors saw in me capacities and desires beyond argumentation, and they taught me how to pursue a different set of goals.

By both accident and miracle, I ended up in a PhD program—politics, New York University—rather than law school. I entered thinking I would study comparative politics. I'd written my undergraduate thesis on the Puerto Rican independence movement and thought I'd be a Latin Americanist focusing on the Caribbean, my crummy Spanish notwithstanding. I also entered thinking I'd get the master's and cut loose—maybe I'd find a way to make a living as a political organizer.

Instead, I found my way to a job organizing our graduate student union with the United Auto Workers, and into the classrooms of the Law and Society Program, where I found my advisor, Professor Christine Harrington, and a desire to understand sociolegal studies. Like Susan Silbey has recently written, I reflect now that "I cannot have been the only naive scholarly initiate with little understanding of what I was doing, as I was learning to do it."[1] Though at the time, I did, indeed, feel like the only one in my cohort learning as I went,[2] it is clear to me that much of the life cycle of mastery, of knowledge transmission and reception, is intuitive, unconscious, embodied, and instinctual; we are all, as it happens, "learning on the job."[3]

I dutifully attended the meetings of the American Political Science Association—but, one year in Miami, as part of the Law and Society Graduate Student workshop—I found my intellectual home. I stayed with several other graduate students at the youth hostel down the street from the opulent conference hotel, only just beginning to realize what a privilege it was to be surrounded by scholars who enjoyed their work. At Law and Society, I saw different disciplinary and cultural norms in practice, and I met people interested in the same questions as me, people using similar methods and pursuing justice-oriented work.

I was so new to the academy, so unaware of how disciplines and subfields worked, so clueless about status and institutional hierarchies. I didn't even really understand, until I left my job at California State University–Long Beach after five years, to teach at Drake University, the actual differences between public and private universities. I still couldn't list for you every school in the Big Ten.

So, though I felt at home in law and society, I didn't always feel at home as a professor. After all, during graduate school, when I worked one day per week as a Kelly Girl, providing temporary clerical staffing to Wall Street traders, my mom said, "Thank goodness you're getting some real world experience." This is the same woman who asks me what I get paid, every time I publish a scholarly article or book. It has only been recently that I don't panic about having money in the bank at the end of the summer, reminding myself that I get paid (and I work) year-round. And, I routinely encounter students whose radical justice-seeking politics are so similar to mine, and also sometimes at odds with the good of the institution where I work—I find that I want to hug them, support them, and, sometimes, ask them to quiet down.

I write all of this in the hopes that you can understand that this process of education—of socialization through conference presentations and scholarly interaction, of giving up a professional goal (lawyering) for immersion into the professionalization provided by the disciplinary field of law and society—has had a profound impact on who I am, what I research, how I write, and how I teach. My students tell me that classes in our major "ruin their lives": They mean that they can't watch movies without seeing law everywhere; they can't interact with their peers without seeing injustice; they can't ignore the speed limit without understanding privilege. They are always—they tell me in exasperation—thinking about, and aware of, law: its limits, its perils, its romance.

Reflecting on my narrative, and on my students' reactions to what and how they learn, helps me keep in mind that midwives and their advocates are very aware of the perils of professionalization and working within regulatory systems; they see the limits (and romance) of law. Some midwives and clients push back, especially against the commodification of childbirth experiences, and their figuring as more "consumers" than "citizens." As one homebirth mom in Alabama told me, at a MANA conference, her objection to regulation was that "It's not the government's place to say what I can and can't do in my home!" She went on to say that she felt she had the *right* to birth at home with the attendant of her choice, a right not adequately captured when she was named as a "consumer."[4] Cherise, a midwife practicing in Washington, DC, interrupted her own comments at the Birth Rights Bar Association meeting to correct herself after she used the word "consumer": "'Consumer' . . . " she shook her head, "I don't like the word . . . "[5]

Later, during the same presentation, Cherise took explicit issue with the links between legitimation, exclusionary practices, and commodification. She asked angrily, "Why don't we have a freaking public registry of CPMs?" Cherise argued that consumers should be able to easily find such a list. She continued:

> There is only one place that has such a registry, and they're not giving it up. . . . We need a transparent, easily accessible list of licensed CPMs. There are 857 NARM-certified midwives and they won't publish a list.[6]

In obvious frustration, she continued, "I want people to use midwives but it's up to [them] to find out who they are—and that can be very difficult." Then she reiterated, shaking her head, "Consumers. These aren't consumers—they are women."[7]

Indeed, as we would expect from neoliberal governance, and in those who seek access to it, citizenship has been replaced by consumer activity, and everything has been commodified. Here, commodification takes the place of well-regulated birth attendants providing safe out-of-hospital births for those not risked out of, and able to afford, the opportunity. It is furthered by movements that seek regulation, not rights—and legitimation through professionalization and accreditation. As Bronwen Morgan has pointed out, activists engage in a complex set of activities in response to neoliberal imperatives: naming, blaming, claiming, as well as rulemaking, monitoring, and enforcement.[8]

As these flashpoints around commodification indicate, professionalism is not emotionally simple for midwives and advocates. When contemporary midwives practicing in states where their profession is neither legal nor regulated begin advocating for licensure, they enter a particularly vulnerable period. Their vulnerability appears in several ways. Individual midwives open themselves to the increased risk of state prosecution of their practice, by virtue of bringing attention to themselves through legislative and social movement activism. They are vulnerable to anti-homebirth campaigns coordinated by nurses, doctors, and hospital associations. And, they may experience changing conceptions of self, practice, calling, and identity that attend their efforts to seek state visibility and legitimacy.

Recognizing that much of their practice is rooted in "explicit" and "tacit" knowledges, "in part embodied, and rule of thumb,"[9] midwives undergoing professionalization also understand that they must "work to conserve themselves" through the codification and standardization of those practices.[10] Raymond DeVries and Rebeca Barroso describe the paradoxical dilemma midwives face when seeking professional status:

> As important as . . . organizational strategies [for legalization and legitimation] are, they form only a part of the re-creation of midwifery. *It is in the everyday practices of midwives where the tradition is given life.* Midwife organizations might preserve the profession, but the profession

loses its meaning if the practices of midwives become indistinguishable from physicians.[11]

And midwives must position themselves as the gatekeepers. As Dvora Yanow writes, "Evaluative measures are a shared property of the practice put into play by masters who seek to maintain self- and other-recognition as such, as well as by novices who seek to become recognized as members of that practice. . . . [Practitioners] evaluate the practice's evaluative criteria" and measure themselves and others against those criteria, even as they change in response to external pressures and demands.[12]

No change has so recently caused as much anxiety about these kinds of identity shifts as when the 2016 change regarding certification requirements for US-MERA went into effect. At MANA meetings and in local organizing sessions, advocates for the US-MERA faced rooms full of midwives and consumers with questions and concerns about the changes, and deep reservations about how the "bridge" proposal would play out. I recall one midwife at a strategy session in Iowa who asked no fewer than three times over the course of two hours, "No more apprenticeship after 2020?" For those midwives already engaged in working toward the CPM through the portfolio (PEP) process, there was concern that they'd be almost done but ineligible for the bridge provided by most new bills, because they couldn't accomplish the required number of births and prenatal/postnatal exams in the time allotted given their low caseload in a given region.

Further, some expressed apprehension that the new certification could limit what we think of as "midwives' knowledge" and that such a legitimation project was "colonizing" and "masculinizing" their expertise. They stressed that the current portfolio evaluation process allows midwives to demonstrate proficiency of care through direct, objective assessment based on ICM and MANA standards, rather than by earning college credit—and that it works just fine, while honoring different learning styles.[13]

The idea that birth attendants learn best *by doing* undergirds the educational approach of midwifery training. Apprenticeship have long been a standard way of achieving midwifery education, and even didactic models put primacy on *doing*. Midwives in MEAC-accredited programs must attend at least fifty births (as well as prenatal, postnatal, and well-baby checks) in varying capacities prior to taking their credentialing exam. Yet, many midwives believe that apprenticeship models, and the traditional ways of learning midwifery, will be gone by the time this book is in your hands.

Presenters at MANA, in a session on the history of the collaboration that led to US-MERA, emphasized both the bridge and the multiple points of collaboration to ease concerns about the outcome. One presenter stressed the "community consensus" and "unifying process" of US-MERA's adoption and argued that the adoption of the standard is "self-regulation" of midwives.[14] These speakers made clear that legislation adopting US-MERA language didn't change the scope of practice for CPMs, didn't infringe upon the autonomy of their practice, and didn't change the best practices already established for standardization and assessment of learning. Adopting US-MERA only impacted the educational route to the credential. Ida Darragh stressed to those gathered, "It is better for us as midwives to have a national standard recognized in every state."[15]

"Professions must be accredited," another MEAC proponent stated. She added that the route to MEAC schooling is "diverse" with a range of schools—from vocational–technical schools and community colleges to four-year programs—in a range of geographic locales (including online learning and hybrid programs), all enabling the degree. While understanding that "accreditation is a cultural thing that is happening now,"[16] some direct-entry midwives (and even those who would seek CPM credentialing under US-MERA guidelines) mourned the loss of traditional ways of knowing and knowledge transmission. They cautioned that the transition to college learning as the only pathway to midwifery could limit who could join the profession and (because of the cost of the education) limit whom they could afford to serve.

These midwives are also clear: To the extent that midwifery offers the opportunity for "everyday acts of resistance" to the "hegemony of obstetrics,"[17] entering into an agreement brokered, in part, with the American College of Obstetricians and Gynecologists doesn't feel very revolutionary or emancipatory.

But, as Darragh told the assembled activists at The Big Push Summit, "The issue about licensure is over. Licensure is the only option for keeping homebirth open."[18]

This reality is changing midwives' perceptions. One midwifery student told my research assistant that, although she'd been initially nervous about finishing her schooling, now that her state had legal status, she was "cautiously excited."[19] That student's preceptor had originally gone to Big Push national meetings to learn how to avoid licensure and stall the movement in her state; she herself "hates politics" but soon realized that "When you're a midwife, you have to be political." At that, she excitedly took her hard copy of Michigan's legalization bill out of her handbag—she is so proud of it that she carries it with her, much like my students sometimes have pocket Constitutions.

In fact, my research assistant was surprised, at MANA Long Beach, at how quickly every conversation turned to legality and licensure, law and politics: Law, politics, and midwifery seem to go hand in hand. And, my assistant's time at MANA clearly showed her, "The ship has sailed on legalization and regulation." Midwifery advocates have seen, as Silbey notes, "Law is powerful, and rules or governs everyday life, because its expectations and ways of organizing . . . are habitual and uncontested."[20] Of course licensure is the only option for keeping homebirth open. Of course law and the market are the paths to legitimacy. Of course they are. It is a matter of common sense.

REGULATION AS DISCIPLINARY, DISCIPLINES AS REGULATORY

The push for regulation and licensure might stem simply from the recognition that "in states without regulation there aren't any choices." As Darragh told attendees at The Big Push Summit, "When you do become regulated there is a choice: You can stay just like you are and suffer the same pressures . . . or, there is a choice to become licensed."[21] Even as they noted that there are drawbacks to becoming visible to the state, members of the Birth Rights Bar Association explained that the benefits of legitimating midwifery through licensure and regulation are significant. Kristin Bumiller found that the "good intentions of social reform" in a public health effort meant to assist survivors of sexual violence have been "swept up in larger processes" of neoliberal governance "that diminish our personal autonomy and freedom."[22] Similarly, midwives find themselves swept into the larger system of health care professionals as they gain a more equal footing and legal status. Certainly, such regulatory governance alleviates their risk of arrest and prosecution; and, it expands the possibilities for reproductive justice and availability of care.[23]

Of course, though, "When lay practitioners become professionals . . . there is usually a price to be paid."[24] Part of professionalization has also meant, in some regards, publicly distancing CPMs and CPM-aspirants from direct-entry, unlicensed women. In one state, an activist was frank: "For twenty-five years we beat down anyone who mentioned the 'L word' . . . lay midwife."[25]

And, the process of becoming a subject of law through licensure disciplines the social forms and professional practices of midwives, who must reorganize those forms and practices as their legal status shifts. I often witnessed, simultaneously, two diametrically opposite reactions among midwives and others to this shift in legal status. One is celebratory—lauding midwives for entering into a meaningful relationship with the state in a way that enables the growth and visibility of their practice. The other is cautious—concerned with the loss of traditional knowledge transfer, the increase of the state's regulatory gaze, and the sacrifice of the radical and feminine traditions of midwifery practice.

Advocates of regulation and licensure acknowledge that there are trade-offs to be made and problems inherent philosophically, with regulation—especially to the extent that regulatory power has tended to prefer hospitals as locales of birth. As one lawyer (also an activist and husband of a midwife) told the Birth Rights Bar Association, "The purpose of the regulatory system in health care is to push everyone into one place."[26] Midwifery, he argued, has the potential to disrupt that purpose by reinforcing the safety and power of homebirth, but it will be difficult. Scholar Robbie Davis-Floyd agrees that place is important—that as long as midwives stay out of hospitals, they should be able to maintain some autonomy and "may be able to successfully limit the degree of change they undergo as they professionalize and commodify."[27] But much relies on the way that the regulatory board is composed and operates. Indra Lusero describes the situation:

> The more medicine is central to the regulatory scheme, the riskier it will be for home birth midwives. . . . When midwives are defined by medicine in their scope of practice an standard of care, they are fundamentally at risk . . . because they are being defined by something they are not.[28]

Ophelia told me, "I agree . . . philosophically," with those who are opposed to regulatory governance, "but there's an unfair advantage if some of us have licenses and others don't." Then, she added, "Some midwives simply aren't good." "Yes," Darragh acknowledged, "Regulation does limit us, but it also is a safeguard" for midwives, and for consumers.[29] Regulatory oversight—not criminal law—becomes the lever by which midwives are held accountable to censure.[30] Most midwives, whether they like it or not, agree that this is a key purpose of achieving legal status.

At its core—and as Ophelia, Lusero, and Darragh make clear in their comments—the move to regulate midwives is a move to facilitate their disciplining: to make sure that people who labor and deliver, and the babies they birth, are not jeopardized by bad practice. To every extent possible, midwives and consumers who advocate for legislation to regulate these practices also advocate that the most effective discipline is self-discipline: Midwives and homebirth consumers should make up the core of the governing body; NARM's credentialing, developed by midwives, should be the gold standard; peer review should be protected and prioritized.

In this way, midwives with established expertise and community support can discipline those members of the profession whose practices are at odds with established norms. This protects consumers, it protects midwives, and draws clear boundaries around appropriate practice. Midwives and advocates recognize that professionalization, regulatory governance, and disciplinary boundary-drawing are co-constitutive. They see that this is, indeed, a key to professional projects: gatekeeping by those who constitute the profession to redirect or exclude those who do not comply.

My observations of the tensions surrounding these issues echo the findings of Scott Barclay and colleagues: "Social movements use the law in their emancipatory struggles to challenge oppressive conditions that are, in turn, so often sustained by legal rules and institutions."[31] Here, midwives and advocates engage in a professional project that is also a movement. It is both regulatory and emancipatory.[32] The pursuit of professional status becomes a comfort with hegemony; in seeking professional status, midwives enable law to sustain medical hegemony over birth, and they remain marginal—but safer.[33] As one participant in a MANA session told attendees, with legalization "You're bringing everyone under the regulatory umbrella—you could say it is disciplinary."[34]

We might want to linger a bit on this definition of discipline. In her examination of equal opportunity law, Linda Hamilton Krieger refers to Lauren Edelman's conceptualization of law's endogeneity and observes that when formal law is initially ambiguous, it "acquires specific meaning only after professional and organizational communities have constructed definitions of violation and compliance."[35] This is certainly the case in midwifery legislation—obviously so, when bills defer the definition of practice to the rulemaking process, where the ambiguity will be defined by professional norms. And it is the case in the professionalization project of midwifery, writ large.

Disciplinary projects are exclusionary—they define violation and compliance. Katherine Beckett and Bruce Hoffman note that

> [T]he process of strategically mobilizing cultural themes and icons in an
> attempt to generate support for their cause transforms birth activists and
> midwives, *a new hegemony—one that excludes* those who do not aspire to
> the creation of a midwifery profession—*is emerging*.[36]

In her presentation at the Birth Rights Bar Association meeting, Deb Fisch acknowledged the pain of this emergence, saying, "It's a sad consequence that licensure means drawing a circle ... but there's no other way to do it."[37] She notes that many midwives in the state will refuse licensure and "go on practicing exactly as they are now, illegally; but, in truth there is a more formal recognition that *that* will be the unauthorized practice of midwifery."[38]

Maureen May and Robbie Davis-Floyd have argued that in midwifery advocacy,

> The political, legislative battles over licensure, credentialing, education,
> and clinical preparation, as well as place of practice, are really about who
> has the right to legally practice and to claim the title *midwife*, which is,
> of course, ultimately all about identity—midwives' social, cultural, and
> historical identity.[39]

When we understand endogeneity and professionalization, though—and the role of legality in creating space for the articulation of discipline-specific knowledge—we see that May and Davis-Floyd are on to something, but their analysis stops short. Discipline boundary-drawing is about *more* than identity—more even than practice. Disciplinarity forms boundaries around what constitutes legitimate knowledge.[40]

Disciplinarity is an epistemology.

Indeed, disciplines can aspire to ideological hegemony, sometimes in processes facilitated by law.

Because disciplinarity draws boundaries not just around identities and practices but around knowledge, midwives and their advocates are correct that the moves toward the state, legitimation, and commodification constituted by disciplinary professionalization could threaten more traditional midwifery practice, centered as it is on women's knowledge and lived experience, apprenticeship models, and word-of-mouth provision of service. They also argue that disciplinary professionalization threatens women, and others who labor and deliver. In response to the US-MERA agreement, one prominent midwife posted a public Facebook status in September of 2019 that was a quote from a 1990 book on midwifery by Ann Oakley and Susanne Houd. The midwife quoted:

> Midwives really should not get involved in the argument for professional status because professionalism has its roots in the patriarchal power and control that alienated women from the birth process in the beginning. The erosion . . . of the autonomous role of the midwife restricts choice for women and promotes birth as a pathological process.[41]

Midwives recognize that legalization schemes may potentially omit direct-entry and apprentice models of midwifery; some see these routes to legalization as colonization and masculinization of knowledge. That they face these concerns while encountering opposition to legalization from both legislators and consumers who are against the expansion of the regulatory state and who refuse to authorize licensing agencies and oversight committees (which conflicts with what hospital associations and medical professionals demand: far-reaching regulation and strict oversight) does not make the epistemological concerns any less pressing. In fact, it might make them even more important.

Understanding that professionalization—and the knowledge construction that occurs within it—happens within contexts of racism, gender oppression, classism, and elitism makes activists and allies wary. This is often expressed in very practical ways. As Ophelia told me about the fight for legal status in Missouri, Black Democratic women were suspicious: "They were worried we were trying to legalize a cheap option and force it on them." Black female legislators "were the most difficult to convince"—precisely because they were operating within a context of racial disparities in birth outcome, laws passed to regulate their reproductive capacities in particular, and a state with structural racism in its criminal justice system. These state representatives were making birth policy choices in a context where Ferguson was about to unfold.

Activists for midwifery often have a deep distrust of the state itself—or, as some put it, "the system." This is because of the way that the medical lobby appears to have coopted legislative decision making in areas of health and well being and because of the ways that state agencies like Child Protective Services often work in tandem with policing functions in anti-narcotics and anti-immigrant capacities, to the detriment of the clients they serve. As one activist recollects about the move toward licensure in her state,

> There were tons of division—lots of politicking—not all midwives were on board. The state was really split, the midwifery committee itself was really split. It was an unusual split among the midwives—people who didn't want to be at risk [for prosecution] *versus people who don't want to be part of a system in any way* because they see themselves as holding an important part *outside of it.* . . . I can't say enough how much I respect that view.[42]

Barbara Katz Rothman is clear about the potential to lose track of the core knowledges that constitute midwifery, as professionalization becomes the focus. She writes, in *Bun in the Oven,*

> I am not about to complain about [midwives'] new focus on evidence-based care. Clearly it is better that practice be based on evidence than not. But *evidence is population-based, it's part of an industrial actuarial model.* Birth is also individual—highly, extraordinarily individual. What one woman with her body, her history, her life, and her baby feels and experiences isn't simply interchangeable with another. Clinical care needs to be artisanal, handcrafted, highly responsive to minute, hard-to-quantify differences. . . . [G]uidelines, suggestions based on evidence, quickly morph into protocols, actions required of clinicians.[43]

Rothman is articulating something that I see as a shared understanding at the core of all of the activism I've witnessed, and cutting across partisan concerns, political arguments, and discomfort with (or desire to be seen by) the state: This shared understanding is that we must attend to knowledge of and about *birth* just as much as we attend to knowledge of and about law.

In her work on grassroots migrant organizing in Canada, Ethel Tungohan notes that the migrants' organizations must take "contradictory actions, whereby members of both groups may be negotiating with government officials on stronger legislation for migrant workers one day and protesting in front of their offices the next."[44] This is the kind of politics and legal mobilization I routinely witnessed in pro-midwifery spaces. In Berkeley, the BirthKeepers evoked eco-feminist norms and practices and then went to San Francisco to protest at an ACOG meeting; some of the very same participants in those actions later sat side by side with their "opponents" seeking understanding and consensus at the Homebirth Summit and US-MERA meetings. Just as Tungohan notes that migrant organizations have a "multi-scalar" approach in terms of being local, national, and transnational,[45] so too are midwifery organizations. Since the 1970s, midwives and advocates have fought locally for visibility, statewide for legislation, nationally for accreditation and organization, and internationally for belonging, community, and legitimacy. Such multi-scalar activism requires nuanced understandings of, and strategic interactions with, politics and law.

Following William Haltom and Michael McCann's classic *Distorting the Law*, I have asked, throughout my research, how the institutions within which midwives and their advocates are located shape access to different framings of law and politics and provide opportunities and constraints related to legal consciousness. I understand that the specific legal struggles for decriminalization, regulation, and licensure are intimately related to, and reliant upon, other cultural fields—popular culture, places of employment, medical conversations—and that law is constitutively related to these other fields.[46]

Law is, as Ewick and Silbey have written, "an embedded and an emergent feature of social life . . . [that] collaborates with other social structures . . . to infuse meaning and constrain social action."[47] But law, as midwives have seen, also has its own distinct rules and requirements. Struggles in the legal and political fields have required legal and political mobilization, as well as skillful implementation of law and politics, in order to be successful. These struggles have required, due to the cultural contexts within which they unfold, compromise.

One of these compromises has centered, until quite recently, on avoiding the reproductive politics that inherently involve birth and people gendered female. As Beckett and Hoffman note, "There are certain cultural categories that birth activists must studiously avoid—namely, feminism."[48] But, we can't avoid feminism when we talk about birth. In fact, as we have seen, rather than resting on legislative success, midwives and their advocates are also engaging in transforming the cultural iconography of motherhood and the cultural institution of birth in order to (re)normalize out-of-hospital, natural childbirth. They understand that anything less will result in legal status coupled with social disapprobation, onerous regulatory requirements, and fear of prosecution for practitioners. In order to achieve true transformation, pro-midwifery advocates are waging a dual-pronged battle: one called "professionalization," which asserts a demand for regulation and licensure, and another called "justice," which refigures birth and mothering in America.

RECLAIMING KNOWING

Midwives believe that self-knowledge is an essential component of women's liberation. The midwives I interviewed stressed the educational role they play in helping expectant parents understand birth, nutrition, wellness, and health. At the BirthKeepers Summit, midwives even hosted a women's health collective that ran workshops on self-care for women, including an evening of cervical self-exams and a discussion of menstrual extraction techniques. In South Dakota, at the Custer weekend workshop, midwives and advocates provided information on holistic fertility management and discussions of cervical mucus. Midwives understand that women (and men) have been trained to be uncomfortable with this knowledge, and around these conversations, and insist that reclaiming that knowledge is essential.

Without knowledge and understanding, they argue, birthing people have no power. Ina May Gaskin puts it this way, "In the United States . . . women have very little, if any, decision-making power about how they will be treated during pregnancy or birth."[49] This insight reminds me of law and society insights into what happens when average people enter the courtroom, or the lawyer's office, or interactions with the police. Time and again, we see that average people have very little understanding of what unfolds during litigation and experience the process as alienating and emotion-laden. Their experiences of legality are fraught with tension, and scholars who undertake the study of legal consciousness, Michael McCann and Tracey March argue, are right to direct their analysis:

[We look at] law's power in the everyday rather than the exceptional, in the routine rather than the rare, in the hardly noticed experiences rather than the high profile disputes over "hard cases" of law. . . . [It is] law's significance in the lives of "ordinary" citizens—especially the working class, the poor, women, and people of color—rather than of "elites" that is the primary concern.[50]

Certainly, sociolegal inquiry has demonstrated again and again that the power of legality stems from "the biased products of past practices and struggles that bound the practical understandings and limit the strategic options available to citizens in ways that tend to sustain privilege and hierarchy throughout society."[51] This focus on law's power must not be accomplished, however, at the expense of a focus on the power of people in constitutive relation to law. McCann and March continue, "Law . . . at once structures the spaces of social life and is reconstructed by citizens' activity within those spaces."[52] Some of the most exciting work in sociolegal studies is about finding ways to recognize when average, everyday people reclaim knowledges of and from law.

The initial impulse behind the legal consciousness literature was to do just that. Susan Silbey has lamented the "domestication" of the concept of legal consciousness in articles that look more for policy recommendations than sites and locales of resistance, counter-hegemony, and ideological formation.[53] My research demonstrates that midwives and their advocates are continually constituting, and story-ing, legal knowledge and knowledge of what is legal—throughout their advocacy at the statehouse, care for clients, direct actions against ACOG, and defense of their profession.

In her study of same-sex couples constitution of law as they seek rights to marry, Kathleen Hull explains that, for her research subjects, "Law is produced in and through commonplace social interactions . . . [which] bear the imprint of law."[54] She argues that "Some of these efforts to enact marriage culturally should . . . be read as attempts to enact legality in the absence of official law."[55] Hull writes that same-sex couples, in talking about marriage and commitment, "choose to assert a reality that simultaneously conflicts with legal reality and draws on terms and concepts that are at least partially inflected with legality."[56] Midwives, as part of a movement toward more holistic practices in medicine, are asserting new realities as well.

Midwifery organizations from the very earliest days in the United States, have mobilized what Charles Rosenberg, in his history of medicine and hospitals in the United States, would call "holistic" understandings and language. This holistic language is not merely rhetorical: It inscribes a way of thinking about the practices the midwives and other holistic health care providers undertake. Rosenberg writes:

> Holistic thinking has drawn its moral edge, intellectual content, and oc-
> casions of social use from its oppositional place in a powerful and widely
> assumed narrative of medical progress. Holism has been a specter at this
> self-congratulatory feast, warning that progress has incurred costs as well
> as provided benefits. Holistic ideas have found their social meaning in
> antagonism to the bureaucracy, specialization, and fragmentation as well
> as the (related) reductionism that have come to dominate twentieth-cen-
> tury medicine.[57]

In cases stemming from criminal prosecution, the courts have continually refused "to acknowledge the skills of the defendant women midwives
and their positive health outcomes," which, to Stacey Tovino, suggests "that
the women midwives' experiential knowledge was both subordinate to the
male physician's new scientific knowledge and rejected as a means of establishing professional and legal standing."[58] As Carol Leonard puts it, "The
keynote address [at the very first MANA in 1983] is a call for midwives to
reclaim the art and science of midwifery, to create *a separate generation of
knowledge and language* by midwives, different from the medical model."[59]
Midwives insist, as Carol Leonard does, "In every birth, the [person in labor]
teaches me a lesson."[60]

WHO ARE THE HEROES?

An astute early reader asked me the other day, "Who is the hero of this
book?" She wondered if it was Ophelia? Or Gina? Or the off-grid doctor
Esther? Could the hero be the state, when it finally regulates the practice
of non-nurse midwifery? Or, perhaps, she wondered, did I imagine that the
hero was me—intrepidly and doggedly collecting narratives that were often
painful to witness.

There are trite—and, nevertheless, honest—answers. I could easily say
"No one is a hero! They're all just doing the work they believe they are meant

to do." And, "Each of them is a hero in their own way . . . " Or even, "Well, I prefer the politics of. . . . And find their work to be the most important. . . . "

But what I want to say is a bit different.

What I find heroic, in all of these stories, is the struggle—the self-aware practices of meaning-making that midwives, their advocates, moms and dads and people who parent (and, yes, scholars) engage in when they tell stories that don't fit neatly, when they live with the contingencies of their realities.

It is heroic to stand, as a pro-life woman, in a room full of radical full-spectrum midwives and claim a space for fetal life. It is heroic to stand, as a Black woman, in a room full of White feminists and claim a space for your knowledge and the knowledge of your predecessors. It is heroic to operate a noncompliant birth center in full view of the state. It is heroic to sit with women who are undergoing abortion or miscarriage and midwife those transitions; and it is heroic to enter women's correctional facilities and attend to those giving birth there. Yes. Sure. Those things take strength and courage of conviction, and maybe a bit of unhinged certainty (this scholar says, with love).

But what is more heroic and more impressive to me—and more potentially transformative—is the willingness of all of those women to be in one room together: to share stories and listen and converse and argue with each other. To stand with their values, while admitting to the tensions. Of her very first International Confederation of Midwives, Carol Leonard remembers this:

> The workshops are informative and educational, but the real event is the storytelling that goes on everywhere until the wee hours of dawn. It is phenomenal that we have all come to the same conclusions, independently, all across the country. Midwives are listening raptly to each other's stories, laughing, crying, eyes dancing with the joy of it. . . . We sit hunkered in hallways, squatting in doorways, lying on beds in clusters of enthusiastically gesturing women, exchanging story after story. This is where the real teaching occurs. We are thirsty for all the powerful knowledge we can finally exchange with our peers.[61]

Reading this reminds me of the hundreds of hours I have spent, apprenticing as a sociolegal scholar, in hotel rooms, restaurants, and bars around the world. Reading Leonard's breathless record of that intellectually vibrant and generative time puts me in mind of the exhilaration I feel in a community of scholars who call themselves "sociolegal," where I live a life I could not have imagined as a teenager, before I knew that being a professor existed as a possibility—where becoming a lawyer was the only common-sense thing I could imagine.

Leonard's text reminds me, too, of a different astute reader of this book. Even earlier in my writing process, this reader sat down with me in a hotel lobby of a Law and Society Association conference and asked, "Is this a story about legal mobilization? Or about pluralism? And, don't you think you should write more about legal consciousness?"

And my answer is yes. It is about all of them.

I deliver this book to readers aware of the contradictions, contestations, gaps, and over-certainties in my own production of knowledge about midwives, their advocates, and people who desire to labor and deliver outside of hospitals. I stand here myself—and with the multitude of voices in this book—aware of the tensions in the narrative. And simultaneously, I am convinced that the space of tensions and elisions, of over-certainty sitting alongside of half-baked ideas, is the space where fruitful scholarly inquiry must live. Susan Silbey has put it this way: "Through our language we suggest homogeneity, generality, and perhaps independence, where upon closer examination, we observe heterogeneity and perhaps concatenation."[62]

Years ago, around the same time that Carol Leonard was hanging signs for a new midwifery organization in hotel elevators, critical legal scholars were beginning to meet in academic community and begin the process of forming a new field. "Attending my first Law & Society Association meeting in 1980," Silbey writes, "I discovered . . . that working within a community of lively exchange and jousting nourishes the scholar and drives the scientific enterprise."[63] When I tell my students about how sociolegal scholarship in the United States was born, I often tell them to imagine it like academic summer camp—a whole bunch of critical, smart, law- and legality-obsessed people gathering—in Madison, Wisconsin; in Amherst, Massachusetts; in Berkeley, California—all helping each other work through their understandings of their experiences with law and legal education.

I tell my students that, soon enough, women and scholars of color entered these academic spaces—publishing, meeting, and expanding our sense of what scholarly inquiry investigates and how it is accomplished—and so did disability scholars and queer scholars and transgender scholars. The community of law and society, of sociolegal inquiry, continues to grow—along with growth in methods, in substantive areas of research, and in overlapping disciplinary perspectives. As the field grows, "The different disciplinary tools (theories, concepts, and methods) become available to us all— . . . [W]e began to see limits in what was taken for granted in our respective disciplines while forming a synthesis across them to encourage new ways to understand how law works."[64]

Midwives—gathering in community, in hotel rooms, and conference halls—and their advocates—gathering in capitol rotundas, at movie screenings, and at Labor Day picnics—are doing similar work: changing common-sense understandings of the legality and law, of locations and practices of birth, bringing multiple perspectives to bear on a new understanding of synthesis in practice merging tradition and apprenticeship models with didactic learning and certification of expertise.

In both settings, self-aware practitioners are attentive to the contradictions, to the messiness, of reality. In both settings, self-aware practitioners are attentive to the ways that their understandings of and ideas about law contribute to its strategic deployment and mobilization, as well as how those same understandings and ideas contribute to their desire to avoid, undermine, or rebel against the law. Legal consciousness is mobilized and constituted simultaneously with legal mobilization; both consciousness and mobilization are shaped by relationships, practices, perceptions, and contexts big and small, local and global. Whether we are midwives, or advocates, or scholars of law and society, our consciousness of and use of law both results from and is an expression of how we make sense of our lived experiences, our relationships with others and self, and our daily—embodied and ongoing—practices. Though the practices are incomplete by virtue of being ongoing, we can story them—provide them a narrative and an interpretation—and use them to create and sustain the production of knowledge, and thus they become authoritative.

This book offers you my take on multiple perspectives. It interweaves the voices of scholars, activists, midwives, and self into the text to demonstrate the importance of multivocal and interdisciplinary work. As midwives, in their horizontal relationships and community with each other, produce knowledge *for* and *about* professionalization and regulation, they stake out space for some measure of autonomy, identity, and justice by insisting that law recognize their knowledge, practices, and lived experience. I hope, too, that our scholarship about law and society does the same.

NOTES

INTRODUCTION

1. Gina is a pseudonym. I have given pseudonyms to every formal interview subject in this book, as well as to the quoted individuals that I recorded during participant-observation. The exceptions to this rule are when I'm speaking about a scholar or activist who is well-known in birth justice circles, and I'm quoting from that person's statements made during public presentations and conferences. If I am quoting from an interview with those people, I have given them pseudonyms.

2. I relate this story almost exactly the way that Gina explained it to me, in order to understand her perspective regarding her interaction with law and practice. But, I must note that Gina did not tell me the child had died; I learned that through press accounts after our interview. I have also, since that interaction, read press accounts, anti-midwife blog accounts, critiques of Gina's practice, and court documents. The reports are inconsistent: Some say the baby lived four days, some say seven. Some indicate there was a dispute about hospital procedure; some blame doctors for overmedicating the infant, others say Gina's incompetence and reliance on faith sealed the child's fate. I do know that, during my fieldwork in South Dakota, Gina was well regarded by homebirth families and often hired by the families that constituted the core of activists around the issue of midwifery in the state.

3. Gina notes, in conversation with me, that the prosecutor was both "the best in the state" and married to the CEO of one of the region's major hospitals.

4. Merry 1990; Moore 1978.

5. De Sousa Santos 1987; Merry 2012.

6. The vast majority of midwives in the United States (and globally) identify as women, and they serve clients who also identify as women. However, not all people who labor and deliver identify as women, and the Midwives Alliance of North American

recognized this in a move for gender-inclusive language within their core competencies. In this book I use both terms ("women" and "people who labor and deliver") as well as "mother" and "client" to denote those people whom midwives serve.

7. Centers for Disease Control and Prevention 2017; see also MacDorman and Declercq 2018.

8. In the United States, medical doctors receive didactic training (medical school) for four years after graduating college; they then enter a residency period, during which they specialize. An ob-gyn residency is typically four years. After residency, doctors sit for board certification exams and must keep current via continuing education.

9. Labor and delivery nurses typically hold a bachelor of science degree in nursing (BSN), a four-year degree; after passing examinations to be certified as a registered nurse (RN), they begin working in labor and delivery while working toward certification in their area of specialty (obstetric nursing).

10. http://www.midwife.org/acnm/files/ccLibraryFiles/Filename/000000005464/CNM-CMAttendedBirthStatisticsJune2015.pdf

11. https://mana.org/about-midwives/state-by-state

12. www.birthcenters.org; www.acnm.org

13. http://www.midwife.org/acnm/files/cclibraryfiles/filename/000000007400/50%20Essential%20Facts%20about%20Midwives.pdf

14. Ibid. An additional ninety-seven practitioners are certified midwives—midwives with a BA in a subject other than nursing, but who have otherwise completed the graduate training required to be certified by ACNM.

15. Rooks 1997; Varney and Thompson 2015.

16. http://narm.org/pdffiles/2016—Job-Analysis.pdf

17. https://pushformidwives.nationbuilder.com/cpms_legal_status_by_state

18. At this point, when I'm giving presentations on midwifery to audiences unfamiliar with the practice, I usually get a question about doulas. Doulas are not midwives, and they do not use medical training in their support of pregnant and laboring people. Doulas may be certified by DONA International or by the Childbirth and Post-Partum Professional Association. Doula certification and licensure are not currently required for practice in any state.

19. Handler 1978.

20. Bell 1992; Crenshaw 1988.

21. Kirkland 2003; McCann 1994; Silverstein 1996.

22. Vanhala 2011.

23. Engel and Munger 2003; Gleeson 2009; Goldberg-Hiller 2002; McCann and Silverstein 2008; Paris 2001; Rosenberg 1991; Sarat and Grossman 1975; Scheingold 1974; Tushnet 1987.

24. Paris 2010.

25. Beckett and Hoffman 2005; Craven 2006, 2010; Davis-Floyd 1993, 2006a, 2006b; Davis-Floyd and Johnson 2006; DeVries 1985; Hoffman 2008; Kline 2019.

26. A rich literature on legal mobilization shows us how frequently social

movement actors mobilize discourses of rights, seek legal recognition, and advance political aims. See Barclay, Jones, and Marshall 2011; Barnes and Burke 2012; Burstein and Monaghan 1986; Engel and Munger 2003; Gleeson 2009; Goldberg-Hiller 2002; Handler 1978; Kessler 1990; Kirkland 2003; McCann 1994; McCann and Silverstein 2008; Paris 2001.

27. Morgan 2003.

28. Shamir 1993, p. 363.

29. Chua and Engel 2019, p. 336.

30. Ibid.

31. Gordon 1984.

32. Ewick and Silbey 1998; Merry 1985, 1990; Sarat 1985, 1990; Trubek 1984.

33. Haney López 2003; Hirsch 2009; Lazarus-Black and Hirsch 1994; McMillan 2011; Merry 2000; Nader 1990.

34. Silbey 2019; see also Nielsen 2004.

35. Bumiller 2008, p. 4; see also Darian-Smith 2015; Morgan 2011.

36. Bumiller 2008, p. 98.

37. Hoffman 2008, p. 90.

38. Fieldnotes, summer 2016.

39. Mazur, McBride, and Hoard 2016, p. 653.

40. Ibid.

41. See Craven 2010 for a discussion of the ways that midwifery advocacy in Virginia and elsewhere are both feminist, and not; see also Spence 2012.

42. See Blackstone, Uggen, and McLaughlin 2009; Dudas 2008; Ewick and Silbey 1998; Fritsvold 2009; Kirkland 2003; Krieger 2000; Lazarus-Black and Hirsch 1994; Marshall 2006; McMillan 2011; Merry 1990, 2000; Nader 1990; Silbey 2005; Wilson 2011, 2013.

43. Ideologies, individuals, and institutions are in constitutive relationship with each other—and such relationships develop out of and reformulate the legal strategies mobilized, and legal consciousness held, by midwives, advocates, and clients alike. See Haltom and McCann 2004.

44. On agency implementation, see Epp 2009; Nielsen 2004; Rosenberg 1991; Valverde 2012. On daily life and legality, see Bourdieu 2000 [1977]; De Certeau, Giard, and Mayol 1998; Lefebvre and Levich 1987; Sarat and Kearns 1993.

45. Indeed, Chua and Engel (2019) argue that the legal mobilization literature is itself a school within the legal consciousness scholarship. See Blackstone, Uggen, and McLaughlin 2009; Dudas 2008; Fritsvold 2009; Kirkland 2003; Knauer 2012; Krieger 2000.

46. Krieger 2000, p. 485.

47. Corrigan 2013; Hampson 2017; Silverstein 2007.

48. Bowen 2005; Creswell et al. 2003; Haltom and McCann 2004; Tarrow 1995.

49. Vedam et al. 2018.

50. McCann 1994; Polletta 2000.

51. Marshall 2005; Nielsen 2004.

52. Barclay, Jones, and Marshall 2011, p. 12.

53. https://www.birthplacelab.org/mapping-collaboration-across-birth-settings/

54. Vedam et al. 2018.

55. See Cramer 2009 on the challenges of finding and interviewing "outlaw" midwives.

56. Yanow 2003, p. 11.

57. Gerring 2003; Meddings et al. 2007.

58. Silbey 2019, p. 14.

59. Ibid.

60. Among them: Castañeda 2019; Coutin 2000; Engel and Munger 2003; Epp, Maynard-Moody, and Haider-Markel 2014; Ewick and Silbey 1995, 1998; Lazarus-Black and Hirsch 1994; Merry 2000.

61. Sarat and Kearns 1993.

62. Silbey 2019, p. 11.

63. Ibid., p. 2.

64. Ahmed 2017; Hemmings 2011; hooks 2014; Moraga and Anzaldua 1983; Williams 1991.

65. Solinger 2007, p. 21.

66. Jordan-Zachery 2007, 2013; Ross and Solinger 2017.

67. Gaskin 2003 [1975], 2011; Kitzinger 2005; Leonard 2008; Rooks 1997; Vincent 2012, 2015.

68. Now, nearly fifteen years later, I ask myself why I didn't look for a practice of nurse midwives—which my HMO certainly did provide for. As educated as I was, I don't even think I was aware that it could be an option.

69. DeVries 1985, pp. xiv–xv. Twenty-five years ago, DeVries embarked on a study very similar to mine. He studied midwifery in three locales: Texas (where there was loose control), Arizona (which had licensure), and California (where there was outright prohibition). He writes (p. xiii):

> I wanted to gather information both on the creation of laws that regulate mid-
> wifery and on the effect of such laws on the way midwives practice. The first
> objective led me to explore how the need for advice from "medical authorities"
> on the part of legal institutions influenced the nature of midwife regulations. The
> second led me to the field itself; I was looking for variations in the quality and
> style of care, the cost of midwifery services, the availability and accessibility of
> midwives, and the willingness of established medical professions to work with
> lay midwives.

70. Barclay, Jones, and Marshall 2011.

71. Marshall 2006, p. 237.

72. Ibid.

73. Rothman 2016, pp. 132–133.

74. Bourdieu 2000 [1977], p. 21.

75. Harrington and Yngvesson 1990, p. 138.

76. Fieldnotes, spring 2018.

CHAPTER 1

1. Throughout my research, I was struck by the equivocations in the language of all of the midwives I interviewed. Many of them have elocutions about time and distance specifically; they say places are "two or three hours away," labor progressed for "a day or so," they began training in "1980 or 81, or 82." I almost edited the equivocations from the text but have come to think of them as important—not as imprecisions that need pointing out, but rather as a linguistic comfort with time's fluidity that is a mark of midwifery care, as distinct from hospital care with laboring women. Doctors and nurses have precise metrics regarding how long a woman can labor, for instance, before additional intervention; these medical professionals time the space between contractions as an indicator of where a woman is in the process of delivery. Although midwives might employ time, they also go much more by "feel" in determining where a labor is, in terms of progression.

2. Fieldnotes, summer 2016. For historical and recent rates of out-of-hospital births, see National Center for Health Satistics, within the Centers for Disease Control and Prevention at cdc.gov/nchs.

3. Lusero 2014, p. 431.

4. *Why Not Home?* 2016 documentary.

5. Silbey 2019, p. 3.

6. Lusero 2014, p. 406.

7. Jamie Wall fieldnotes, fall 2017.

8. Centers for Disease Control and Prevention 2018.
The CDC points out that it may very well be that better surveillance of these deaths, and improved reporting processes, are the reasons for this seeming increase in recent years and that it is not necessarily the case that in-hospital birth has gotten more dangerous.

9. Owens 2017, p. 21.

10. Oparah et al. 2018, p. 45.

11. https://data.unicef.org/topic/maternal-health/maternal-mortality/; see also www.who.int.

12. Ibid.

13. For US rates, see Centers for Disease Control and Prevention 2018; for other country rates, see www.who.int and https://data.unicef.org/topic/maternal-health/maternal-mortality/

14. Centers for Disease Control and Prevention 2018.

15. America's Health Rankings analysis of CDC WONDER Online Database, Mortality files, United Health Foundation, AmericasHealthRankings.org.

16. Price 2020.

17. Amnesty International 2011.

18. WHO et al. 2014.

19. WHO et al. 2018.

20. Kitzinger 2005, p. 2.

21. Block 2007, p. 139.

22. Ibid.
23. Declercq et al. 2013.
24. Williams 1997, p. 234.
25. Kukura 2018, p. 730.
26. Declercq et al. 2013.
27. Block 2007, p. xiii.
28. Rooks 1997, pp. 448–449.
29. Fisher and Todd 1993, p. 8.
30. Rothman 2016, p. 37.
31. Ibid.
32. Cramer 2015.
33. Bridges 2011, p. 96.
34. Ibid., pp 83–89.
35. Vincent 2015, p. 85.
36. Davis-Floyd 2018.
37. Gaskin 2003 [1975].
38. Mitler, Rizzo, and Horwitz 2000.
39. Rothman 2016, p. 192.
40. Cheyney et al. (2014) show no increase in adverse outcome for mom or baby, with lower rates of intervention. These findings are consistent with studies from Britain, Canada, Australia, Belgium, Sweden, France, and Denmark—all countries with longer histories of tracking statistics related to in-home birth attended by midwives.
41. Vincent 2015, p. 1.
42. Marland and Rafferty (1997) have compiled an excellent cross-cultural study of midwives—with the exception of a chapter by Irvine Louden that is devoted to midwives in the United States, which unthinkingly reiterates exceptionally racializing and marginalizing language around "granny midwives" in the South. Louden lays the high rates of infant and maternal mortality at the midwives' feet, rather than pointing out a lack of prenatal care, unwillingness of White physicians to treat or care for the mothers, lack of access to medical care in general, and lives lived in poverty. He also unthinkingly repeats lore that immigrant midwives in urban areas "provided an appallingly low standard of maternal care [and] [m]any had turned to abortion as a means of making a living. What they lacked was support, supervision, and above all a sense of self-respect and pride in their occupation" (p. 189). I do not cite him further.
43. Forbes 1966.
44. Federici 2004.
45. Murphy 2012, pp. 13–14.
46. Marland and Rafferty 1997, p. 5; see also DeVries 1985; Rooks 1997.
47. Marland and Rafferty 1997, p. 7.
48. Rooks 1997, p. 3.
49. Marland and Rafferty 1997, p. 2.
50. Solinger 2007. In their introduction to *Reproductive Justice (2017)*, Loretta

Ross and Rickie Solinger write, "*Every* government depends on the reproductive capacity of people who can give birth" (pp. 14–15). And they argue that the reproductive capacity of women of color and women in poverty has been easy to control through the use of law.

51. Cramer 2015, p. 27.

52. Rosenberg 2007, p. 118.

53. Ibid., p. 39.

54. The AMA was founded in Philadelphia by a group of 250 delegates. Doctors consolidated themselves professionally thirty-one years before lawyers did; the American Bar Association was founded in Saratoga Springs, New York, by 100 constituting members, in 1878.

55. Rosenberg 2007, p. 119.

56. Ibid., pp. 117–120.

57. Luker 1984.

58. Owens 2017, p. 3.

59. Ibid., p. 46.

60. Ibid., p. 54.

61. Leavitt 1986.

62. Luker 1984, p. 274 n19.

63. Lusero 2014, p. 414, citing AMA timeline and Rooks.

64. Ibid., p. 415.

65. Tovino 2004, p. 83.

66. Rothman 2016, p. 210.

67. DeLee 1933; see also *Why Not Home?* 2016 documentary.

68. Leavitt 1986, p. 71.

69. Varney and Thompson 2015, p. 34.

70. Rooks 1997, p. 449.

71. DeVries and Barroso 1997, p. 254

72. DeVries 1985, pp. 60, 79.

73. Thrower 2016.

74. Tovino 2004, p. 77.

75. https://www.washingtonmidwives.org/

76. Fieldnotes, fall 2016.

77. Spence 2012, p. 26.

78. Lusero 2014, pp. 410–413; Wertz and Wertz 1989. See also Romlid (1997, p. 47), who states that in 1940 65 percent of US births were in the hospital; by 1950, 94 percent of all births took place in the hospital.

79. Varney and Thompson 2015, p. 45.

80. The documentary *The Business of Being Born* (2008) has powerful clips of women under the influence of twilight sleep.

81. Varney and Thompson 2015, p. 144.

82. Lusero 2014, p. 411.

83. Davis-Floyd 1993; Kitzinger 2005; Rothman 1982; Solinger 2007.

84. Murphy 2012, p. 4.

85. Rooks 1997.

86. https://www.aafp.org/news/blogs/leadervoices/entry/20190709lv-ruralhealth
matters.html

87. Rooks 1997, p. 59.

88. Vincent 2015, p. 45.

89. Rothman 2016, p. 61. (emphasis added)

90. See Adamson and Glare 1980; McQuarrie 1980.

91. Leonard 2008, p. 118.

92. Davis-Floyd 2006a, p. 60.

93. Vincent 2015, p. 156.

94. Kitzinger 2005, p. 156.

95. Declercq et al. 2013, p. x.

CHAPTER 2

1. I've been at three meetings where midwives and advocates have created a messaging grid. The one I present here is not taken directly from any of those meetings, but is an amalgamation of those three.

2. DeVries and Barroso 1997, p. 253.

3. Gaskin 2003 [1975], p. 468.

4. Michelle Murphy (2012) has written an excellent critical history of the feminist self-help movement, showing it to be "animated by and entangled with histories of medicine, subjectivities, race, governance, and capitalism in the late twentieth century,"(p. 3) and unpacking the ways that the movement did indeed "responsibilize" women for their health care, turning it into self-management while rearranging "the material, technical, and social conditions by which the responsibility for governing sex could be bound to women as individuals" (p. 2).

5. Vincent 2015, p. 59.

6. Murphy 2012, p. 72.

7. Todd and Fisher 1993c, p. 8.

8. Todd 1993a, pp. 183–212.

9. Davis 1993, pp. 246–247.

10. Rothman 2016, p. 25.

11. Leonard 2008.

12. Gaskin 2003 [1975], p. 6.

13. Leonard 2008, pp. 23, 22.

14. Ibid., p. 77.

15. Davis-Floyd 2006a, p. 39.

16. Osterholzer 2018, pp. 58–59.

17. Ibid., pp. 78–79.

18. Ibid., p. 46.

19. Runes 2004.

20. Fieldnotes, summer 2013.

21. See Cramer (2012) for a history of the first birth center in the state of Iowa.

22. Varney and Thompson 2015, p. 127.

23. Oparah et al. 2018, p. 13. (emphasis added)

24. Davis-Floyd 2006a, p. 39.

25. Leonard 2008, p. 189.

26. Rooks 1997, p. 228.

27. Fieldnotes, summer 2009.

28. Rothman 2016.

29. DeVries and Barroso 1997, p. 259.

30. Rothman 2016, pp. 5–8.

31. Davis-Floyd 2006b, p. 165.

32. Coutin, Maurer, and Yngvesson 2002.

33. Garriott 2018.

34. Beckett and Hoffman 2005; Block 2007; Craven 2010; Davis-Floyd and Johnson 2006; Hoffman 2008.

35. This list differs slightly from the list of "organizational strategies of re-creation used by American midwives" who are "faced with the extinction of their profession" provided by DeVries and Barroso (1997)—but it does not disagree with them on the four essential points: (1) alliance with an existing profession; (2) the creation of programs to train and certify the competency of midwives; (3) the establishment of organizations to represent the interest of midwives; and (4) the creation of new forms of delivering maternity care.

36. Leonard 2008, p. 84.

37. Ibid., p. 225.

38. DeVries and Barroso 1997, p. 256.

39. Leonard 2008, p. 263.

40. Rothman 2016, p. 127.

41. Leonard 2008, p. 283.

42. Ibid.

43. Ibid., p. 285.

44. DeVries and Barrosso 1997, p. 256.

45. Davis-Floyd 2006a, p. 30.

46. Ibid., p. 43.

47. Fieldnotes, fall 2016.

48. Ibid.

49. Kitzinger 2005, p. 213.

50. Davis-Floyd 2006a, p. 61.

51. I thank Sarah Hampson for pointing this out, using these words, in personal communication.

52. *Why Not Home?* 2016 documentary.

53. As this book goes to press, in 2020, advocates and midwives on The Big Push list are talking about how to get rid of the "2020" designation in boilerplate bills and how to change the timeline for US-MERA in states where CPMs don't yet have legal status.

54. Fieldnotes, fall 2016.

55. Fieldnotes, fall 2017. The 2015 Homebirth Summit was comprised of fifty delegates with overlapping interests in US-MERA, and it was key to reaching agreement.

56. Fieldnotes, winter 2010.

57. Fieldnotes, fall 2016.

58. Fieldnotes, spring 2017.

59. Jamie Wall fieldnotes, fall 2017. A different advocate from Missouri expressed significant regret about the way that the US-MERA agreement played out in her state. The agreement facilitated the bill's passage, but the final language did not include the 2020 bridge that PEP-educated midwives had been promised. "A lot of midwives in Michigan are PEP educated and I feel a lot of regret about [not having bridge language written into the bill]. Had we known that it wouldn't make it in . . . "

60. Rothman 2016, p. 208.

61. Yang, Attanasio, and Kozhimannil 2016, p. 262.

62. Kitzinger 2005, p. 104.

63. Rothman 2016, pp. 3, 9.

64. This is similar to the processes Garriott notes occurred regarding the legalization, regulation, and commodification of marijuana in Colorado.

65. Cramer 2015.

66. Davis-Floyd 2006b, p. 165.

67. Ibid., p. 184.

68. Rothman 2016, p. 123.

69. Ferreira and Teixeira 2013; Pine and Gilmore 1998.

70. Daviss relegates this part of the conversation about commodification to a footnote; she acknowledges that often the commodification of birth becomes "a service to be sold to the highest bidder" (Daviss 2006, p. 400, n3).

71. *Why Not Home?* 2016 documentary.

72. Rothman 2016, pp. 18–19.

73. *Why Not Home?* 2016 documentary.

74. Rothman 2016, p. 10.

75. Ibid., p. 17.

76. Personal communication with Robbie Davis-Floyd.

77. Fieldnotes, fall 2017.

78. Rothman 2016, p. 23.

79. Chapter 6 of this book discusses some of that pushback.

80. Leonard 2008, pp. 74–75.

81. Ibid., pp. 220–221.

82. Vincent 2015, p. 185.

83. Ibid., p. 158.

84. Jamie Wall fieldnotes, fall 2017.

85. Fieldnotes, winter 2010.

86. Leonard 2008, p. 194.

87. Fieldnotes, summer 2009.

88. Indeed, the search for legitimation and recognition is one that groups engage in routinely, as they seek rights and access from governing bodies.

89. DeVries 1985.

90. Davis-Floyd and Johnson 2006.

91. Hoffman 2008, p. 7.

CHAPTER 3

1. Munz 2008.

2. Leonard 2008, p. 294.

3. Ibid., p. 295.

4. The National Association of Certified Professional Midwives (NACPM) was not actively engaged in pushing for legal status for CPMs until the very last years of my fieldwork. I did not attend any NACPM meetings, though I was present on one organizing call of state-level advocates working with NACPM. No one in Iowa, Missouri, or South Dakota mentioned NACPM to me as important in their organizational strategy. And my research assistant Jamie (Wall) Hanna was told, in Michigan,

> ACNM didn't give support until the last day. MANA and NARM sent letters, but US-MERA did not. . . . NARM and MANA were "super helpful and supportive." Eventually, a final effort included MEAC, MANA, NARM, and ACNM. We were told that NACPM representatives said it would ruin their relationship with nurse midwives, so NACPM did not publicly support the bill.

5. Beckett and Hoffman 2005, p. 127.

6. Ibid.

7. Wisconsin State Code 440.982 provides that no person shall practice midwifery unless licensed under Wisconsin law after having provided proof of credentialing through either NARM or ACNM, and providing proof of their training in using a defibrillator.

8. Fieldnotes, winter 2010.

9. Jamie Wall fieldnotes, fall 2017.

10. Fieldnotes, summer 2009.

11. Fieldnotes, spring 2018.

12. Ibid.

13. Leonard 2008, p. 156.

14. Fieldnotes, winter 2010.

15. Fieldnotes, spring 2018.

16. Jamie Wall fieldnotes, fall 2017.

17. Cramer 2009.

18. Fieldnotes, winter 2010.

19. Leonard 2008, p. 199. Carol Leonard herself, though, is explicitly pro-choice. Her memoir contains this extended passage on abortion:

> Although our ancient craft is to preserve the sanctity and holiness of birth—and therefore, life—the title midwife still means 'with woman.' To me, this means that

midwives are beholden to honor and respect a woman's decision, no matter what side of the abortion question she ends up on. We are charged to support and aid her in all phases of her reproductive journey not just childbirth. This needs to be done with a clear heart, without judgment. Midwives of antiquity often helped women procure abortions, either induced with abortifacient herbs or otherwise. The midwives of old used "quickening" or the first perceptible fetal movements felt by the mother, as the indicator that it was too late to abort. They believed that the soul entered the body at quickening (roughly 16 weeks).

. . . In keeping with midwives' ancient traditions, Ken [Leonard's husband, and an ob-gyn] taught me how to safely perform the technique commonly known as ME, or menstrual extraction, for early termination of unwanted pregnancies. Now, with the availability of very accurate pregnancy tests only ten days post conception, the more appropriate term for the procedure is EUE, or early uterine evacuation. This is a relatively simple suction technique that can be done safely up the seventh week of pregnancy. It is nontraumatic, relatively painless, and because of the flexibility of the canula, or extraction tube, it carries little risk. . . . Ken is firmly committed to women's freedom of choice and authority over their own bodies. . . . He wants to be sure that I am skilled in the technique, in case *Roe v. Wade* is ever overturned and we are denied legal recourse. I have since taught the technique to some of my sister midwives, who are prepared to go underground to safely help women, if this ever becomes necessary (pp. 199–200).

20. Fieldnotes, spring 2018.
21. Fieldnotes, winter 2016.
22. Fieldnotes, summer 2009.
23. Jamie Wall fieldnotes, fall 2017.
24. Fieldnotes, summer 2017.
25. Fieldnotes, spring 2018.
26. This is similar to what I heard from advocates in Maryland (Fieldnotes, summer 2009). One told me, "Absent a problem, no one is organized. We're all complacent." But, in 2009, at the Big Push Summit, this person told the group that in Maryland, "there is one person legally doing homebirths in Maryland, but there are 200–300 people getting homebirths in the state—and no way is one person attending all 300 births per year." Some of the births were undoubtedly attended by midwives who were operating legally out of Virginia, but clearly some unauthorized practitioners must be at play in the state. She, and others, felt it would be safer to have CPM credentialing and state regulation, even though there weren't present problems.
27. Jamie Wall fieldnotes, fall 2017.
28. Fieldnotes, spring 2018.
29. Ibid.
30. Fieldnotes, winter 2010.
31. Fieldnotes, summer 2016.
32. Fieldnotes, summer 2009.

33. Fieldnotes, summer 2010.

34. This created some confusion in Iowa, when marriage equality activists also handed out M&M candies.

35. Fieldnotes, spring 2018.

36. Fieldnotes, winter 2016.

37. Fieldnotes, summer 2016.

38. Ibid.

39. Fieldnotes, winter 2016.

40. American Medical Association H-420–998.

41. Amicus brief submitted by the American Medical Association on behalf of Respondents (Missouri State Medical Association), 2007.

42. The most recent ACOG statement dates from 2017 and has a more moderate tone: https://www.acog.org/clinical/clinical-guidance/committee-opinion/articles/2017/04/planned-home-birth. It states, in part:

> In the United States, approximately 35,000 births (0.9%) per year occur in the home. Approximately one fourth of these births are unplanned or unattended. Although the American College of Obstetricians and Gynecologists believes that hospitals and accredited birth centers are the safest settings for birth, each woman has the right to make a medically informed decision about delivery. Importantly, women should be informed that several factors are critical to reducing perinatal mortality rates and achieving favorable home birth outcomes. These factors include the appropriate selection of candidates for home birth; the availability of a certified nurse–midwife, certified midwife or midwife whose education and licensure meet International Confederation of Midwives' Global Standards for Midwifery Education, or physician practicing obstetrics within an integrated and regulated health system; ready access to consultation; and access to safe and timely transport to nearby hospitals. The Committee on Obstetric Practice considers fetal malpresentation, multiple gestation, or prior cesarean delivery to be an absolute contraindication to planned home birth.

43. https://pediatrics.aappublications.org/content/131/5/1016

44. The most recent ACNM statement on planned out-of-hospital birth can be found at: https://www.midwife.org/acnm/files/ACNMLibraryData/UPLOADFILE-NAME/000000000251/Planned-Home-Birth-Dec-2016.pdf

45. Fieldnotes, summer 2009.

46. Leonard 2008, p. 145.

47. Fieldnotes, spring 2018.

48. Ibid.

49. Fieldnotes, summer 2009.

50. Fieldnotes, summer 2016.

51. Fieldnotes, winter 2010.

52. Tovino 2004, p. 101.

53. Fieldnotes, spring 2018.

54. Jamie Wall fieldnotes, fall 2017.

55. Fieldnotes, spring 2018.

56. Jamie Wall fieldnotes, fall 2017.

57. Fieldnotes, spring 2018.

58. Fieldnotes, winter 2010.

59. Ibid.

60. Fieldnotes, summer 2009.

61. Jamie Wall fieldnotes, fall 2017.

62. Fieldnotes, winter 2015.

63. Ibid.

64. Fieldnotes, spring 2018.

CHAPTER 4

1. *Missouri State Medical Association v Missouri* (2008).

2. Bertelson 1994.

3. Bryant 1994.

4. Handler 1978.

5. Boutcher 2013; Hilbink 2004; Marshall and Hale 2014; Sarat and Scheingold 1998, 2001, 2006; Scheingold and Sarat 2004.

6. http://birthrightsbar.org/

7. Fieldnotes, spring 2018.

8. Fisch and Lusero have also offered a plenary on the theme of "Choose Your Own Adventure." That session touched on similar topics and had similar advice regarding interacting with the law.

9. This session was hosted before US-MERA went into effect and at a time when there were still considerable tensions between ACNM and MANA regarding licensure, at the national level.

10. Fieldnotes, fall 2017.

11. Personal communication.

12. Fieldnotes, fall 2017.

13. Ibid.

14. Ibid.

15. Mendoza 2002.

16. Munz 2008.

17. Beckett and Hoffman 2005, p. 126.

18. Associated Press 2007.

19. Liptak 2006.

20. Iowa Code 147.2.

21. https://wiki.uiowa.edu/display/stories/Push+to+legitimize+midwifery+in+Iowa%2C+by+Lindsey+Moon

22. Block 2020.

23. Greenfield 2020.

24. Fieldnotes, spring 2018.

25. Jamie Wall fieldnotes, fall 2017.

26. Fieldnotes, summer 2009.

27. Fieldnotes, spring 2018.

28. See Kukura 2018; Spence 2012.

29. Fieldnotes, spring 2016.

30. Ibid.

31. Kitzinger 2005, pp. 100–104.

32. Kukura 2018, p. 758.

33. https://birthmonopoly.com/obstetric-violence/

34. Kukura 2018, p. 790.

35. *Pemberton v Tallahassee*, 667 Supp 2d 1247, 11th Circuit Court, 1999. In this case, the state of Florida compelled a mother to comply with medically ordered bed rest at twenty-five weeks and to eventually to undergo a C-section.

36. The same article (Redden 2017) reports that in 2004, "A Pennsylvania hospital obtained a court order allowing doctors to perform a C-section on a woman over her objections. The woman checked out of the hospital and delivered her daughter vaginally, without any complications, at another hospital."

37. Paltrow and Flavin 2013.

38. Ibid.

39. Ibid.

40. Chavkin and Diaz-Tello 2017, p. 6.

41. McClain-Freeney 2018. See *Rinat Dray v Staten Island University Hospital*, Supreme Court of New York, Appellate Division, Second Judicial Department, argued December 4, 2017.

42. Kukura (2018, p. 794) notes that "when confronted with a conflict over forced medical treatment, courts often turn to the Supreme Court's abortion rights doctrine. . . . [T]he state's interest in the fetus will outweigh the mother's liberty interest after viability."

43. Grose 2014; Shire 2017; Valeii 2018; Weiss 2017.

44. Birth Rights Bar Association n.d., pp. 14–15, 27.

45. Ibid.

46. Paltrow and Flavin 2013.

47. https://birthmonopoly.com/caroline/

48. Some studies have indicated that there is a "strong association between coercion [during childbirth] and postpartum PTSD" (Kukura 2018, p. 760).

49. McCann 2019.

50. Vollers 2017; Webb-Hehn 2018.

51. http://governor.alabama.gov/news/press-releases/governor-ivey-signs-midwives-bill

52. Paris 2010.

53. Fieldnotes, spring 2016.

54. Fieldnotes, summer 2009.

55. Fieldnotes, spring 2017.

56. Fieldnotes, spring 2018.
57. Fieldnotes, fall 2016.
58. Fieldnotes, summer 2009.
59. Leonard 2008, p. 156.
60. Ibid., pp. 156–157.
61. Jamie Wall fieldnotes, fall 2017.
62. Ibid.
63. Fieldnotes, summer 2009.
64. Ibid.
65. Fieldnotes, spring 2016.
66. Ibid.
67. Yang et al. 2016, p. 5.
68. Ibid.
69. Fieldnotes, summer 2009.
70. Jamie Wall fieldnotes, fall 2017.
71. Fieldnotes, summer 2018.
72. Jamie Wall fieldnotes, fall 2017.
73. Fieldnotes, summer 2009.
74. Fieldnotes, spring 2017.

CHAPTER 5

1. Fieldnotes, spring 2005.
2. Tovino 2004, p. 95.
3. California's Business and Professions Code, Section 2508 (a)(2).
4. This phenomenon is well documented in the recent literature and not limited to CPMs by any means. Robinson (1986) found that malpractice insurance requirements put the profession of nurse-midwifery in a "fight for survival" (p. 1001). The American College of Nurse-Midwives responded quickly to the crisis, developing a plan to self-insure midwives through the professional organization. Still, Jevitt and Johnson's (2007) study of certified nurse midwives found, "The price of private liability insurance is a disincentive for students to study midwifery and for clinical preceptors to work with students." They further argue, "Midwifery program directors and academic administrators must advocate for affordable liability coverage" (p. 278). And, Cohain (2007) argues that medical malpractice coverage requirements decrease access to planned homebirth. There are similar parallels to be made with other non-allopathic health care providers like chiropractors, naturopaths, homeopaths, and massage therapists.
5. Fieldnotes, spring 2005.
6. Here, I find myself in the interesting position of disagreeing with a previous statement that I made, in print in 2018, to the effect that such an omission *was* odd; conversations with midwifery advocates since then made clear to me that with the NARM standard in place, they, at least, didn't find it odd that apprenticeship wasn't directly addressed by the legislature; *they assumed that it was assumed.*

7. Osterholzer 2018, pp. 327–328.

8. Ellickson 1991; Engel 1984; Greenhouse, Yngvesson, and Engel 1994.

9. Kukura 2018, p. 772.

10. Fieldnotes, fall 2016.

11. Ibid.

12. Ibid.

13. Ibid.

14. Ibid.

15. Lusero 2014, p. 428.

16. As this book goes to publication, a case in upstate New York is making waves, potentially changing how liability and vicarious liability are determined. CNM Sadie Moss Jones has been charged in the death of a client and her stillborn baby, after a failed VBAC attempt. The state has named Dr. Keith Lescale as a co-defendant in the case, after he performed ultrasound on the mother during her prenatal care. In late 2019, the lower court ruled against Lescale's motion for dismissal, on the grounds that Jones considered him a "collaborating physician" and that he had a duty of care to warn her client of the risks associated with out-of-hospital VBAC.

17. Jenkins 1994.

18. Fieldnotes, fall 2015.

19. Lusero 2014, pp. 428–429.

20. Simon 1988, p. 772.

21. California's Business and Professions Code, Section 2507 (a), states that "The license to practice midwifery authorizes the holder, *under the supervision of a licensed physician and surgeon*, to attend cases of normal childbirth and to provide prenatal, intrapartum, and postpartum care, including family-planning care, for the mother, and immediate care for the newborn." Section 2507 (b) further states, "As used in this article, the practice of midwifery constitutes the furthering or undertaking by any licensed midwife, *under the supervision of a licensed physician and surgeon who has current practice or training in obstetrics*, to assist a woman in childbirth so long as progress meets criteria accepted as normal." And Section 2507 (d) stipulates that "the ratio of licensed midwives to supervising physicians and surgeons shall not be greater than four individual licensed midwives to one individual supervising physician and surgeon." (all emphasis added)

22. Munz 2008.

23. Birth Rights Bar Association n.d.

24. Yang et al. 2016.

25. Trachman n.d., amicus brief in support of Kolodji. BRBA brief available on their website: birthrightsbar.org/brba-resources

26. Davis-Floyd is a valuable resource on the medicalized worldview (1993, 2006, 2018); see also Heimer 1999; Kitzinger 2005; Luker 1984; McGregor 1998; Rooks 1997; Rooks et al. 1989; Rothman 1982.

27. Munz 2008.

28. Aviram 2019, p. 13.

29. Ibid., p. 15.

30. Fieldnotes, fall 2015.

31. Ibid.

32. Ibid.

33. Silbey 2019, p. 8.

34. Bumiller 1987, p. 435.

35. Certainly, homebirth midwives are not the only alternative health care providers met with suspicion by members of the medical profession and the general public. Again, chiropractors, osteopaths, naturopaths, and homeopaths are met with a similar mix of curiosity, suspicion, and disapprobation.

36. Fisher and Todd 1993.

37. Fieldnotes, summer 2014.

38. Lusero 2014, p. 418.

39. Fieldnotes, summer 2011.

40. Vedam et al. 2018.

41. Silbey 2019, p. 4.

42. Ibid., p. 8.

43. Ewick and Silbey 1998.

44. Midwives' views of law mirror those of activists and citizens in other realms, as detailed by: Blackstone, Uggen, and McLaughlin 2009; Ewick and Silbey 1995; Marshall 2006; Silbey 2005; Wilson 2011.

45. Bell 1992; Crenshaw 1988; Engel and Munger 2003; Gleeson 2009; Goldberg-Hiller 2002; Handler 1978; Hull 2006; Klarman 2006; Kostiner 2003; McCann and Silverstein 2008; Paris 2001; Polletta 2000; Scheingold 1974; Tushnet 1987.

46. McCann 1994.

47. Kirkland 2003; Vanhala 2011.

48. Fieldnotes, spring 2017.

49. Paris 2010.

50. Ibid.

51. Fieldnotes, fall 2016.

52. Fieldnotes, fall 2015.

53. Lusero 2014, p. 418.

54. Calavita 2010.

55. Cramer 2018.

56. Burstein and Monaghan 1986; Kessler 1990; Sarat 1985; Silverstein 1999, 2007.

57. Barnes and Burke 2012; Lipsky 1980; Nielsen 2004.

58. Haider-Markel 1998; Keiser 2001.

59. Cottrol, Diamond, and Ware 2003; Klarman 2006.

60. Kessler 1990, p. 121.

61. Corrigan 2013; Marshall 2005; McCann 1994; McCann and Silverstein 2008; Silverstein 2007.

62. Wilson 2011, 2013.

63. Kostiner 2003.

64. Sarat and Kearns 1993.

65. Marshall 2006.

66. Krieger 2000, p. 488.

67. Ibid., p. 485.

CHAPTER 6

1. The term "birthkeeper" comes from Jeannine Parvati Baker, a well-known midwife and feminist, who died prior to the conference coming to fruition.

2. There were many times during interviews and writing fieldnotes that I disagreed strongly with my informants, or with what I was hearing; I have not noted that disagreement in this text—preferring to focus on what the informants/events can tell us. However, my fieldnotes from this portion of the BirthKeepers Summit indicate that I found Odent's commentary *extremely* problematic—to the point that I had to struggle to take notes that detailed his remarks, more than my reactions to them. To my ears, there were portions of his talk that veered at times dangerously close to eugenics and at other times to mother-blaming.

3. Fieldnotes, spring 2015.

4. Ibid.

5. Ibid.

6. Fieldnotes, summer 2009.

7. Ibid.

8. Fieldnotes, summer 2016.

9. The river in question is the Missouri, which neatly bisects the state near the capital, Pierre. West River is sparsely populated and contains the majority of the state's American Indian reservations. The families tend to be ranchers, and the politics tend toward libertarianism. East River is more urban and populated (with the state's largest city, Sioux Falls). The homebirth community in East River tend to be more Mennonite, Evangelical, or Catholic ("church people" this doctor told me). East River folks also were the drivers behind the eventually successful bill.

10. Cramer 2015.

11. This was not uncontroversial. The crowd at MANA was a bit uneasy, and midwives near me murmured about how going after elite clients wouldn't allow them to serve their communities, or birth justice. They do, though, need to eat and pay their bills.

12. Osterholzer 2018, p. 46.

13. Ibid., p. 68.

14. Levine and Mellema 2001.

15. Biss 2014, p. 95.

16. Ross and Solinger 2017, p. 9.

17. Ibid., p. 10.

18. Fieldnotes, spring 2017.

19. Ross and Solinger 2017, p. 11.

20. Ibid., p. 17.

21. Solinger 2007, p. 248.

22. Bridges 2011, p. 92.

23. Haskell 2018.

24. Villarosa 2018.

25. Ibid.

26. Haskell 2018.

27. Villarosa 2018.

28. Ibid.

29. Ibid.

30. Oparah et al. 2018.

31. Solinger 2007, pp. 12–13.

32. Owens 2017, p. 125.

33. Ibid., p. 124. Sims is widely known as the father of modern gynecology.

34. Villarosa 2018.

35. My previous work on celebrity pregnancy as a locale of responsibilization makes this point. Even when causes of harm are structural, women are made responsible for avoiding the hazards: "More and more, individuals are the focal point of the responsibility" (Cramer 2015, p. 125). "This exhortation to take responsibility often occurs absent an understanding of structural constraints on women's ability to do so" (p. 126).

36. Oparah et al. 2018, p. 14.

37. Ibid., p. 93.

38. Ibid., p. 94.

39. Ibid., p. 92.

40. Ibid.

41. Ibid., p. 93.

42. Ross and Solinger 2017, p. 71.

43. Bridges 2011, p. 107. (emphasis added)

44. Ibid.

45. Oparah et al. 2018, p. 5.

46. Fieldnotes, summer 2009.

47. Preece 2015, p. 17.

48. Fieldnotes, fall 2015.

49. Fieldnotes, fall 2016.

50. Fieldnotes, spring 2016.

51. Fieldnotes, fall 2015.

52. Ibid.

53. Ibid.

54. Spence 2012, p. 24.

55. Spence (2012) writes that "support for midwives . . . is understood as a critical part of the reproductive justice framework" (p. 21).

56. Trachman n.d., amicus brief in support of Kolodji. BRBA brief available on their website: birthrightsbar.org/brba-resources

57. Hampson 2017, p. 6.

58. Ibid., p. 5.

59. Ibid.

60. DeVries and Barroso 1997, p. 264.

61. Kostiner 2003, p. 354.

62. Ibid.

63. Readers will note that there is an entire literature on social movements and direct action that I do not engage directly in this discussion.

CONCLUSION

1. Silbey 2019, p. 2.

2. Re-reading this, hours after finally reading Susan Silbey's beautiful 2019 *Annual Review* piece, I am struck by the similarities in our trajectories and self-reflections.

3. Yanow 2015, p. 273.

4. Fieldnotes, fall 2017.

5. Fieldnotes, spring 2018.

6. Ibid.

7. Ibid.

8. Morgan 2011, p. 28.

9. Yanow 2015, p. 278.

10. Ibid., p. 275.

11. DeVries and Barroso 1997, p. 264. (emphasis added)

12. Yanow 2015, p. 284.

13. Fieldnotes, fall 2017.

14. Ibid.

15. Ibid.

16. Ibid.

17. May and Davis-Floyd 2006, p. 86.

18. Fieldnotes, fall 2017.

19. Jamie Wall fieldnotes, fall 2017.

20. Silbey 2019, p. 3.

21. Fieldnotes, summer 2009.

22. Bumiller 2008, p. 166.

23. Fieldnotes, spring 2018.

24. Davis-Floyd 2006b, p. 185.

25. Fieldnotes, summer 2009.

26. Fieldnotes, spring 2018.

27. Davis-Floyd 2006b, p. 195.

28. Lusero 2014, p. 420.

29. Fieldnotes, summer 2009.

30. Lusero 2014, p. 418.

31. Barclay et al. 2011, p. 2; see also Ewick and Silbey 1995.

32. I am grateful for a conversation with Liz Chiarello, who pushed me in my thinking here.

33. Heimer and Staffen, 1998.

34. Fieldnotes, fall 2017.

35. Krieger 2000, p. 486.

36. Beckett and Hoffman 2005, p. 128. (emphasis added)

37. Fieldnotes, spring 2018.

38. Ibid.

39. May and Davis-Floyd 2006, p. 83.

40. Certainly, readers have noticed the multiple ways that "discipline" is defined and used in this text. It means, of course, to punish and regulate in the Foucauldian sense. It means, as well, a set of practices and habits in the way that Bourdieu used the term. And, it stands for what we academics call the boundaries around fields and knowledge.

41. Fieldnotes, fall 2019.

42. Fieldnotes, spring 2018.

43. Rothman 2016, pp. 198–199. (emphasis added)

44. Tungohan 2016, p. 349.

45. Ibid., p. 355.

46. Harrington 1994; Harrington and Yngvesson 1990.

47. Ewick and Silbey 1998, p. 22.

48. Beckett and Hoffman 2005, p. 127.

49. Gaskin 2003 [1975], p. 3.

50. McCann and March 1995, p. 210.

51. Ibid.

52. Ibid.

53. Silbey 2005.

54. Hull 2003, p. 630.

55. Ibid., 629.

56. Ibid., 645.

57. Rosenberg 2007, p. 140.

58. Tovino 2004, p. 106.

59. Leonard 2008, p. 263. (emphasis added)

60. Ibid., p. 35.

61. Ibid., p. 85.

62. Silbey 2019, p. 14.

63. Ibid., p. 6.

64. Ibid., p. 7.

BIBLIOGRAPHY

Adamson, G. David, and Douglas J. Glare. May 2, 1980. "Home or Hospital Births?" 243 *Journal of the American Medical Association* 17: 1732–1736.

Ahmed, Sara. 2017. *Living a Feminist Life.* Durham, NC: Duke University Press.

All My Babies: A Midwife's Own Story. 1953. Documentary directed by George C. Stoney.

Amnesty International. 2011. "Deadly Delivery: The Maternal Health Care Crisis in the USA." https://www.amnestyusa.org/reports/deadly-delivery-the-maternal-health-care-crisis-in-the-usa/

Associated Press, September 28, 2007. "State Medical Board Issues $11,000 Fine to Unlicensed Pa. Midwife." *The Sentinel.*

Aviram, Hadar. 2019. "Standing Trial for Lily: 'Criminal Legal Consciousness' and Legal Mobilization Strategy Among Open Rescuers from Factory Farms." Unpublished.

Barclay, Scott, Lynn C. Jones, and Anna-Maria Marshall. 2011. "Two Spinning Wheels: Studying Law and Social Movements." In Austin Sarat (ed.), *Special Issue: Social Movements/Legal Possibilities* (Studies in Law, Politics, and Society) 54: 1–16.

Barnes, Jeb, and Thomas F. Burke. 2012. "Making Way: Legal Mobilization, Organizational Response, and Wheelchair Access." 46 *Law & Society Review* 1: 167–198.

Beckett, Katherine, and Bruce Hoffman. 2005. "Challenging Medicine: Law, Resistance, and the Cultural Politics of Childbirth." 39 *Law & Society Review* 1: 125–170.

Bell, Derrick. 1992. "Racial Realism." 24 *University of Connecticut Law Review* 363.

Bertelson, Christine. May 31, 1994. "Truly Outrageous: Raid on Midwife Upsets Court, Too." *St. Louis Post-Dispatch* (MO).

Birth Rights Bar Association. [n.d.] "Exhibit A, Brief of Human Rights in Childbirth et al. as Amicus Curiae in Support of Plaintiff Rinat Dray." https://birthrightsbar.org/resources/Documents/dray-brief.pdf

Biss, Eula. 2014. *On Immunity: An Inoculation*. Minneapolis: Graywolf Press.

Blackstone, Amy, Christopher Uggen, and Heather McLaughlin. 2009. "Legal Consciousness and Responses to Sexual Harassment." 43 *Law & Society Review* 3: 631–668.

Block, Jennifer. 2007. *Pushed: The Painful Truth About Childbirth and Modern Maternity Care*. Philadelphia: Perseus Books.

———. 2019. *Everything Below the Waist: Why Health Care Needs a Feminist Revolution*. New York: St. Martin's Press.

———. 2020. March 2020. The Criminalization of the American Midwife. *Longreads*. https://longreads.com/2020/03/10/criminalization-of-the-american-midwife/

Bourdieu, Pierre. 2000 [1977]. *Outline of a Theory of Practice*. New York: Cambridge University Press.

Boutcher, Steven. 2013. "Lawyering for Social Change: Pro Bono Publico, Cause Lawyering and the Social Movement Society." 18 *Mobilization: An International Quarterly* 2: 179–196.

Bowen, John. 2005. "Zones of Methodological Convergence in Qualitative Social Science Research," contribution to Michele Lamont and Patricia White, *Workshop on Interdisciplinary Standards for Systematic Qualitative Research*. Washington, DC: National Science Foundation.

Bridges, Khiara M. 2011. *Reproducing Race: An Ethnography of Pregnancy as a Site of Racialization*. Berkeley: University of California Press.

———. 2017. *The Poverty of Privacy Rights*. Stanford, CA: Stanford University Press.

Bryant, Tim. May 27, 1994. "Judges Reinstate Suit by Couple in Raid of Birth Clinic." *St. Louis Post-Dispatch* (MO).

Bumiller, Kristin. 1987. "Victims in the Shadow of the Law: A Critique of the Model of Legal Protection." 12 *Signs: Journal of Women in Culture and Society* 3: 421–439.

———. 2008. *In an Abusive State: How Neoliberalism Appropriated the Feminist Movement Against Sexual Violence*. Durham, NC: Duke University Press.

Burstein, Paul, and Kathleen Monaghan. 1986. "Equal Employment Opportunity and the Mobilization of Law." 20 *Law & Society Review* 3: 355–388.

The Business of Being Born. 2008. Documentary directed by Abby Epstein.

Calavita, Kitty. 2010. *Invitation to Law and Society: An Introduction to the Study of Real Law*. Chicago: University of Chicago Press.

Cassidy, Tina. 2007. *Birth: The Surprising History of How We Are Born*. New York: Grove Press.

Castañeda, Heide. 2019. *Borders of Belonging: Struggle and Solidarity in Mixed-Status Immigrant Families*. Stanford, CA: Stanford University Press.

Centers for Disease Control and Prevention. January 20, 2017. "Births and Natality." https://www.cdc.gov/nchs/fastats/births.htm

———. 2018. "Pregnancy Mortality Surveillance System." https://www.cdc.gov/reproductivehealth/maternal-mortality/pregnancy-mortality-surveillance-system.htm

Chavkin, Wendy, and Farah Diaz-Tello. March 6, 2017. "When Courts Fail: Physicians' Legal and Ethical Duty to Uphold Informed Consent." 1 *Columbia Medical Review* 2: 6–9.

Cheyney, Melissa, Marit Bovbjerg, Courtney Everson, Wendy Gordon, Darcy Hannibal, and Saraswathi Vedam. 2014. "Outcomes of Care for 16,924 Planned Home Births in the United States: The Midwives Alliance of North America Statistics Project, 2004 to 2009." 59 *Journal of Midwifery and Women's Health* 1: 17–27.

Christ, Carol P. 2008. "Embodied Embedded Mysticism: Affirming the Self and Others in a Radically Interdependent World." 24 *Journal of Feminist Studies in Religion* 2: 159–167.

Chua, Lynette, and David M. Engel. 2019. "Legal Consciousness Reconsidered." 15 *Annual Review of Law and Social Science* 335–353.

Cohain, Judy Slome. 2007. "Management or Care: Different Outcomes." *Midwifery Today* 82: 19–21.

Corrigan, Rose. 2013. *Up Against a Wall: Rape Reform and the Failure of Success.* New York: New York University Press.

Cottrol, Robert, Raymond Diamond, and Leland Ware. 2003. *Brown v. Board of Education: Caste, Culture, and the Constitution.* Lawrence: University of Kansas Press.

Coutin, Susan. 2000. *Legalizing Moves: Salvadoran Immigrants' Struggle for US Residency.* Ann Arbor: University of Michigan Press.

——, Bill Maurer, and Barbara Yngvesson. 2002. "In the Mirror: The Legitimation Work of Globalization." 27 *Law & Social Inquiry* 4: 801–843.

Cramer, Renée Ann. 2009. "Sharing in Community While Interviewing 'Outlaws' Methodological Challenges and Opportunities." 1 *International Review of Qualitative Research* 4: 453–479.

——. 2012. "The Des Moines Birth Place: Iowa's First Birth Center." 71 *Annals of Iowa* 1: 39–73.

——. 2015. *Pregnant with the Stars: Watching and Wanting the Pregnant Celebrity Body.* Stanford, CA: Stanford University Press.

——. September 2018. "The Limits of Law in Securing Reproductive Freedoms: Midwife-Assisted Homebirth in the United States." 8 *Global Discourse* 3: 493–509.

Craven, Christa. 2006. "Every Breath Is Political, Every Woman's Life a Statement: Cross-Class Organizing for Midwifery in Virginia." In Robbie Davis-Floyd and Christine Barbara Johnson (eds.), *Mainstreaming Midwives: The Politics of Change* (pp. 311–345). New York: Routledge.

——. 2010. *Pushing for Midwives: Homebirth Mothers and the Reproductive Rights Movement.* Philadelphia: Temple University Press.

Crenshaw, Kimberle. 1988. "Race, Reform, and Retrenchment: Transformation and Legitimation in Antidiscrimination Law." 101 *Harvard Law Review* 1331.

Creswell, J. W., V. L. Plano Clark, M. L. Gutmann, and W. E. Hanson. 2003. "Advanced Mixed Methods Research Designs." In A. Tashakkori and C. B. Teddlie (eds.), *Handbook of Mixed Methods in Social and Behavioral Research* (pp. 209–240). Berkeley, CA: Sage.

Darian-Smith, Eve. 2015. "Global Studies—The Handmaiden of Neoliberalism?" 12 *Globalizations* 2: 164–168.

Davis, Kathy. 1993. "Nice Doctors and Invisible Patients: The Problem of Power in Feminist Common Sense." In Alexandra Dundas Todd and Sue Fisher (eds.), *The Social Organization of Doctor–Patient Communication* (pp. 243–267). Norwood, NJ: Ablex Publishing.

Davis-Floyd, Robbie. 1993. *Birth as an American Rite of Passage.* Berkeley: University of California Press.

———. 2006a. "ACNM and MANA: Divergent Histories and Convergent Trends." In Robbie Davis-Floyd and Christine Barbara Johnson (eds.), *Mainstreaming Midwives: The Politics of Change* (pp. 29–80). New York: Routledge.

———. 2006b. "Qualified Commodification: The Creation of the Certified Professional Midwife." In Robbie Davis-Floyd and Christine Barbara Johnson (eds.), *Mainstreaming Midwives: The Politics of Change* (pp. 163–201). New York: Routledge.

———. 2018. *Ways of Knowing About Birth: Mothers, Midwives, Medicine & Birth Activism.* Long Grove, IL: Waveland Press.

———, and Christine Barbara Johnson. 2006. "Renegade Midwives: Assets or Liabilities?" In Robbie Davis-Floyd and Christine Barbara Johnson (eds.), *Mainstreaming Midwives: The Politics of Change* (pp. 447–468). New York: Routledge.

———, and Carolyn F. Sargent. 1997. *Childbirth and Authoritative Knowledge: Cross-Cultural Perspectives.* Berkeley: University of California Press.

Daviss, Betty-Anne. 2006. "From Calling to Career: Keeping the Social Movement in the Professional Project." In Robbie Davis-Floyd and Christine Barbara Johnson (eds.), *Mainstreaming Midwives: The Politics of Change* (pp. 413–445). New York: Routledge.

Declercq, Eugene, Carol Sakala, Maureen P. Corry, Sandra Applebaum, and Ariel Herrlich. 2013. "Listening to Mothers III: Pregnancy and Birth." New York: Childbirth Connection. https://www.nationalpartnership.org/our-work/resources/health-care/maternity/listening-to-mothers-iii-pregnancy-and-birth-2013.pdf

De Certeau, Michel, Luce Giard, and Pierre Mayol. 1998. *The Practice of Everyday Life: Volume 2: Living and Cooking* Timothy J. Tomasik (trans.). Minneapolis: University of Minnesota Press.

DeLee, Joseph B. 1933. *The Principles and Practice of Obstetrics.* New York: W. B. Saunders.

De Sousa Santos, Boaventura. 1987. "Law: A Map of Misreading. Toward a Postmodern Conception of Law." 14 *Law & Society Review* 3: 279–302.

DeVries, Raymond G. 1985. *Regulating Birth: Midwives, Medicine, and the Law.* Philadelphia: Temple University Press.

———, and Rebeca Barroso. 1997. "Midwives Among the Machines: Re-Creating Midwifery in the Later Twentieth Century." In Hilary Marland and Anne Marie Rafferty (eds.), *Midwives, Society, and Childbirth: Debates and Controversies in the Modern Period* (pp. 248–272). London: Routledge.

Dick-Read, Grantly. 2013 [1942]. *Childbirth Without Fear*. London: Pinter & Martin.

Didion, Joan. 2006. *We Tell Ourselves Stories in Order to Live: Collected Nonfiction*. New York: Everyman's Library.

Dudas, Jeffrey. 2008. *The Cultivation of Resentment: Treaty Rights and the New Right*. Stanford, CA: Stanford University Press.

Ehrenreich, Barbara, and Deirdre English. 1973. *Witches, Midwives, and Nurses: A History of Women Healers*. Old Westbury, NY: Feminist Press.

Ellickson, Robert. 1991. *Order Without Law: How Neighbors Settle Disputes*. Cambridge, MA: Harvard University Press.

Engel, David. 1984. "The Oven Bird's Song: Insiders, Outsiders, and Personal Injuries in an American Community." 18 *Law & Society Review* 4: 551–582.

———, and Frank Munger. 2003. *Rights of Inclusion: Law and Identity in the Life Stories of Americans with Disabilities*. Chicago: University of Chicago Press.

Epp, Charles. 2009. *Making Rights Real: Activists, Bureaucrats, and the Creation of the Legalistic State*. Chicago: University of Chicago Press.

———, Steven Maynard-Moody, and Donald Haider-Markel. 2014. *Pulled Over: How Police Stops Define Race and Citizenship*. Chicago: University of Chicago Press.

Epstein, Jessica. 2014. "Scientizing Food Safety: Resistance, Acquiescence, and Localization in India." 48 *Law & Society Review* 4: 893–920.

Ewick, Patricia, and Susan S. Silbey. 1995. "Subversive Stories and Hegemonic Tales: Toward a Sociology of Narrative." 29 *Law & Society Review* 2: 197–226.

———. 1998. *The Common Place of Law: Stories from Everyday Life*. Chicago: University of Chicago Press.

———. 2003. "Narrating Social Structure: Stores of Resistance to Legal Authority." 108 *American Journal of Sociology* 6: 1328–1372.

Federici, Silvia. 2004. *Caliban and the Witch: Women, the Body, and Primitive Accumulation*. Brooklyn, NY: Autonomedia.

Ferreira, Hélder, and Aurora A. C. Teixeira. January 2013. "'Welcome to the Experience Economy': Assessing the Influence of Customer Experience Literature Through Bibliometric Analysis." FEP Working Papers. Portugal: University of Porto.

Fisher, Sue, and Alexandra Dundas Todd. 1993. "Introduction: Communication and Social Context—Toward Broader Definitions." In Alexandra Dundas Todd and Sue Fisher (eds.), *The Social Organization of Doctor–Patient Communication* (pp. 1–14). Norwood, NJ: Ablex Publishing.

Forbes, Thomas. 1966. *The Midwife and the Witch*. New Haven, CT: Yale University Press.

Fritsvold, Erik. 2009. "Under the Law: Legal Consciousness and Radical Environmental Activism." 34 *Law & Social Inquiry* 4: 799–824.

Garriott, William. 2019. Unpublished paper presented at Law and Society Association meetings. On file with author.

Gaskin, Ina May. 2003 [1975]. *Spiritual Midwifery*, 4th ed. Summertown, TN: Book Publishing Company.

———. 2011. *Birth Matters: A Midwife's Manifesta*. New York: Seven Stories Press.

Gerring, John. 2003. "Interpretations of Interpretivism." 1 *Qualitative Method: Newsletter of the American Political Science Association Organized Section on Qualitative Methods* 2: 2–6.

Gleeson, Shannon. 2009. "From Rights to Claims: The Role of Civil Society in Making Rights Real for Vulnerable Workers." 43 *Law & Society Review* 3: 669–700.

Goldberg-Hiller, Jonah. 2002. *The Limits to Union: Same-Sex Marriage and the Politics of Civil Rights*. Ann Arbor: University of Michigan Press.

Gordon, Richard. 1984. "Critical Legal Histories." 36 *Stanford Law Review* 57–125.

Greenfield, Beth. January 29, 2020. "Arrested Rural Midwife Heads to Trial on 95 Felony Counts." https://news.yahoo.com/arrested-rural-midwife-heads-to-trial-on-95-felony-counts-182148503.html

Greenhouse, Carol, Barbara Yngvesson, and David Engel. 1994. *Law and Community in Three American Towns*. Ithaca, NY: Cornell University Press.

Grose, Jessica. May 21, 2014. "Woman Sues a New York Hospital for Forcing a C-Section. Can Doctors Do That?" *Slate*. https://slate.com/human-interest/2014/05/rinat-dray-sues-for-forced-c-section-says-doctors-at-staten-island-university-hospital-performed-the-procedure-against-her-will.html

Haider-Markel, Donald P. March 1998. "The Politics of Social Regulatory Policy: State and Federal Hate Crime Policy and Implementation Effort." 51 *Political Research Quarterly* 1: 69–88.

Haltom, William, and Michael McCann. 2004. *Distorting the Law: Politics, Media, and the Litigation Crisis*. Chicago: University of Chicago Press.

Hampson, Sarah Cote. 2017. *The Balance Gap: Working Mothers and the Limits of Law*. Stanford, CA: Stanford University Press.

———. September 2018. "Mothers Do Not Make Good Workers: The Role of Work/Life Balance Policies in Reinforcing Gendered Stereotypes." 8 *Global Discourse* 3: 510–531.

Handler, Joel. 1978. *Social Movements and the Legal System: A Theory of Law Reform and Social Change*. New York: Academic Press.

Haney López, Ian F. 2003. *Racism on Trial: The Chicano Fight for Justice*. Cambridge, MA: Harvard University Press.

Harrington, Christine B. 1994. "Outlining a Theory of Legal Practice." In Maureen Cain and Christine Harrington (eds.), *Lawyers in a Postmodern World: Translation and Transgression* (pp. 49–70). New York: New York University Press.

———, and Barbara Yngvesson. 1990. "Interpretive Sociolegal Research." 15 *Law & Social Inquiry* 1: 135–148.

Haskell, Rob. January 10, 2018. "Serena Williams on Motherhood, Marriage, and Making Her Comeback." *Vogue*. https://www.vogue.com/article/serena-williams-vogue-cover-interview-february-2018

Heimer, Carol A. 1999. "Competing Institutions: Law, Medicine and Family in Neonatal Intensive Care." 33 *Law & Society Review* 1: 17–66.

———, and Lisa R. Staffen. 1998. *For the Sake of the Children: The Social Organization of Responsibility in the Hospital and in the Home.* Chicago: University of Chicago Press.

Hemmings, Clare. 2011. *Why Stories Matter: The Political Grammar of Feminist Theory.* Durham, NC: Duke University Press.

Hilbink, Thomas. 2004. "You Know the Type . . . : Categories of Cause Lawyering." 29 *Law and Social Inquiry* 3: 657– 698.

Hirsch, Susan. 2009. *In the Moment of Greatest Calamity.* Princeton, NJ: Princeton University Press.

Hoffman, Bruce. 2008. "Minding the Gap: Legal Ideals and Strategic Action in State Legislative Hearings." 33 *Law & Social Inquiry* 1: 89–126.

hooks, bell. 2014. *Outlaw Culture: Resisting Representations.* New York: Routledge.

Hough, Carolyn A. 2006. "I'm Living my Politics: Legalizing and Licensing Direct-Entry Midwives in Iowa." In Robbie Davis-Floyd and Christine Barbara Johnson (eds.), *Mainstreaming Midwives: The Politics of Change* (pp. 347–374). New York: Routledge.

Hull, Kathleen. 2003. "The Cultural Power of Law and the Cultural Enactment of Legality: The Case of Same-Sex Marriage." 28 *Law & Social Inquiry* 3: 629–657.

———. 2006. *Same-Sex Marriage: The Cultural Politics of Love.* New York: Cambridge University Press.

Jenkins, Susan M. March 1994. "The Myth of Vicarious Liability. Impact on Barriers to Nurse-Midwifery Practice." 39 *Journal of Nurse Midwifery* 2: 98–106.

Jevitt, Cecilia, and Peter Johnson. 2007. "Liability Insurance in Midwifery Education: Faculty and Student Needs Versus Academic Realities." 23 *Journal of Professional Nursing* 5: 278–284.

Johnson, Christine Barbara. 2006. "Creating a Way Out of No Way: Midwifery in Massachusetts." In Robbie Davis-Floyd and Christine Barbara Johnson (eds.), *Mainstreaming Midwives: The Politics of Change* (pp. 375–407). New York: Routledge.

———, and Robbie Davis-Floyd. 2006. "Why Midwives Matter: Overcoming Barriers to Caretake the Power of Birth." In Robbie Davis-Floyd and Christine Barbara Johnson (eds.), *Mainstreaming Midwives: The Politics of Change* (pp. 507–538). New York: Routledge.

Jordan-Zachery, Julia. 2007. "Am I a Black Woman or a Woman Who Is Black? A Few Thoughts on the Meaning of Intersectionality." 3 *Politics and Gender* 2: 254–263.

———. 2013. "Now You See Me, Now You Don't: My Political Fight Against the Invisibility/Erasure of Black Women in Intersectionality Research." 1 *Politics, Groups, and Identities* 1: 101–109.

———. 2017. *Shadow Bodies: Black Women, Ideology, Representation and Politics.* Camden, NJ: Rutgers University Press.

Keiser, Lael R. 2001. "Street-Level Bureaucrats, Administrative Power, and the Manipulation of Federal Social Security Disability Programs." 1 *State Politics & Policy Quarterly* 2: 144–164.

Kessler, Mark. 1990. "Legal Mobilization for Social Reform: Power and the Politics of Agenda Setting." 24 *Law & Society Review* 1: 121–144.

Kirkland, Anna. 2003. "Victorious Transsexuals in the Courtroom: A Challenge for Feminist Legal Theory." 28 *Law & Social Inquiry* 1: 1–37.

Kitzinger, Sheila. 2005. *The Politics of Birth*. London: Elsevier Books.

Klarman, Michael. 2006. *From Jim Crow to Civil Rights: The Supreme Court and the Struggle for Racial Equality*. New York: Oxford University Press.

Kline, Wendy. 2019. *Coming Home: How Midwives Changed Birth*. New York: Oxford University Press.

Knauer, Nancy J. 2012. "Legal Consciousness and LGBT Research: The Role of the Law in the Everyday Lives of LGBT Individuals." 59 *Journal of Homosexuality* 5: 748–756.

Kostiner, Idit. June 2003. "Evaluating Legality: Toward a Cultural Approach to the Study of Law and Social Change." 37 *Law and Society Review* 323.

Krieger, Linda Hamilton. 2000. "Afterword: Socio-Legal Backlash." 21 *Berkeley Journal of Employment and Labor Law* 1: 476–520.

Kukura, Elizabeth. 2016. "Contested Care: The Limitations of Evidence-Based Maternity Care Reform." 31 *Berkeley Journal of Gender, Law, and Justice* 1.

———. 2018. "Obstetric Violence." 106 *Georgetown Law Review* 721–801.

Lazarus-Black, Mindie, and Susan Hirsch. 1994. *Contested States: Law, Hegemony, and Resistance*. New York: Routledge.

Leavitt, Judith Walzer. 1986. *Brought to Bed: Childbearing in America, 1750–1950*. New York: Oxford University Press.

Lefebvre, Henri, and Christine Levich. 1987. "The Everyday and Everydayness." *Yale French Studies* 73: 7–11.

Leonard, Carol. 2008. *Lady's Hands, Lion's Heart: A Midwife's Saga*. Hopkinton, NH: Bad Beaver Publishing.

Levine, Kay, and Virginia Mellema. 2001. "Strategizing the Street: How Law Matters in the Lives of Women in the Street Level Drug Economy." 26 *Law & Social Inquiry* 1: 169–207.

Lipsky, Michael. 1980. *Street Level Bureaucrats: Dilemmas of the Individual in Public Services*. New York: Russell Sage Foundation.

Liptak, Adam. April 3, 2006. "Prosecution of Midwife Casts Light on Home Births." *New York Times*.

Litoff, Judy Barrett. 1978. *American Midwives: 1860 to the Present*. Westport, CT: Greenwood Press.

Luker, Kristin. 1984. *Abortion and the Politics of Motherhood*. Berkeley: University of California Press.

Lusero, Indra. 2014. "Making the Midwife Impossible: How the Structure of Maternity Care Harms the Practice of Home Birth Midwifery." 35 *Women's Rights Law Reporter* 4: 406–434.

MacDorman, Marian F. August 2010. "Trends and Characteristics of Home and Other Out-of-Hospital Births in the United States, 1990–2006." 58 *National*

Vital Statistics Reports 11. www.cdc.gov/nchs/data/nvsr/nvsr58/nvsr58_11 .PDF

———, and Eugene Declercq. December 10, 2018. "Trends and State Variations in Out-of-Hospital Births in the United States, 2004–2017." 46 *Birth* 2: 279–288.

Marland, Hilary, and Anne Marie Rafferty (eds.). 1997. *Midwives, Society, and Childbirth: Debates and Controversies in the Modern Period.* London: Routledge.

Marshall, Anna-Maria. 2005. "Idle Rights: Employees' Rights Consciousness and the Construction of Sexual Harassment Policies." 39 *Law & Society Review* 1: 83–124.

———. 2006. "Communities and Culture: Enriching Legal Consciousness and Legal Culture." 31 *Law and Social Inquiry* 1: 229–249.

———, and Daniel Hale. 2014. "Cause Lawyering." 10 *Annual Review of Law and Social Science* 301–320.

May, Maureen, and Robbie Davis-Floyd. 2006. "Idealism and Pragmatism in the Creation of the Certified Midwife: The Development of Midwifery in New York and the New York Midwifery Practice Act of 1992." In Robbie Davis-Floyd and Christine Barbara Johnson (eds.), *Mainstreaming Midwives: The Politics of Change* (pp. 81–158). New York: Routledge.

Mazur, Amy, Dorothy E. McBride, and Season Hoard. 2016. "Comparative Strength of Women's Movements over Time: Conceptual, Empirical, and Theoretical Innovations." 4 *Politics, Groups, and Identities* 4: 654–676.

McCann, Adam. August 12, 2019. "Best & Worst States to Have a Baby." *WalletHub.* https://wallethub.com/edu/best-and-worst-states-to-have-a-baby/6513/

McCann, Michael W. 1994. *Rights at Work: Pay Equity and the Politics of Legal Mobilization.* Chicago: University of Chicago Press.

———, and Tracey March. 1995. "Law and Everyday Forms of Resistance: A Socio-Political Assessment." In Austin Sarat and Susan S. Silbey (eds.), *Studies in Law, Politics, and Society* (vol. 15, pp. 207–236). JAI Press: Greenwich, CT.

———, and Helena Silverstein. 2008. "Rethinking Law's Allurements: A Relational Analysis of Social Movement Lawyers in the United States." In Austin Sarat and Stuart Scheingold (eds.), *Cause Lawyering: Political Commitments, and Professional Responsibilities* (pp. 261–292). New York: Oxford University Press.

McClain-Freeney, Lisa. April 23, 2018. "Rinat Dray Decision Proves How Hard It Is for Women Subjected to Forced Surgeries to Get Justice." National Advocates for Pregnant Women. http://advocatesforpregnantwomen.org/blog/2018/04/rinat_dray_decision_proves_how.php

McGregor, Deborah Kuhn. 1998. *From Midwives to Medicine: The Birth of American Gynecology.* New Brunswick, NJ: Rutgers University Press.

McQuarrie, Howard G. May 2, 1980. "Home Delivery Controversy." 243 *Journal of the American Medical Association* 17: 1747–1748.

McMillan, L. Jane. 2011. "Colonial Traditions, Co-Optations, and Mi'kmaq Legal Consciousness." 36 *Law & Social Inquiry* 1: 171–200.

Meddings, Fiona, Fiona MacVane Phipps, Melanie Haith-Cooper, and Jacque-
lyn Haigh. 2007. "Vaginal Births After Caesarean Section (VBAC): Exploring
Women's Perceptions." 16 *Journal of Clinical Nursing* 1: 160–167.

Mendoza, Martha. December 22, 2002. "Prosecutions Thin Ranks of Midwives."
Washington Post.

Merry, Sally Engle. 1985. "Concepts of Law and Justice Among Working Class
Americans: Ideology as Culture." 11 *Legal Studies Forum* 59–71.

———. 1990. *Getting Justice and Getting Even: Legal Consciousness Among Working
Class Americans.* Chicago: University of Chicago Press.

———. 1998. "Global Human Rights and Local Social Movements in a Legally Plural
World." *Canadian Journal of Law and Society* 12: 247–271.

———. 2000. *Colonizing Hawai'i: The Cultural Power of Law.* Princeton, NJ: Princeton University Press.

———. 2012. "Legal Pluralism and Legal Culture: Mapping the Terrain." In Brian
Z. Tamanaha, Caroline Mary Sage, and Michael J. V. Woolcock (eds.), *Legal
Pluralism and Development: Scholars and Practitioners in Dialogue* (pp. 66–82).
New York: Cambridge University Press.

Mitler, Lloyd K., John A. Rizzo, and Sarah M. Horwitz. 2000. "Physician Gender
and Cesarean Sections." 53 *Journal of Clinical Epidemiology* 10: 1030–1035.

Moore, Sally Falk. 1978. *Law as Process: An Anthropological Approach.* New York:
Routledge.

Moraga, Cherrie, and Gloria Anzaldua. 1983. *This Bridge Called My Back: Writings
by Radical Women of Color.* London: Persephone Press.

Morgan, Bronwen. 2003. *Social Citizenship in the Shadow of Competition: The Bureaucratic Politics of Regulatory Justification.* London: Routledge.

———. 2011. *Water on Tap: Rights and Regulation in the Transnational Governance
of Urban Water Services.* New York: Cambridge University Press.

Munz, Michele. April 16, 2008. "Midwifery Bill Runs into Issues in Senate." *St.
Louis Post-Dispatch* (MO).

Murphy, Michelle. 2012. *Seizing the Means of Reproduction: Entanglements of Feminism, Health, and Technoscience.* Durham, NC: Duke University Press.

Nader, Laura. 1990. *Harmony Ideology: Justice and Control in a Zapotec Mountain
Village.* Stanford, CA: Stanford University Press.

Nielsen, Laura Beth. 2004. *License to Harass: Law, Hierarchy, and Offensive Public
Speech.* Princeton, NJ: Princeton University Press.

Norsigian, Judy. 1970. *Our Bodies, Ourselves.* Boston: Boston Women's Health Book
Collective.

Oparah, Julia Chinyere, Helen Arega, Dantia Hudson, Linda Jones, and Talita Os-
eguera. 2018. *Battling over Birth: Black Women and the Maternal Health Care
Crisis.* Amarillo, TX: Praeclarus Press.

Osterholzer, Kim Woodard. 2018. *A Midwife in Amish Country: Celebrating God's
Gift of Life.* Washington, DC: Salem Books.

Owens, Deirdre Cooper. 2017. *Medical Bondage: Race, Gender, and the Origins of American Gynecology*. Athens: University of Georgia Press.

Paltrow, Lynn, and Jeanne Flavin. 2013. "Arrests of and Forced Interventions on Pregnant Women in the United States, 1973–2005: Implications for Women's Legal Status and Public Health." 38 *Journal of Health Politics, Policy, and Law* 2: 299–343.

Paris, Michael. 2001. "Legal Mobilization and the Politics of Reform: Lessons from School Finance Litigation in Kentucky, 1984–1995." 26 *Law & Social Inquiry* 3: 631–684.

———. 2010. *Framing Equal Opportunity: Law and the Politics of School Finance Reform*. Stanford, CA: Stanford University Press.

Pine, B. Joseph, II, and James H. Gilmore. July–August 1998. "Welcome to the Experience Economy." *Harvard Business Review*. https://hbr.org/1998/07/welcome -to-the-experience-economy

Polletta, Francesca. 2000. "The Structural Context of Novel Rights Claims: Southern Civil Rights Organizing, 1961–1966." 34 *Law & Society Review* 2: 367–406.

Pound, Roscoe. 1910. "Law in Books and Law in Action." *American Law Review* 44: 12.

Preece, Bronwyn (ed.). 2015. *In the Spirit of Homebirth: Modern Women, An Ancient Choice*. Vancouver: Seven Stories Press.

Price, Sean. 2020. "Maternal Deaths: First U.S. Data Since 2007 Shows Serious Problems Persist." Texas Medical Association. https://www.texmed.org/Texas MedicineDetail.aspx?id=52424

Redden, Molly. October 5, 2017. "New York Hospital's Secret Policy Led to Woman Being Given C-Section Against Her Will." *The Guardian*. https://www. theguardian.com/us-news/2017/oct/05/new-york-staten-island-university-hos- pital-c-section-ethics-medicine/

Rinat Dray v Staten Island University Hospital, Supreme Court of New York, Appellate Division, Second Judicial Department, argued December 4, 2017.

Robinson, Gail. 1986. "Midwifery and Malpractice Insurance: A Profession Fights for Survival" 134 *University of Pennsylvania Law Review* 1001–1034.

Romlid, Christina. 1997. "Swedish Midwives and Their Instruments in the Eighteenth and Nineteenth Centuries." In Hilary Marland and Anne Marie Rafferty (eds.), *Midwives, Society, and Childbirth: Debates and Controversies in the Modern Period* (pp. 38–60). London: Routledge.

Rooks, Judith P. 1997. *Midwifery and Childbirth in America*. Philadelphia: Temple University Press.

———, Norman L. Weatherby, Eunice K. M. Ernst, Susan Stapleton, David Rosen, and Allan Rosenfield. 1989. "Outcomes of Care in Birth Centers: The National Birth Center Study." *New England Journal of Medicine* 321: 1804–1811.

Rosenberg, Charles E. 2007. *Our Present Complaint: American Medicine, Then and Now*. Baltimore, MD: Johns Hopkins University Press.

Rosenberg, Gerald N. 1991. *The Hollow Hope: Can Courts Bring About Social Change?* Chicago: University of Chicago Press.

Ross, Loretta, and Rickie Solinger. 2017. *Reproductive Justice: An Introduction.* Berkeley: University of California Press.

Rothman, Barbara Katz. 1982. *In Labor: Women and Power in the Birthplace.* New York: Norton.

———. 1989. *Recreating Motherhood: Ideology and Technology in Patriarchal Society.* New York: Norton.

———. 2016. *A Bun in the Oven: How the Food and Birth Movements Resist Industrialization.* New York: New York University Press.

Runes, Valerie Vickerman (ed.). April 2004. *From Calling to Courtroom: A Survival Guide for Midwives.* http://www.fromcallingtocourtroom.net/default.htm

Sarat, Austin. 1985. "Legal Effectiveness and Social Studies of Law." 9 *Legal Studies Forum* 23.

———. 1990. "The Law Is All Over: Power, Resistance, and the Legal Consciousness of the Welfare Poor." 2 *Yale Journal of Law and the Humanities* 2.

———, Lawrence Douglas, and Martha Merrill Umphrey. 2005. *The Limits of Law.* Stanford, CA: Stanford University Press.

———, and William Felstiner. 1995. *Divorce Lawyers and Their Clients: Power and Meaning in the Legal Process.* New York: Cambridge University Press.

———, and Joel Grossman. 1975. "Courts and Conflict Resolution: Problems in the Mobilization of Adjudication." 69 *American Political Science Review* 4: 1200–1217.

———, and Thomas Kearns. 1993. *Law in Everyday Life.* Ann Arbor: University of Michigan Press.

———, and Stuart A. Scheingold. 1998. *Cause Lawyering: Political Commitments and Professional Responsibilities.* New York: Oxford University Press.

———. 2001. *Cause Lawyering and the State in a Global Era.* New York: Oxford University Press.

———. 2006. *Cause Lawyers and Social Movements.* Stanford, CA: Stanford University Press.

Scheingold, Stuart. 1974. *The Politics of Rights.* New Haven, CT: Yale University Press.

———, and Austin Sarat. 2004. *Something to Believe In: Politics, Professionalism, and Cause Lawyering.* Stanford, CA: Stanford University Press.

Shamir, Ronen. 1993. "Professionalism and Monopoly of Expertise: Lawyers and Administrative Law, 1933–1937." 27 *Law & Society Review* 2: 361–398.

Shire, Emily. July 12, 2017. "The Mom Forced to Have a C-Section." *Daily Beast.* https://www.thedailybeast.com/the-mom-forced-to-have-a-c-section

Silbey, Susan S. 2005. "After Legal Consciousness." *Annual Review of Law and Social Science* 1: 323–368.

———. 2019. "The Every Day Work of Studying the Law in Everyday Life." 15 *Annual Review of Law and Social Science* 5: 1–18.

Silverstein, Helena. 1996. *Unleashing Rights: Law, Meaning, and the Animal Rights Movement*. Ann Arbor: University of Michigan Press.

———. 1999. "Road Closed: Evaluating the Judicial Bypass Provision of the Pennsylvania Abortion Control Act." 24 *Law & Social Inquiry* 1: 73–96.

———. 2007. *Girls on the Stand: How Courts Fail Pregnant Minors*. New York: New York University Press.

Simon, Jonathan. 1988. "The Ideological Effects of Actuarial Practices." 22 *Law & Society Review* 4: 771–800.

Solinger, Rickie. 2007. *Pregnancy and Power: A Short History of Reproductive Politics in America*. New York: New York University Press.

Spence, Rebecca. 2012. "Abandoning Women to Their Rights: What Happens When Feminist Jurisprudence Ignores Birthing Rights." 19 *Cardozo Journal of Law and Gender* 1: 101–123.

Tarrow, Sidney. 1995. "Bridging the Quantitative-Qualitative Divide in Political Science." 89 *American Political Science Review* 2: 471–474.

Taylor, Catherine. 2002. *Giving Birth: A Journey into the World of Mothers and Midwives*. New York: Penguin Putnam.

Thrower, Eileen J. B. 2016. "A Timeline of Midwifery in Georgia." http://georgia midwife.org/wp-content/uploads/2018/05/A-Timeline-of-Midwifery-in-Georgia .pptx.pdf

Todd, Alexandra Dundas. 1993a. "A Diagnosis of Doctor–Patient Discourse in the Prescription of Contraception." In Alexandra Dundas Todd and Sue Fisher (eds.), *The Social Organization of Doctor–Patient Communication* (pp. 183–212). Norwood, NJ: Ablex Publishing.

———. 1993b. "Exploring Women's Experiences: Power and Resistance in Medical Discourse." In Alexandra Dundas Todd and Sue Fisher (eds.), *The Social Organization of Doctor–Patient Communication* (pp. 267–286). Norwood, NJ: Ablex Publishing.

Tovino, Stacey A. 2004. "American Midwifery Litigation and State Legislative Preferences for Physician-Controlled Childbirth." *Scholarly Works* 394.

Trachman, Ellen. [n.d.]. *"Amici Curiae* on Behalf of Birth Rights Bar Association et al., in Support of Petitioner Yelena Kolodji," in *Kolodji v Board of Registered Nursing*, et al., Superior Court of the State of California for the County of San Francisco, Case No. CPF-15-514098. BRBA brief available on their website: birthrightsbar.org/brba-resources

Trubek, David. 1984. "Where the Action Is: Critical Legal Studies and Empiricism." 36 *Stanford Law Review* 1/2: 575–622.

Tungohan, Ethel. September 2016. "Intersectionality and Social Justice: Assessing Activists' Use of Intersectionality Through Grassroots Migrants' Organizations in Canada." 4 *Politics, Groups, and Identities* 3: 347–363.

Tushnet, Mark V. 1987. *The N.A.A.C.P.'s Legal Strategy Against Segregated Education, 1925–1950*. Chapel Hill: University of North Carolina Press.

Valeii, Kathi. June 18, 2018. "Birth Needs a #MeToo Reckoning." *Dame*. https:// www.damemagazine.com/2018/06/18/birth-needs-a-metoo-reckoning/

Valverde, Marina. 2012. *Everyday Law on the Street: City Governance in an Age of Diversity*. Toronto: University of Toronto Press.

Vanhala, Lisa. 2011. "Social Movements Lashing Back: Law, Social Change, and Intra-Social Movement Backlash in Canada." In Austin Sarat (ed.), *Special Issue: Social Movements/Legal Possibilities* (Studies in Law, Politics, and Society) 54: 113–140.

Varney, Helen, and Joyce Beebe Thompson. 2015. *The Midwife Said Fear Not: A History of Midwifery in the United States*. New York: Springer.

Vedam, Saraswathi, Kathrin Stoll, Marian MacDorman, Eugene Declercq, Melissa Cheyney, Timothy Fisher, Emma Butt, Y. Tony Yang, and Holly Powell Kennedy. February 21, 2018. "Mapping of Integration of Midwives Across the United Sates: Impact on Access, Equity, and Outcomes." 13 *PLoS One* 2. https:// doi.org/10.1371/journal.pone.0192523

Villarosa, Linda. April 11, 2018. "Why America's Black Mothers and Babies Are in a Life-or-Death Crisis." *New York Times Magazine*. https://www.nytimes.com /2018/04/11/magazine/black-mothers-babies-death-maternal-mortality.html

Vincent, Peggy. 2012. *Baby Catcher: Chronicles of a Modern Midwife*. New York: Scribner.

———. 2015. *Midwife: A Calling*. Ant Press.

Vollers, Anna Claire. March 6, 2017. "Mothers Stage Sit-In at Statehouse Tonight to Demand Senate Vote on Midwife Bill." *Alabama.com*. https://www.al.com /news/2017/05/mothers_stage_sit-in_at_stateh.html

Webb-Hehn, Katherine. September 3, 2018. "Midwifery Makes a Comeback in Alabama." *Scalawag Magazine*. https://www.scalawagmagazine.org/2018/09/alabama -homebirth-reproductive-justice/

Weiss, Suzannah. November 8, 2017. "These New Moms Say They Were Forced to Have C-Sections Without Their Consent." *Glamour*. https://www.glamour.com /story/new-moms-c-sections-without-consent

Wertz, Richard, and Dorothy Wertz. 1989. *Lying In: A History of Childbirth in America*. New Haven, CT: Yale University Press.

Weschler, Toni. 2002. *Taking Charge of Your Fertility: The Definitive Guide to Natural Birth Control, Pregnancy Achievement, and Reproductive Health*, rev. ed. New York: HarperCollins.

WHO, UNICEF, UNFPA, World Bank, and United Nations Population Division. 2014. "Trends in Maternal Mortality: 1990 to 2013." https://apps.who.int/iris /bitstream/handle/10665/112682/9789241507226_eng.pdf?sequence=2

———. 2018. "Maternal Mortality in 2000–2017." https://www.who.int/gho/maternal_health/countries/usa.pdf

Why Not Home? 2016. Documentary directed by Jessica Moore.

Williams, Jan. 1997. "The Controlling Power of Childbirth in Britain." In Hilary Marland and Anne Marie Rafferty (eds.), *Midwives, Society, and Childbirth: Debates and Controversies in the Modern Period* (pp. 232–248). London: Routledge.

Williams, Patricia. 1991. *Alchemy of Race and Rights: Diary of a Law Professor.* Cambridge, MA: Harvard University Press.

Wilson, Joshua C. 2011. "Sustaining the State: Legal Consciousness and the Construction of Legality in Competing Abortion Activists' Narratives." 36 *Law & Social Inquiry* 2: 455–483.

———. 2013. *The Street Politics of Abortion: Speech, Violence, and America's Culture Wars.* Stanford, CA: Stanford University Press.

Yang, Y. Tony, Laura B. Attanasio, and Katy B. Kozhimannil. 2016. "State Scope of Practice Laws, Nurse-Midwifery Workforce, and Childbirth Procedures and Outcomes." 26 *Women's Health Issues* 3: 262–267.

Yanow, Dvora. 2003. "Interpretive Empirical Political Science: What Makes This Not a Subfield of Qualitative Methods." 1 *Qualitative Method: Newsletter of the American Political Science Association Organized Section on Qualitative Methods* 2: 9–13.

———. 2015. "After Mastery: Insights from Practice Theorizing." In Raghu Garud, Barbara Simpson, Ann Langley, and Haridimos Tsoukas (eds.), *The Emergency of Novelty in Organizations* (pp. 272–317). New York: Oxford University Press.

Young, Kathryne M. 2014. "Everyone Knows the Game: Legal Consciousness in the Hawaiian Cockfight." 48 *Law & Society Review* 3: 499–530.

INDEX

AABC, *see* American Association of Birth Centers

AAP, *see* American Academy of Pediatrics

Abortion: avoiding issue, 104–5; medical decisions, 45; midwives and, 171–72, 176, 226n42, 231–32n19; pro-choice activism, 59–60, 105; pro-life groups and individuals, 60, 105, 167, 172, 181, 184; standing of providers, 122; state laws, 35, 122

ACNM, *see* American College of Nurse-Midwives

ACOG, *see* American College of Obstetricians and Gynecologists

African Americans: care from midwives and doulas, 191–92; civil rights movement, 166–67; concerns about midwife legalization, 211–12; enslaved, 44, 45–46, 187; forced sterilizations, 45; infant mortality rates, 190; maternal health disparities, 191, 193, 226n42; middle-class, 50; midwives, 43, 45–46, 48, 49, 152, 171, 178, 193,

226n42; in midwives' organizations, 78; structural racism and, 211–12; as test subjects, 44, 45, 46; treatment in hospitals, 131, 188–90; views of homebirths, 192. *See also* Racial disparities; Reproductive justice movement; Women of color

Alabama: Big Push Summit, 19, 29, 58–59, 69; C-section rate, 134–35; legal status of midwives, 11, 18 (table), 69, 135; legislature, 135; midwifery laws, 49, 104, 135; number of midwives, 135; obstetric violence cases, 134; prosecutions of midwives, 69; Tuskegee Institute, 49

Alabama Birth Coalition, 135

Alabama Board of Midwifery, 135

Allemann, Elizabeth, 103

All My Babies: A Midwife's Own Story, 178

Alternative health care providers, 76, 137, 216, 236n4, 238n35

AMA, *see* American Medical Association

American Academy of Family Physicians, 53–54

CPSIA information can be obtained
at www.ICGtesting.com
Printed in the USA
JSHW021409220421
13828JS00001B/25

9 781503 614499